APPROACHING
THE APOCALYPSE

APPROACHING THE APOCALYPSE:

A SHORT HISTORY OF CHRISTIAN MILLENARIANISM

John M. Court

I.B. TAURIS

LONDON · NEW YORK

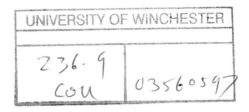
Published in 2008 by I.B.Tauris & Co Ltd
6 Salem Road, London W2 4BU
175 Fifth Avenue, New York NY 10010
www.ibtauris.com

In the United States of America and Canada
distributed by Palgrave Macmillan, a division of St Martin's Press
175 Fifth Avenue, New York, NY 10010

ISBN: 978 1 84511 759 7 (pb)
       978 1 84511 758 0 (hb)

A full CIP record for this book is available from the British Library
A full CIP record is available from the Library of Congress

Library of Congress Catalog Card Number: available

Typeset in Adobe Garamond Pro by Sara Millington, Editorial and
Design Services
Printed and bound in Great Britain by T.J. International Ltd, Padstow,
Cornwall

Biblical quotations in this volume have been taken from the New Revised
Standard Version.

This wide-ranging and accessible study of millennial thought and its implications for Christian history is part of the necessary rehabilitation of a doctrine whose significance for the intellectual history of Christianity has too often been relegated to the margins of scholarly concern. John Court's broad knowledge and thorough treatment make a welcome contribution to a better appreciation of this important feature of Christian theology. His book spans two thousand years and focuses on a number of the key issues, such as the biblical origins of millennialism, Montanism, the significance of the marking of the first millennium, the impact of Joachite ideas and the millennial dynamic of North American Christianity. Christian theologians down the centuries may have liked to think that they had dispensed with the doctrine of the millennium by showing how it misrepresented the New Testament. The widespread influence of such ideas only demonstrates the impossibility of pinning down such an allusive apocalyptic image and the pervasiveness of themes with millennial import in the foundation texts of Christianity.

Christopher Rowland, Dean Ireland Professor of the Exegesis of Holy Scripture,
University of Oxford

From the book of Daniel to the *Left Behind* novels of Tim LaHaye and Jerry Jenkins, John M. Court's *Approaching the Apocalypse* offers a fascinating history of the startling idea of the end of days within Western cultural history. Covering a wealth of different historical and textual material, and opening a window onto 2000 years of Christian eschatological thinking, this lively survey ought to be recommended reading for undergraduate and graduate courses in both apocalyptic ideas and millenarian movements.

John Walliss, Director, Hope Centre for Millennialism Studies and Senior
Lecturer in the Sociology of Religion, Liverpool Hope University

With the modern-day interpreters of the book of Revelation that it generates, the colourful language that it uses of Rapture and Armageddon and its preoccupation with the state of Israel, Christian millenarianism makes a major impact on contemporary politics and religion. Millenarianism is as intriguing to general readers as it is to students of the Bible and Christian history. This short book usefully explains key elements of its discourse and the diversity of ideas within it. John Court helps interested non-specialists, as well as undergraduate students new to the field, to negotiate both the history of apocalyptic expectation in the West and otherwise confusing terms such as pre- and postmillenarian. Without overloading the reader with information, he has succeeded in writing an accessible, compact introduction to selected millenarian themes, personages and movements from the Bible to the present day.

Christine Trevett, Professor of Religious and Theological Studies, University of
Cardiff and author of Montanism: Gender, Authority and the New Prophecy

*We are to remove mountains and bring the millennium, because
then we can have a quiet moment to discuss whether
the millennium is at all desirable.*

G.K.Chesterton, *Charles Dickens*

*I can't see why there's all this fuss about the human race
perhaps being wiped out in the near future.
It certainly deserves to be.*

Attributed to Philip Larkin, at least by Kingsley Amis

*When mankind's number is up there may be some bangs, but for
all our artistically epic fantasies, we'll shuffle off with a whimper.*

Marina Hyde on Armageddon, *Guardian*, 13 December 2005

*To those that teach a personall comming of Christ, and a
resurrection of the just, to live and raigne with Christ a thousand
yeares, before the resurrection of the uniust and end of the world.
Of which there bee severall sorts, who are commonly
called Millinaries.*

Part of the title of a work by 'I.E.', London, 1641

CONTENTS

PREFACE

N ow that the fervour of excitement and the threat of fanaticism associated with the dawn of the new **Millennium** has practically subsided, it is a good time to attempt an overview of **millenarian** expectation over the two millennia of Christian history. This account provides a series of snapshots of particular situations in which millenarian ideas were dominant. As a narrative of these phenomena it is critical (in the academic sense) without being judgemental. This approach allows for a brief analysis of the main trends, and invites comparison with **apocalyptic** beliefs and activity in other religious traditions. Nevertheless it is essentially an account of the Christian phenomena, examining the Biblical roots of the different ideas about the end of the world, particularly the expectation of the return of Jesus Christ, which is linked to the establishment of a messianic Kingdom that will last for a thousand years. This work investigates examples of such thinking from the early Fathers of the Christian church, through the Middle Ages (with particular reference to ideas associated with the year 1000), the Black Death and other plagues, to nineteenth-century millenarian movements in various parts of the world and the most recent enthusiasms for the third Millennium in America and Israel.

This project does not seek to provide an exhaustive survey but rather a short historical review, focussed on Christian traditions and with a selected range of examples. The intention is to explore both the continuity of ideas associated with the Thousand Year Reign (the

Millennium) of Christ, and also the ways in which the themes are varied, affected as they are by a diversity of historical contexts in which the expectation comes to the forefront. This study will also engage with the range of motifs that are found frequently in association with millenarian expectation – themes such as the **Rapture**, **Utopia**, plagues, the interpretation of **Biblical prophecies** and the building of the **New Jerusalem**.

This work is intended as a serious critical study built on firm academic foundations but is designed to be accessible, as an introductory text, explaining the terminology used and offering a clear narrative line. It should appeal to the general reader with an interest in understanding such matters. Linked with a suitable reader, such as *Radical Christian Writings* (edited by Christopher Rowland and Andrew Bradstock, published by Blackwell, 2002), it could provide a textbook for a student course in this area of religion or the sociological study of religion.

The recurrently literal readings of texts such as the book of **Revelation** – especially those popular in the second century CE and the later Middle Ages – never found as much favour within the traditions of the mainstream churches as they did in more radical movements. The mainstream tendency was to stress the allegorical rather than the literal meaning of the text. In such allegorical interpretation the Millennium symbolises the temporal lifespan of the church throughout those ages (as many as there may be) which last from the resurrection of Christ to the **Last Judgement**. So the descriptions of a **Second Coming** and the Millennium, no longer taken literally or as a prophetic projection, are to be regarded as metaphorical variations on a theme, conveying the same spiritual truth.

For a particular kind of reader this avoids controversies and lets them off any apparently Biblical commitment to **premillennialism** (the doctrine that Christ's return will mark the beginning of the Millennium). Ironically, other types of literary-critical reading, applied to these texts in Revelation, can yield different results. One theory, which had wide appeal in the first half of the twentieth century, saw those texts as damaged and corrupted, for example by the pages being jumbled and reassembled in the wrong order. This made it the responsibility of the commentator, as in the classic two-volume commentary on Revelation by R.H. Charles,[1] to reconstruct the text so that the events occurred more consistently and in the correct order. The texts as they stand provide a series of snapshots for the theological album, which can be reassembled in any preferred order on the album pages. However, to achieve this result the commentator must employ not only the corrupted text but also his preconceived ideas as to what constitutes the correct order. Thus a premillennialist text can become an example of **postmillennialism** (the doctrine that the Millennium culminates with the return of Christ), or vice versa.

It is possible to suggest that what these texts actually represent is a more haphazard and uncoordinated set of impressions of this religious experience of the end of time. As such they have permitted (or even encouraged) throughout history the diversity of theories that are examined here. It would only be by the application of our own subjective instincts and preconceived ideas that they could allow us to declare prophetically that one theory is right and all the rest must be wrong. However, even now there are groups of believers who wait for an imminent verification of their prophecies, and at the time of writing, in 2007, the Christian church in Ethiopia is celebrating (according to their calculations) the end of two millennia since Christ's birth.

I

INTRODUCTION

But this I know, the skies will thrill with rapture,
And myriad, myriad human voices sing.
And earth to heaven, and heaven to earth, will answer:
'At last the Saviour, Saviour of the world, is King.'[1]

Scrupulous accuracy and attention to detail is properly regarded as the hallmark of good, academic scholarship. It has also been the hallmark of those who avidly searched the Bible for detailed information about God's plans for the future of this world, for good or ill. Among such information, the idea of the millennial **Kingdom of God** has probably attracted the greatest fascination among the widest variety of intellects. This topic is the subject of the present volume.

Millenarianism is a term that can be applied loosely or strictly. Use of the word in a looser sense is not necessarily to be discouraged or regarded as unhelpful, because this can at least serve to focus attention on the wider relevance of what can be – at its narrowest – an extreme position. For our purposes, looking at a short history of Christian millenarianism, the term has two principal dimensions: one is a rather literal view of the future of the world as it approaches the **Apocalypse**; the other is a sociological usage widely applied to sects (by a process of extension from the characterisation of early Christian groups that were dominated by Biblical prophecies).

The tightest definition of millenarianism applies to numerous small, often sectarian, groups throughout Christian history. These groups are often called 'chiliastic' because of their preoccupation with the thousand (Greek: *chilioi*) years of Christ's reign. They concentrate on the literal realisation of the end of the world, where Biblical prophecies are to be fulfilled within the immediately projected future of the group.

However, the definition of millenarianism can also be extended to refer to any future-dominated or eschatological belief that is cast in literal and material terms. This is to generalise away from the particular beliefs of specific chiliastic sects. In this sense, literal readings of apocalyptic ideas are to be compared and contrasted with other ways of seeing the future: for example, either with the allegorising of future hope into moral and spiritual truths, or the conviction that a new world has already been realised in the present as a result of the resurrection of Christ. Taken as one element of Christian doctrine among many others, futurist kinds of belief are valuable in emphasising the incompleteness or unsatisfactory nature of the present state of things. The extremist position emerges when the futurist view takes over the whole ground. An uncompromisingly literal 'vision' of the Biblical future, often coupled with a rigorist view of ethics, in the face of the Last Judgement, can dominate people's lives totally and even determine the affairs of nations.

The main Biblical text that sets the programme for the millennial Kingdom, the reign of Christ with the saints for a thousand years, is Revelation 20.2–7. Although a long period, this thousand years is conceived as an interim time during which Satan is imprisoned and those who have a share in the resurrection of Christ also fulfil a priestly kind of ministry. It resembles an earthly triumph and vindication of the deaths of both Christ himself and the Christian martyrs. The traditional doctrines of Roman Catholicism consider it an error to concentrate on the literal period of one thousand years for this earthly Kingdom, rather seeing it as a symbol for the prolonged but indefinite time of the church (the interval between the resurrection of Christ and the Last Judgement).

Whilst only a small part of the wider content of the book of Revelation, these visions of the end have given rise to much speculative rearrangement. It is no surprise that there is disagreement on the literal nature of the Millennium, or its temporal relationship to the Second Coming of Christ. For some, who follow closely the order of the events described in Revelation, the Second Coming of Christ (19.11–16) precedes the Millennium, and the last events are established by divine cataclysm. For others, who associate the Second Coming only with the Last Judgement (20.11–15), the Millennium must come first; for them this earthly reign of the Christian saints is the climax, and yet the natural outcome, of the gradual but sustained activity of the church in the world.

Both these interpretations of the book of Revelation have been widely influential through the centuries. They may be labelled 'premillennialist' and 'postmillennialist' respectively, according to whether the Second Coming is believed to occur before or after the Millennium. In this way Christians have assumed the structure of the Jewish dream as recounted in Daniel 7, a dream of two ages (this age and the age to come), which occur either side of the coming of a mysterious but glorious figure called a 'son of man' and, simultaneously, the point at which the saints are to receive the Kingdom (Dan. 7.18). So the Millennium can face both ways: it is a divine vindication demonstrated on earth and also an earthly anticipation of heavenly conditions. In the book of Daniel, however, it does seem that the Kingdom of the Saints is God's final word, and not an interim situation.

Thoughts about the Millennium are inspired by, but not confined to, the book of Revelation. All kinds of Biblical material are employed (as well as other related ideas from non-Biblical sources, such as the Sibylline Oracles) to elaborate the picture and apply it to a wide variety of practical circumstances. The principal traditions come from Jewish and Christian apocalyptic texts (of which Daniel and Revelation are the only representatives within the Biblical canon) and the prophetic books of the Old Testament contribute visions of a new Eden and paradise regained. The words of Jesus, from such Gospel texts as Mark 9.1 ('Truly I tell you, there are some standing here who will not taste death until they see that the kingdom of God has come with power'), add both authority and a sense of urgency. The text of 2 Peter 3.8 ('But do not ignore this one fact, beloved, that with the

Lord one day is like a thousand years, and a thousand years are like one day') must also be relevant, if only for the specific reference to 'a thousand years'. In its context this text might be seen as revisionist, offering an explanation for the delay in Christ's return, but it also shows (such is the flexibility in Christian interpretation) that the doctrine of the Second Coming is non-falsifiable by anything short of a global catastrophe.

The key figure for any millenarian group has been the **messianic leader** or **charismatic** prophet. He claimed to be the awaited **Messiah**, or anointed one, who was often thought to be a warlike saviour (as in the Sibylline tradition), or the forerunner who prophesied the imminent return of Christ. Usually the prophet would claim to have received a special revelation. He therefore exercised a creative role for the group, assembling the traditional prophecies and interpreting them for application to the group's immediate situation. He was often a priest from a mainstream church who was overwhelmed with apocalyptic fervour and thereby set himself apart, or who exploited others in his disillusionment with conventional attitudes. Such a charismatic person typically becomes the focus for a group of people in high tension or undergoing traumatic change.

An early example of such a prophetic figure was Montanus, who was responsible for a revival of apocalyptic ideas in second-century Christianity. In 156 CE in Phrygia (Asia Minor) he claimed to be the incarnation of the Holy Spirit, who the Bible says will reveal the things to come (see John 16.13). The book of Revelation (especially the letter to the church in Philadelphia in Rev. 3.7–13) was a major influence on the birth of the movement called Montanism in this region. Montanism did not remain a local cult, however: it spread widely under the pressures of persecution. It became a threat to the established church authorities, whose rather static view was confronted by a prospect of immediate change. The eminent Christian theologian Tertullian was converted to its apocalyptic literalism and rigorist ethics. He described a vision of a walled city in the morning sky of Judaea, heralding the descent of the New Jerusalem.

Jewish and Christian apocalypses use a schematic view of history to calculate the calendar and to focus attention on the imminent events of this world's end. In the same spirit, later generations (instead of discarding once-failed prophecies) reuse the apocalyptic traditions to provide a once-for-all interpretation of the current crisis. A highly sophisticated example of this is provided by Joachim of Fiore (1145–1202 CE) who claimed prophetic inspiration, in the form of a key to interpret the Bible, as providing a pattern of world history. In his view, a genealogy as symbolic and structured as that to be found in St Matthew's Gospel (1.1–17) shows the generations of the world as apparently grouped into three ages, each presided over by a member of the Trinity. After the ages of Law (the Father) and the Gospel (the Son), the world was awaiting the imminent age of the Holy Spirit. Saint Benedict and the new monastic orders were seen as 'midwives' for the birth of this new age, which was expected early in the thirteenth century.

With the emergence of the Franciscan orders, some friars appropriated this prophecy to themselves as 'Spirituals'. Whether for Joachim or the Franciscan friars, this view of the coming third age was at odds with the received (Augustinian) tradition that the Kingdom of God is represented by the present church on earth. Resistance to these established structures could lead to revolution and to explicit antinomianism (the notion that Christians are released by grace from an obligation to observe the moral law) – even to the 'sanctification of sin' among the Brethren of the Free Spirit, the lay Christian movement of the thirteenth and fourteenth centuries. Nevertheless the language of the third age long survived, in a different if equally revolutionary form: the German 'Third Reich' was set to last for a thousand years.

The revolutionary aspect of millenarianism seems to be one of its most consistent features for groups who are variously motivated to change the world. It can be a social struggle, or a peasants' revolt – but with cosmic aims. The use of apocalyptic language ensures that the struggle is not for limited objectives, but rather that it claims 'uniqueness' in the endeavour to transform the world. The upheaval in which such groups are engaged is often held to be the apocalyptic battle of **Armageddon** (see Rev. 16.16): that is, the ultimate purification of society. Clearly, this is a mechanism of protest for people unsure of their place in existing society, or with no other means to express grievances. These uprisings are often provoked at a time of national crisis or a terrifying natural disaster (such as during the Black Death). Alternatively, they may be a 'protestant' reaction to the luxury or laxity of the church, characterised by a drive for rigorous asceticism.

The long history of millenarian 'happenings' is echoed today in revolutionary movements, especially in developing countries (or what is often referred to, rather patronisingly, as the Third World). There the impact and consequences of modern colonialism (the culture and supposedly superior 'civilisation' of the Western world) are either welcomed as salvation or, more likely, rejected with every means that a primitive (or even preliterate) tribe can command. Such millennial movements may be expressions of **cargo cults**, they may rely on trance-inducing drugs, or may perhaps relate to vestiges of Judaeo-Christian traditions left by missionaries.

The common feature is a dissatisfaction with the current order of things, which in many cases develops as a result of cross-culture contact. Threatened or tantalised groups seek powerful religious remedies for their helplessness. (Similarly, increasing use of apocalyptic rhetoric in modern political utterances during party conferences or election campaigns may simply be a feature of fashionable 'spin', but it may inadvertently reveal a growing consciousness of being disadvantaged or marginalised.) However, revolutionary millenarianism is not always a protest of the impoverished and the lower classes. Often the prophetic leader, who creates the group's faith, will come from the educated elite. And some groups, like the Franciscans who were influenced by Joachim, were people from the wealthy classes who voluntarily embraced poverty for the sake of spiritual mysticism.

Edward Irving (1792–1834 CE) was a Church of Scotland minister with a fashionable London congregation. From 1825 he was engrossed in studying the prophecies of the book of Revelation as applied to the years after the French Revolution. (At this time there was an upsurge of literary and artistic interest in the themes of Romantic millenarianism.) Irving preached that the climactic seventh bowl (Rev. 16.17) was about to be poured. The Irvingites are a good example of a middle-class, and more intellectual, involvement in popular millenarian revival. They 'rapidly developed gifts of prophesyings, glossolalia, spiritual healing, automatic writing and telepathy'.[2] When Irving was expelled from the church, the group met at the Owenite socialist headquarters (one might say that clearly the group was no longer acceptable in the eyes of the world!), before they formed the Catholic Apostolic Church.

The complex of millenarian phenomena over the centuries can be explained in various ways. The social factors relating to the emergence of an insecure group on the margins of society and the historical reasons of a time of crisis (such as the Age of Revolution in the latter half of the eighteenth century and the Napoleonic Wars) can be supplemented by psychological explanations. Sectarian movements can have a desperate and paranoid nature: there is a leader (who is sure that he is right, offers present religious experiences and promises future bliss); an enemy (society, the establishment, anyone who does not subscribe to the doctrine as promulgated) who can be labelled as the **Antichrist**; and a group of followers who (because of circumstances or their own psychology) are so disadvantaged or insecure as to need to be attached to such a leader. There can also be a positive theological explanation for the appeal of millenarian beliefs, in that they analyse the contemporary situation in terms of Biblical revelation and seem to account for the present state of the world.

Social anthropological study of modern millenarian groups has shown how resilient they are to the apparent failure of their specific prophecies relating to the Second Coming. This cognitive dissonance, which might be expected to lead to the group's disintegration, is often apparently overcome by a revised form of the message, with antinomianism and increased missionary activity in compensation.

The millenarianism that depends on a certain particular reading and interpretation of the Bible might itself be used as an analogy to explain the existence of the New Testament and the rise of Christianity. Thus for a theory such as John G. Gager's,[3] the wheel has turned full-circle: the early church engaged in a vigorous mission because the belief in Jesus as Messiah was disconfirmed by his death and the eschatological hopes of his return were unfulfilled. However, the problem is that Gager's analogy is very general, while his millenarian model is based on very precise data. It would be necessary to establish that the early Christians were (as a social category) proletarian poor and that Jesus clearly perceived his fate and finely calculated the date of his return for the theory of cognitive dissonance to apply. It is not just the mission of Jesus' followers that needs to be explained, but the whole context of realistic future hope which underpins Christianity and its many millenarian offshoots.

* * *

Although the focus of the present book is on movements within Christianity, it could be illuminating to consider briefly, as a comparison within religious studies, a possible analogy from within another religious tradition such as Islam:

> Both Sunnis and Shias shared the belief that at the end of days a messiah-figure known as the *Mahdi*, or the 'expected one', would come to the rescue of Islam. He would return to Mecca at the head of all the forces of righteousness to take on the forces of evil in one final, apocalyptic battle, after which he and the lesser prophet Jesus would proceed to Jerusalem to kill the devil. Thereafter the world would submit to his rule until the sounding of the last trumpet, and Judgement Day.[4]

Sunnis and Shias differ in the view they take of the origins of the Mahdi. The Shias regard him as the twelfth and final imam of early Islam. They believe that this twelfth imam, unlike those before him, had neither died nor gone to heaven, but had disappeared from human sight and had become the 'Hidden Imam'. It was thought that he was concealed in some mountain cave, to wait until he should be summoned by the righteous: then he would reappear as the 'great king' in order to lead the faithful to victory.

Muslim India blurred these and other distinctions in Islam, and a quintessential Shia belief became entrenched in Sunni beliefs in India. In the mid-sixteenth century a Sunni mullah proclaimed himself as the Mahdi. His followers, the Mahdawis, were not discouraged by his early death. However, the violence endemic in their cult caused it to be condemned officially as a heresy.

Nevertheless the belief in a messiah figure who would appear from the mountains to the west as the King of the West took hold among all sections of the Muslim community in India, becoming increasingly popular as Muslim power there waned.[5]

The modern parallel might be Osama bin Laden, whom Charles Allen describes as

> idealist and romantic, and perhaps harbouring apocalyptic visions of martyrdom, a Wahhabi Arab at heart but fully conscious of Islam's ache for a Mahdi, well aware that already he was adored by his 'Arabs' and by many Afghans and Pathans as the personification of Islamic resistance to Western imperialism.[6]

* * *

The tendency of sociological and psychological theorists on millenarianism is reductionist, arguing for a universal comparability and a single explanation of the phenomena instanced in historical and modern examples. Anthony Stevens and John Price emphasise, from their perspective of evolutionary psychology, a broad congruence in the behaviour of charismatic prophets and those whom the world terms 'mad'.[7] In contrast Albert I. Baumgarten stresses the diversity of millenarian experience, so that any millennial movements must be characterised by their individual nature, by their perception of time, and by the ways in which these groups confront inevitable disappointments and then return to 'normal' time. He acknowledges 'that there is no single standard millenarian vision in Judaism, Christianity or any other major religious tradition as one of the hallmarks of contemporary research on the topic'.[8]

Different disciplinary approaches are adopted, therefore, in order to analyse millennial movements from the three Abrahamic faiths, as well as those from the East. Only then is it possible, with specific data established, to offer comparative views of the phenomena and appropriate theoretical reflection. Accordingly, in the interests of such comparative study of religious phenomena, Baumgarten outlines four stages in the life of a typical millennial group. He labels these: arousal; a search for the signs of the times; 'upping the ante'; and disconfirmation and its aftermath. Baumgarten insists that the millenarian phenomena take a variety of forms, and are found (in social terms) not only among the dispossessed, but also in triumphalist and elitist versions.[9]

The first stage of 'arousal' occurs when the millennial message attracts a responsive audience rather than disdain. There is a process of mutual validation between the messenger (the charismatic prophet) and the community group that accepts the message as authoritative. People whose place in life has undergone some form of drastic change are usually interested in a message that speaks of cosmic change, so that the anomalies of their present situation can be resolved.

In the second stage, the 'search for the signs of the times', there is search for confirmation of the millennial message in a variety of contexts (in particular events, or a chronological sequence, and in interpreting the Biblical texts). 'Triangulation' (to use a metaphor from map-making) is desired; confirmation of the millenarian position is sought from many different lines of argument. There is obvious awareness of earlier disappointments, where hopes have been dashed, so it is necessary to confront criticisms and find assurance that now it is 'for real'.

Baumgarten uses a gambling metaphor to describe the third stage as 'upping the ante'. To remain in the game one must increase the wager – so members of the group are forced to accept an increased risk. There are social implications in such a joint acceptance of the risk: apostates must be removed from the group, and 'floaters' and 'freeloaders' must be confirmed in their commitments or ejected. There may be a fresh commitment to violence, revolution or criminal involvement (illustrating the antinomian aspects of many millenarian movements). Increased pressures of this kind may be a way of responding to small-scale events that seemed like disconfirmations of the original message. The group thus reasserts commitment to what otherwise would seem the rather elusive promises of their leaders. All are thereby assured that the sequence of millennial time is still effective, and the desired outcomes appear realistic.

The fourth and final stage is that of 'disconfirmation and its aftermath'. This negative conclusion is one which the group member, the 'insider', avoids by reinterpretation. By such means what appears to the 'outsider' as disconfirmation can become for the insider an important mark of truth, since such setbacks are only to be expected. It is important to note that Festinger's exposition of the theory of cognitive dissonance (as outlined in his book *When Prophecy Fails*[10]) is more accurate as a reflection of the perspective naturally expected by the outsider.[11] The experienced pleasures of living in millennial time are not so easily relinquished. If ultimately the disillusionment becomes decisive, the individuals or the group as a whole will need a process of transformation in order for them to re-enter 'normal time'. There may even be socially creative outcomes from the experience, if constructive changes can now be made to the problematic situation, the 'bad old world' from which they had originally sought to escape. In this way the dreams of a new heaven can come to shape normal time.

This study follows a suitable interval proceeding a major turning point in our calendar, the inauguration of a new Millennium (whether it is dated in the year 2000 or 2001). The media reported avidly on a variety of group expectations in the period prior to the new Millennium. Particularly one might cite the expectation of trouble from extremist Christian sects who would seek to reach Jerusalem by the promised time, and the counter moves adopted by Israeli government security. As students of these phenomena, we now have an excellent opportunity to look at these millennial expectations of our own time and to see the extent to which these particular hopes were confirmed or disappointed by actual events.

The approach of this book is broadly chronological, ranging from the Biblical periods to the start of the twenty-first century. The examples chosen should be regarded not as constituting a completely comprehensive or encyclopaedic portrait of millenarian thinking (which would be impossible to achieve in one volume), but rather as stepping-stones to take the reader across the wilder marshland of Christian history. The emphasis falls within the varieties of the Christian tradition and, because of the limitations of space, it is only possible to notice in passing the intriguing comparisons with other religions such as Judaism and Islam.

As stepping-stones the significant stages of the millennia and half-millennia demand attention, so there are chapters on the years 1000, 1500 and 2000 CE. Beyond these milestones, the aim has been to select the widest variety of examples, revealing different millenarian preoccupations. These range from questions of place (the New Jerusalem, utopias and the Holy Land) and of the building of the Kingdom of God (quite literally in the case of Jezreel's Tower), to calculations of time in the eras of Christian history in order to predict and determine the End, and to considerations of leadership figures (such as Shiloh in Joanna Southcott's pregnancy, and the Messiah of Jonestown or of Waco).

My hope is that students of Christian history, Biblical studies and apocalyptic thinking will find in this overview a useful starting-point and a platform from which to pursue further study in the directions of their choice. With this overtly pedagogical aim in mind, the book is supplemented with a glossary explaining those concepts and theological ideas referred to in the text that might otherwise seem obscure or unfamiliar to readers coming to the subject for the first time.

II

THE ROOTS OF THE IDEA

My father awaited with anxious hope 'the coming of the Lord', an event he still frequently believed to be imminent. He would calculate, by reference to the prophecies of the Old and New Testaments, the exact date of this event; the date would pass without the expected Advent, and he would be more than disappointed – he would be incensed. Then he would understand that he must have made some slight error in calculation, and the pleasures of anticipation would recommence.

Edmund Gosse, *Father and Son*[1]

I f we investigate the roots of such a deeply felt and passionately expressed motive of apocalyptic speculation, we may well find some kind of natural explanation, or at least an analogy in the natural order of things. An illuminating text is found in the New Testament letter of James (see 5.7–8):

> Be patient, therefore, beloved, until the coming of the Lord. The farmer waits for the precious crop from the earth, being patient with it until it receives the early and the late rains. You also must be patient. Strengthen your hearts, for the coming of the Lord is near.

Few of those who do not rely on subsistence farming for their survival appreciate the full intensity, and the tremendous amount of patience, involved in this waiting for the arrival of the rains; it is an integral relationship between the human being and the weather. In Denis Baly's words:

The Palestinian longs for the rain with an intensity which cannot be put into words, and when 'there is no rain on the land, the farmers are ashamed, they cover their heads' (Jer. 14.4). Even 'the poor of the earth' who 'lie all night naked, without clothing, and have no covering in the cold' (Job 24.4, 7), stand shivering in the pitiless downpour, repeating again and again, 'Thank God for the rains! Thank God for the rain!' so thoroughly has it been drummed into their thinking that without the rain they die.[2]

So the natural order of human experience in the created world may well provide some explanation of (or at least an analogy to) the climactic expectation of a millennial hope. One can see a parallel in the yearning for the monsoon rains in the Indian subcontinent. In our search for the roots of the millennial idea, it seems a comparatively small step from this natural expectation to a more structured scheme of time, and therefore of a time of waiting.

The notion of the thousand years may depend upon a way of interpreting the seven days of Creation within Jewish thought. The opening chapter of Genesis, with its account of the timescale of Creation, is structured in terms of the days of the week, perhaps influenced originally by the Babylonian calendar and refined in accordance with Jewish temple liturgy. Creation (or the 'first things') then becomes a model for the expectation of the End (the 'last things') in a cyclic world view. The days of Creation are taken by some as a forecast of a cosmic World Week of history, within which each day is calculated to represent a thousand years. The climax of this scheme must therefore come on the Sabbath, or seventh age. As Jack Fruchtman suggests, 'The idea of a millennium is at least as old as the ancient Hebrews who envisioned a coming age of messianic perfection that was to sweep away all earthly problems, although not necessarily the earth itself.'[3]

In Jewish thinking about the future hope, this age is assimilated to the expected reign in this world of the Messiah (or anointed King, the descendant of David) as foretold by the Old Testament prophets. The original Jewish thinking on this subject concentrated on the establishment of an age of blessing in this world; the reason simply being that there was, at that point, no concept or expectation of either resurrection or an afterlife. In later Jewish thought, once ideas of a state beyond time had developed, it was possible for Jewish commentators to envisage the Millennium as an anticipatory period of fruitfulness and peace, to take place in the interim before world history itself came to an end.

Consider, as examples of this later thought:

> For my son the Messiah shall be revealed with those who are with him, and those who remain shall rejoice four hundred years [or thirty, or one thousand years]. And after these years my son the Messiah shall die, and all who draw human breath. And the world shall be turned back to primeval silence for seven days, as it was at the first beginnings; so that no one shall be left. (4 Ezra 7.28–30)

and a quotation from the Talmud:

> The world is to exist for 6000 years.
> The first 2000 are to be void.
> The next 2000 are the period of the Torah.
> And the following 2000 are the period of the Messiah.
> (Babylonian Talmud, *Avodah Zara* 9A)

QUESTIONS ABOUT THE CALCULATION OF TIME

Until now we have not mentioned the fundamental question of how time is calculated, and there is a serious danger that we shall assume the temporal perspective as a given amid our excitement about the interpretation and classification of Biblical and historical data. Most of the time we take the presence of a timescale and the accuracy of time-keeping for granted. At the forefront of modern technology is the atomic clock; such timekeeping devices are regulated by the periodic processes that occur regularly in atoms. Hydrogen maser clocks (based on radiation from hydrogen atoms) are among the most accurate; such a clock is estimated to lose one second in a time span of 1.7 million years. Such technology provides for the future regulation (and correction) of domestic clocks by means of radio signals communicated from a central point of reference and control. Small wonder then that the calculation of time is taken for granted.

Just as previous ages could not come near to this level of accuracy in the measurement of time, so also there is great discrepancy in the way time has been conceived historically, when compared with modern, self-confident assumptions. Philosophers in the ancient world were very interested in time, not least because of the conceptual problems concerned with the creation of the world and the measuring of its development. Philo of Alexandria, for example, classified the existing schools of philosophy into three categories:

- the world is created and is subject to decay (Epicureans and Stoics)
- the world is uncreated and not subject to decay (Aristotle)
- the world is created and not subject to decay (Plato, Hesiod, Moses).

The triumph of this particular analysis is the parallel that is drawn between the influential Greek philosophy of Plato and the authoritative traditions of the Jews found in Genesis and attributed to Moses as the spokesman for God. Equally attributed to Moses is the idea, fundamental to the first chapter of Genesis, of the measurement of the world's creation and of subsequent time in terms of night and day, moon and sun, and the ensuing seasons and years.

From the Christian perspective, a most significant advance came with the coordination of time measured in terms of salvation history from the birth of Jesus Christ (as recorded in the annals of the Roman Empire). St Luke's Gospel (at the start of chapter 3) and his Acts of the Apostles indicate his intention to relate the events of Christ and his Church to the context of the Roman Empire. Roman administration measured time from the foundation of the city of Rome, or by the years spent under the control of particular emperors or client kings, or by the annual appointment of civic officers or provincial governors by the Senate. It was only with the Emperor Constantine in the third century CE, when the Roman world became Christian, that a connection could really be made between political and religious scales of measurement.

For a long time Christian history and classical history had little in common, and classical history remained a pagan preserve. Christians, on the other hand, did concern themselves with a particular sequence of historical events: those associated with Jesus of Nazareth. However, new converts from paganism did not really know how or where the history of Jesus fitted in with the history they had learnt at school. Comparative frameworks of dates were of some limited help. A significantly new order of historical activity came into being with the tradition of Church history, developed by Eusebius of Caesarea (*c.*260–*c.*340 CE) in the eastern half of the Empire. He begins his *Ecclesiastical History* with this plan of the project:

> The chief matters to be dealt with in this work are the following: the lines of succession from the holy apostles, and the periods that have elapsed from our Saviour's time to our own; the many important events recorded in the story of the Church...[4]

It is rightly observed that the original works of Luke's Gospel and Acts had 'antiquated the apologetically intentioned portrayals of church history in the second century even before they appeared' and 'drew the author of Acts intellectually closer to Eusebius' in the fourth century.[5] Eusebius explains that Christ was 'the living Word...; before anything was created and fashioned ... He was the first and only begotten of God.' Nonetheless Eusebius begins his history,

> with the appearance of our Saviour in the flesh ... It was the 42nd year of Augustus's reign, and the 28th after the subjugation of Egypt and the deaths of Anthony and Cleopatra, the last of the Ptolemaic rulers of Egypt, when our Saviour and Lord, Jesus Christ, at the time of the first registration, when Quirinius was governor of Syria ... was born in Bethlehem, in Judaea.[6]

One further step was needed, beyond the design of Eusebius' history, orientated upon the Church. In the fifth century Augustine, bishop of Hippo in North Africa, became conscious of the need for a new kind of Christian historical apologetic, where Christians and pagans could meet on common ground. He therefore commissioned from Orosius his *Seven Books of Histories Against the Pagans*. Augustine's own thinking on the subject of time is reflected in his *City of God*, in which he states that 'the world was in fact made with time, if at the time of its creation change and motion came into existence' (Book XI, chapter 4). Rejecting the cyclical theories of recurrence that he associated with ancient Greek philosophers, he saw a single, linear progress in time, anchored in the historical event of Christ's Incarnation, and proceeding to an ultimate point of 'eternal felicity'.

It is scarcely surprising that in the century after Augustine, an unassuming monk from Scythia, styled as Dionysius Exiguus, was responsible for inventing the dating system for the 'Christian era' (known as AD or *Anno Domini*). It happened because he was called upon to construct a new Easter cycle. To do so he abandoned the Era of Diocletian (the Era of Martyrs, reckoned from the year of Emperor Diocletian's accession in 284 and still observed in the Coptic Church) and accepted (erroneously) the date of 753 AUC (*Ab Urbe Condita* – years after the foundation of Rome) for the date of the Incarnation. His dating system for the Christian era was accepted for England by the Synod of Whitby in the year 664 (according to that system) and is still in use. A more secular age has retained the system of calculation, but relabelled AD as CE for reasons of historical neutrality or political correctness. One can still interpret the abbreviation as 'Christian Era' rather than 'Common Era' if preferred.

The Biblical ideas of time – the past, the future and eternity – can be quite different from those expressed in secular thought. Philosophers can speak of time as the dimension of change, where change happens, and as a fourth dimension alongside the three dimensions of space. But is the language of temporal change more than a metaphor, especially when the theory of relativity might seem to deny the notion of an absolute 'now', and instead claim that distinctions between past and future are only subjective? There is a long-standing tradition, going back to Parmenides and Zeno, which adopts a 'static' view of time, in which temporal change is regarded as an illusion. By contrast there is an alternative tradition, a 'dynamic' view of time, going back to Aristotle and ultimately to Heraclitus, in which the future lacks the reality of past and present, although reality is added with the passage of time. In both these contexts any statements about the future are therefore not determinately true or false.

Lines of argument about the future tend to be of four distinct kinds. There is the Doomsday argument, which declares that our future will be brief. Second, there is the argument focussed upon the Omega Point, namely that the future will be long and ultimately triumphant. Third, there is the cyclical view of recurrence in a continuous loop of time. Fourth, there is the view that can be called loosely the 'Platonist Argument' – that future ages are no closer to ideal perfection than any other, and 'all such stories are only metaphors for present-day experiences and desires'.[7]

The Doomsday scenario can be illustrated by a quotation from Robert Browning's poem 'Christmas Eve and Easter Day':

> A final belch of fire like blood,
> Overbroke all heaven in one flood
> Of doom. Then fire was sky, and sky
> Fire, and both, one brief ecstasy,
> Then ashes. But I heard no noise
> (Whatever was) because a Voice
> Beside me spoke thus, 'Life is done,
> Time ends, Eternity's begun
> And thou art judged for evermore.'

What remains open to interpretation is the extent to which this doomsday is described literally as an ultimate event, or whether it is intended as a nightmare allegory of life with ethical implications for the present.

Zoe Oldenbourg captured the prevailing attitude of the Middle Ages to such ultimate issues, particularly at the time of the Crusades, in this vivid extract from her novel *The Corner-Stone*:

> The blinded man's head was full of Brother Humbert's words concerning the end of the world. He told himself that since, after all, nobody knew the day nor the hour, it could just as well happen immediately. An immense cross would appear, spanning the heavens like a flash of lightning from orient to occident. But would he be able to see it? He could not but believe that he would, since even the dead were to see it and quit their graves. He thought that he would have wished, when the time came, to be in Acre graveyard, near the tomb of his son.

And it seemed to him that it would be happiness far surpassing all earthly joys to see God himself appear with His Cross in the heavens. Maybe I shall die first. But the dead, too, will see it.[8]

The twentieth-century's development of the nuclear deterrent brought about an insight, closer to realism than nightmare, of what the End might look like in the form of a 'nuclear winter' and the annihilation of all sentient life. Some lines from A.C. Swinburne's 'The Garden of Proserpine' anticipate this poetically:

Then star nor sun shall waken,
Nor any change of light:
Nor sound of waters shaken,
Nor any sound or sight:
Nor wintry leaves nor vernal,
Nor days nor things diurnal;
Only the sleep eternal
In an eternal night.

This can be compared with words from a novel written in 1805, entitled *The Last Man*:

[The Last Man will] behold the plains and mountains stripped of verdure, dry and barren like a rock; the trees in decay and covered with a whitish bark; the sun, whose fire was grown dim, casting on every object a livid and gloomy light; … the earth had undergone the common destiny. After having for ages struggled against the efforts of time and men, who had exhausted it, she bore the melancholy features of decay.[9]

Words that began as poetic metaphor or as science fiction may take on reality in the face of issues such as actual and threatened genocide, terrorism and the mass-destruction of the planet.

A much more optimistic perspective is provided by the idea of progress toward an ultimate Omega Point – a time when all powers and intelligences come together in a conclusive synthesis. Not all such prospects, enhanced as they may be by projections from Darwinian evolution, are necessarily theological. But there may be a foundation text in St Paul's first letter to the church at Corinth:

For God has put all things in subjection under his feet ... When all things are subjected to him, then the Son himself will also be subjected to the one who put all things in subjection under him, so that God may be all in all.' (1 Cor. 15.27–8)

The argument of the Omega Point can be represented by Teilhard de Chardin's work *The Phenomenon of Man* (1955), which is a classic attempt to incorporate the theory of evolution into a constructive religious world view, tending towards the ultimate Omega Point:

Because it contains and engenders consciousness, space–time is necessarily *of a convergent nature*. Accordingly its enormous layers, followed in the right direction, must somewhere ahead become involuted to a point which we might call *Omega*, which fuses and consumes them integrally in itself ... It is therefore a mistake to look for the extension of our being or of the noosphere in the Impersonal. The Future-Universal could not be anything else but the Hyper-Personal – at the Omega Point.[10]

In the context of religious fiction, C.S. Lewis sketched something similar:

And for us this is the end of all the stories, and we can most truly say that they all lived happily ever after. But for them it was only the beginning of the real story. All their life in the world and all their adventures in Narnia had only been the cover and the title page: now at last they were beginning Chapter One of the Great Story which no one on earth has read: which goes on for ever: in which every chapter is better than the one before.[11]

The third option is the cyclical view of recurrence. Although it might seem to be most at home within ideas of reincarnation, developed in the context of Indian religion, there is also a basis in ancient Greek philosophy (among the pre-Socratics) and, most significantly of all, it can be seen as a broad presupposition of the Biblical view of the relationship between End and Beginning, Creation and Re-creation. Early Christians inherited from Judaism the belief that history would come to a climax with the renewal of the world, envisaged in terms of the raw materials of the creation myth. In the historical life of Jesus there was a climactic event of history and a summing up of the significance of Israel's mythology and cultic practice. The understandings that developed of the role of Christ emphasised the claim that with him the new creation had begun (2 Cor. 5.17).

The mythological complex centred on Creation includes reference to divine agencies in creation (such as Word and Wisdom), stories of Adam and Eve as the first human pair, and the use of cosmological models such as Jerusalem and the tower of Babel to describe the world inhabited by men and deities. Early Christian thought reflects this in referring to the divine Word (*Logos*); describing Christ's work as that of the Second Adam; referring to Jerusalem in cosmographical as well as geographical terms; and seeing the beginnings of the Christian church at Pentecost as the reversal of events at the tower of Babel.

The story of creation was commemorated in the traditions of worship; it was re-enacted in rituals, prefiguring in these actions the future renewal, for which Israel had longed. The cyclic view of creation depended on the cycle of nature in the seasons of the year: where this existed alongside a linear idea of history, the two schemes together were developed into an idea of eschatological re-creation. The End was envisaged as a return to the Beginning. Whether this was conceived as a sudden event or as a gradual transformation, in both cases it was a renewal of Creation, within a structure of sequential world-ages (Creation, Present and New Creation).

The fourth viewpoint is that stories about the Beginning or the End are really about present experience. In Stephen Clark's words:

> By this account, Creation and Judgement both alike are not events far off, but present experiences of eternal truth. To believe that God made the world is to live by the Covenant; to think that Christ will come to judge the living and the dead is to see ourselves in the light of his life and death.[12]

He goes on to quote from Jurgen Moltmann's *Theology of Hope*:

> The Christ event can here be understood in a wholly non-eschatological way as epiphany of the eternal present in the form of the dying and rising *Kyrios* [Lord] of the cultus.[13]

Clark does not say that Moltmann is here referring specifically to the negative effect on Paul's message as a result of contact with the Hellenistic ideas that were prevalent at Corinth. The extreme philosophical sceptic would say that talk of the futuristic world represents an 'improper' view of time, just as the view of paradise as a heavenly rather than an earthly location is an 'improper' view of space. At Corinth it would have been on the grounds that all of these religious ideas corresponded to their (misguided) view of present experience (see 1 Cor. 15.19).

Perhaps the Christian tradition of interpreting such matters that comes closest to this 'common sense' view belongs to the Quakers. Their strength is in a spiritual internalisation of their faith. The Coming of Christ is in this way applied to the spirit of each individual believer. The 'war of the Lamb' is a spiritual warfare against evil. The corollary of this in terms of international and interpersonal relations is a complete pacifism. Similarly, there are also Muslims who believe that *jihad* is an interior and not an exterior fight against evil.

One of the most noticeable, and yet surprising, features of this kind of comparison between the ways of reading 'deep time' is the ease with which one finds oneself crossing the boundaries of intellectual disciplines. So the reader should reflect on the real nature of the relationship between the languages used – the language of the mythological systems that furnish the raw materials of apocalyptic; the language of scientific studies of cosmology concerned with the beginning and ending of the universe; the language of literature and poetry, which might include the category of science fiction; and the language of philosophy, which seeks to make some sense of it all.

III

THE BIBLICAL BASIS

WHICH ARE THE PRIMARY TEXTS?

How did the earliest Christians understand the divinely given salvation in which they hoped to share? For clarity, but at some risk of oversimplification, there appeared to be two distinct options: one understanding was more intellectual and spiritual, and the other was more immediate and practical, affecting the present material world. The former is seen at its most eloquent and metaphysical in the Prologue to St John's Gospel (John 1.1–18): in the person of Christ is given a full revelation of God, who is the ultimate Truth. Salvation therefore exists in an intellectual or a spiritual knowledge of God; this includes the gift of eternal life, and all the privileges and joys of the highest spiritual illumination.

The second option, and the one more relevant to the particular concerns of this history, is the view of salvation in terms of membership of the Kingdom of God. This Kingdom is eagerly awaited; it is thought to be on the point of inauguration when Christ will return to earth in his **Parousia** or Second Coming. This reign of God represents a new order of material things, a renewal of creation. The new heaven and the new earth, whose institution is thus awaited, may be anticipated by a millennial Kingdom in which Christian disciples will share the blessings of human life under the happiest of conditions. Alternatively, another way of looking at this Millennium (or period of one thousand years) was to see this period as in itself the first stage of the new world order, the anteroom or vestibule of the new creation:

> The Christian millennialist belief centered on a future moment when time as men knew and understood it would end, and Christ would return to raise the dead and then rule over an everlasting, paradisiac kingdom. The politicization of this idea occurred early in its history when its theological elements became linked to the dual ideas of legitimacy and authority. Its roots in Christendom extended to the … Hebraic belief that the future messiah would descend from the line of King David. This belief legitimized the authority of David's successors and was readily inculcated in the later [Christian] theory of papal rule. The Christian idea was, however, [initially] apolitical, for in holding that the kingdom of Christ was 'not of this world' … the Christian-millennialist forecast a place for Christianity beyond all earthly social and political affairs.[1]

Already, in this quotation, we see the interplay between this-worldly and other-worldly concepts of God's Kingdom. Jack Frucht-man has prioritised the tradition of the Gospel of John, in drawing attention to the saying that the Kingdom is 'not of this world'. The larger quotation comes from the discussion about the ultimate source of power between Jesus and Pontius Pilate, the local representative of the Roman Empire, in John 18.36:

> Jesus answered, 'My kingdom is not from this world. If my kingdom were from this world, my followers would be fighting to keep me from being handed over to the Jews. But as it is, my kingdom is not from here.'

A particular political point is being made here: the traditions of the Kingdom of God in the other three Gospels would not be seen as so other-worldly.

How is this millennial Kingdom visualised, then, in the earliest generations of Christianity? In many instances it differed little from preceding Jewish expectations, so graphically described in the apoca-lyptic writings, which begin with the book of Daniel in the Hebrew Bible and are followed through in later Jewish apocalypses (those outside of the canon but nonetheless highly influential in Jewish thought, among Orthodox rabbis as well as among Jewish sectarians, such as the Dead Sea Scroll community at Qumran). Often only the constituents of the Kingdom have changed; instead of the people of Israel, the membership is exclusively Christian. If this clearly defined category represents those who are included, it is equally clear that the enemies of Christ (of whatever kind), and all who reject him as Lord, are to be left out. The benefits of the Kingdom are a reward for loyal service: an uninterrupted vista of joy and recreation (or re-creation). The glorious Second Coming of Christ was essentially linked to the resurrection of the dead. The Last Judgement – for Christ comes as judge – involves both the living and the dead, and the outcome of that judgement determines participation in (or exclusion from) the millennial Kingdom and whatever may follow it. In this understanding the highest importance is inevitably attached to the physically conceived idea of bodily resurrection. This idea is advocated at an early stage, and as a matter of urgency, in Paul's correspondence with the Thessalonians. They were afraid that their relations and friends who had already died since they became Christians would for this reason be excluded from any share in the messianic Kingdom. Not so, says Paul reassuringly, because all will be resurrected when the time comes. Many early Christians will have regarded this resurrection and judgement as an imminent event. The immediacy of such an expectation would have proved a reassurance in periods of trial and persecution, brought about by the enemies of the Christian communities. Such suffering must have been infinitely easier to endure, when the prospect of an imminent millennial reward provided recompense.

A typical interpretation of this chain of prophecy anchored to the book of Revelation, in terms of the patterns of world history, is the following (from an anonymous text headed 'An eye for the future' that was circulated as unsolicited mail in spring 2002):

> The 1260-year period equals 'three and a half times' (Rev. 12.6, 14; Dan. 7.25), and the word time is here used as another large unit, *years* of years (one 'time' = 360 years). In a final fulfilment the 'seven times' corresponds to 2520 years, after which the peoples of the world were to realize 'that the Most High rules over the kingdoms of men and that he gives them to whom he will' (Dan. 4.13–14

or 4.16–17). 2520 years is the period from King Nebuchadnezzar and the Neo-Babylonian Empire (when the prophecy was given) to 1948 when, after a resolution of the United Nations, the land that God gave the Israelites (Gen. 35.10–12) was restored to them and they began to return in great numbers (Isa. 11.12; Jer. 23.7–8; Ezek. 39.28; Zech. 10.9).

Some were negative to the new state and to those supporting Israel. When the 1260-year (and the 2520-year) period had passed and Israel was founded in 1948, several of its neighbours declared war. The present era of recurrent conflicts and worldwide terrorist acts started (Rev. 11.7) and has not yet come to an end (11.8–13; see also for example 9.13–21; 16.1–11; Zech. 12). One day the world is called to an extensive and decisive battle (Rev. 16.12–14) with predicted end (Rev. 19.19–21; Dan 7.11, 26, and see Rev. 2.27–28, 11.4–6, 17.14, 19.11–16; Mic. 5.1–5 or 5.2–6; and also John 14.20; 1 Cor. 12.27).

Few can fail to notice the Old Testament echoes that resonate through the chapters of the Christian Apocalypse, the book of Revelation. However, the precise origination of those echoes is by no means universally agreed; sources that have been identified (usually unilaterally, not multilaterally) include the prophecies of Isaiah, Ezekiel, Joel, Zechariah and, even more, the apocalyptic book of Daniel. For instance, during my earliest researches into Revelation, some 40 years ago, a postgraduate from the USA came to Durham to work on the use of Ezekiel's prophecies in Revelation; I read some of his thesis then, but I do not think it was ever published.

As well as the chariot vision of chapter 1 (which became the foundation of Merkabah mysticism), Ezekiel's book recorded other highly charged dramatic scenes. These visions include those of the army of dry bones, prefiguring the ideas of restoration and resurrection, in Ezekiel 37; the great climactic battle of chapters 38–9, involving the mysterious figures Gog and Magog, which invites comparison with Armageddon in Revelation 16.16; the rebuilding of the Temple in Ezekiel 40; and finally the millennial capital of Israel, featured in chapters 45 and 48, which resembles the Holy City of Revelation 21.[2] According to Ezekiel's vision of the last days (chapters 38–9) Gog of the land of Magog, chief prince of Meshech and Tubal (see also Gen. 10.2), is the enemy of Israel, against whom God will rain fire and brimstone. A similar apocalyptic scenario is presented in Revelation 20.7–8 when Satan leads Gog and Magog from the four corners of the earth against the New Jerusalem.

THE OLD TESTAMENT CONTEXT

There was a future aspect to Israel's belief throughout much of the Old Testament. This 'looking forward' is not eschatology (as it is not strictly defined by the last and ultimate things), but it is the area of thought from which eschatology is a development. However, this may run deeper than simple prophecies of the outcome of human action and state policies. Israel could believe that, while there was a brief period of innocence and bliss at the opening of history, and while also their present situation as a community or nation was of vital importance, the real climax and crown of history lay in the future. There was a firm assurance that 'the best is yet to be'. This assurance was rooted in belief in Yahweh, and was not the mere expression of human optimism. Such an element of belief can be traced back to quite an early period. In J.M.P. Smith's words:

> The development of the idea of the Day of Yahweh … was marked, not so much by the addition from time to time of new features, as by the expansion and deepening of elements already present, at least in germ, at the time of the origin of the prophetic conception.[3]

Apocalyptic literature brings this process of the development of beliefs to a head, with its remarkable growth and elaboration of the concepts of the last things (*ta eschata*).

One key concept to consider is that of the final judgement of God. This can be expressed in the terms of the book of Deuteronomy (see Deut. 28.1–68) where it is expounded by thinkers, wise after the event of the Babylonian Exile and concerned to point up its warning lessons. Realism is combined with ideal elements. In the ideal version of God's final judgement all peoples are to be subjected to the chosen nation; but in reality there is the potential of divine judgement over Israel just as much as over other peoples. This could be a neglected aspect in popular thought, which is highly resistant to self-evaluation; so in the eager anticipation of the Day of the Lord (exposed, for example, in Amos 5.18–20) the popular hope was for divine revenge upon Israel's neighbours, to pay them back for 'wrongs' done to Israel.

On the other side of the judgement was the idea of a Golden Age, fulfilling God's purpose through a reign of prosperity and peace. Here is the concept of a coming Kingdom, frequently associated with the restoration of the Davidic line of kings. It continues to be reflected today through the Jewish daily prayer (the *Shemoneh Esrei*): 'Rebuild Jerusalem soon in our days as an everlasting building, and speedily set up therein the throne of David.' In its earlier form this expectation was seen in historical and nationalistic terms, possibly with a transformation of the present world order. Within later apocalyptic texts these ideas were substantially developed, not so much as representing the end of a historical era, but the end of history itself.

The Jewish perspective on the goodness of the original Creation by God was not abandoned, although the ensuing Jewish world view was modified in terms of a pessimistic dualism. This earth, the scene of so much distress and disaster, is dominated for the time being by evil spirits under the leadership of Satan. The power of darkness makes war on the power of light. However, darkness is not eternal and static; instead darkness is transient, so the present state of affairs will come to an end and God will vindicate his kingly rule. According to the *Assumption of Moses*, 'then shall his kingdom appear throughout all his creation, and then Satan shall be no more, and sorrow shall depart with him' (10:1). In this modified dualism the course of the world is divided into two ages, this age and the age to come. The conviction is that the turning point between the ages is imminent: 'Creation is already grown old, and is already past the strength of youth' (4 Ezra 5.55).

The epochs of world history are presented as predetermined in the purposes of God (although this may not be a literal belief, but rather a metaphorical expression of the confidence of faith). See, for example: the imagery of the four metals and clay in the five-part statue of Daniel 2; the tree at the centre of the earth, symbolising the ruler's greatness in Daniel 4; the four beasts representing world empires in Daniel 7 and the future resolution in terms of the fifth Kingdom of the 'saints of the Most High' (Dan. 7.18); and finally the climax with the resurrection of the dead in Daniel 12. Much was made of these texts in the later history of interpretation, particularly by the Fifth Monarchy Men and the movement known as Dispensationalism.

The third complex of ideas concerns an intermediary figure associated with the new Kingdom of God. Where eschatological ideas are more political and nationalistic, there may be an anointed Messiah figure – not a supernatural agent of redemption, but rather a human figure who will restore the Davidic dynasty. The Messiah was by no means an essential element, for the Jewish people the real hope was vested in the kingly rule of God. In some of the texts from Qumran there is a priestly figure standing alongside the Davidic leader, but taking precedence over him. In the Song of Solomon the Messiah is a warrior-hero to restore Israel's sovereignty, but the war is decided by supernatural powers:

> For he shall not put his trust in rider and bow, nor shall he multiply for himself gold and silver for war, nor shall he set his hope upon the multitude for the day of battle. The Lord himself is his King ... All nations shall be in fear before him. (S. of S. 17.37–8)

The Jewish rabbis made the wealth of imagery within such eschatological expectation somewhat more systematic. Their view was that the function of the Messiah, and of the messianic age, was as a prelude to the new age of God. At this point the doctrine of the intermediate Kingdom was developed: it was to be ruled over by the Messiah and the saints, and it was expected to last for four hundred or, alternatively, a thousand years. Their belief is that when the new age of God finally dawns there will be no place for national kings such as the Messiah. The descriptions of this age may well include a new figure, a supernatural agent, who can bear a variety of enigmatic titles, such as 'Man', 'Primal Man' or 'Son of Man'. The figure who comes on the clouds of heaven in Daniel 7.13 is identified in context as a collective representation of 'the saints' of Israel. It is likely that Jesus himself, or the early Christians influenced by him, developed the term 'Son of Man' to apply exclusively to Jesus in the new context of Christian expectation.

TEXTS FROM THE NEW TESTAMENT

MARK 13

This chapter of Mark's Gospel appears almost self-contained, and is referred to as the 'Little Apocalypse'. It may have been formulated in response to the declared plan of the Roman Emperor Caligula (Gaius) to set up his image in the Temple in Jerusalem. This action was not carried out, after the emperor was assassinated in January 41 CE, but the very idea evoked strong echoes of the actions of the Seleucid ruler Antiochus IV Epiphanes in 167 BCE. Those earlier circumstances are reflected in the quotation from Daniel 9.27 in Mark 13.14: 'the desolating sacrilege set up where it ought not to be'.

A modern political reading of Mark's Gospel offers an interesting insight, as it emphasises the evangelist's equal opposition to both the Jews and the Roman occupiers:

> Not only does Mark disapprove of those currently in power, he condemns the desire for power, and promises a return of the resurrected Jesus. This Parousia will rearrange the present political power, and result in the destruction of all who have shamed, or been ashamed of, Jesus. Mark's apocalyptic understanding further leads him to denounce other traditional authorities like family, ethnicity and ritual regulations.

> Short of God's direct intervention, Jesus is presented by Mark as God's last, and best, attempt to call people to repentance, and to replace Satan's rule with God's Kingdom … For Mark, the suffering and death of Jesus and his followers will move God to intervene directly. Such an intervention will lead to Jesus' Parousia in authority and power, as well as human salvation.[4]

The eschatological discourse of Mark 13 in itself reflects a traditional view of the sequence of apocalyptic expectations. Events follow a preordained pattern as they build to the climax in the coming of the Son of Man figure (see Mark 13.26). However awry the world may seem to be, God is still in absolute control of the timetable (13.20). This text shows that one should expect suffering and persecution, as well as false claims associated with the coming prophet and the Messiah (13.21–22).

Timothée Colani claimed that Mark 13 represented 'a very complete summary of the apocalyptic views spread among the Jewish Christians of the first century, such as we know them by John's book [Revelation]'.[5] His conclusion was based on two features of this text: the threefold structure of expectations, and the use of three technical terms with eschatological connotations – 'birth pains' (also found at 1 Thess. 5.3); 'afflictions'; and 'end'/'climax'. These special terms function as signposts, one for each of the three proposed subdivisions of the text. Colani's analysis made use of the work of H.J. Holtzmann on the Synoptic Gospels, published in Leipzig in 1863. Holtzmann worked on the presumption of a threefold understanding of the Parousia: woes in world history and the mission of God's Kingdom (Mark 13.5–13); affliction including the destruction of Jerusalem (13.14–23); and, third, the coming of Christ (13.24–27).

I would accept the idea of a threefold structure, marked by these technical terms, but would draw the boundaries somewhat differently. In Mark's Gospel the traditional ideas are applied by the evangelist to current circumstances in his readers' experience, pointing to their real significance as 'signs of the end'. (The same thing happened in rather different ways in Luke's Gospel, in chapter 21.) The first stage of affliction includes 'wars and rumours of wars' (13.7), that is, international strife of various kinds. Natural disasters, including earthquakes and outbreaks of famine, are only the beginning of the woes or birth pains, which leads to anticipation of a full range of cosmic signs and supernatural portents heralding the appearance of the Messiah. The third and final stage is the climax when the Son of Man comes 'with great power and glory' (13.26). When the Judgement takes place, 'he will send out the angels, and gather his elect from the four winds' (13.27).

LUKE 21.7–36

Luke 21.20 introduces a new element into the picture seen in Mark's Little Apocalypse: 'When you see Jerusalem surrounded by armies, then know that its desolation has come near.' The wider prophecy has been qualified by a specific reference to the historical fact of the fall of Jerusalem to the Romans in 70 CE, following the siege in the Jewish

War. The prophetic hope concerned with the last days has not been extinguished. It has a living and strongly spiritualised relevance as part of the Christian message in Luke's day. There is still an eager and earnest expectation of the fulfilment of God's promises and the completion of the divine plan, but the urgency and the imminence have been transformed by the establishment of an extended sequence of time in which particular events of world history can (and must) be included.

1 THESSALONIANS 4.13–5.11[6]

This text reveals particular perspectives among some early Christians about the ideas of resurrection from the dead and the Second Coming of Christ. From Paul's position, for whom the end of the world was an imminent expectation, the basis of Christian hope can provide words of comfort for the Thessalonians. He seeks not so much to inform his readers as to console them, in much the same way as tombstone epitaphs are intended to encourage those left behind (see 1 Thess. 4.18). They should not grieve (4.13); talk about dying is scaled down in the Greek to the idea of 'falling asleep'.

Questions arose for the Thessalonians because a significant number of Christians had died; it seems likely that they were the casualties of mob violence, victims of social uprisings against the Christian community (as indicated in Acts 17). The problem was that nothing had happened in consequence – not even a divine thunderbolt of vengeance – and the victims might sink without trace. However, the Christian hope is in Jesus, who can be regarded as the prototype of Christian martyrs (see Rev. 1.5; 2.13). The message is that God will redeem his faithful witnesses, those who do his will, even though the whole world is disintegrating.

Paul's answer has both negative and positive aspects. Negatively, Christians should 'not grieve as others do who have no hope' (1 Thess. 4.13). In Ramsay MacMullen's words:

> In all the 'Oriental' cults ... the element of resurrection has received emphatic attention ... It should really not be taken for granted ... that people who believe a god might rise from death also believed in such a blessing for themselves as well. The conjecture needs support – and finds none.[7]

Positively, Paul refers to the shared Christian faith that 'Jesus died and rose again' (4.14). Then most relevantly he interprets this faith in the tradition of Christian prophecy (the 'word of the Lord' in 4.15) to mean that, when Christ's Second Coming takes place, the earliest Christian martyrs will first be resurrected, so that they may share with the surviving witnesses in the glorious and unending life of God (4.17; see also 1 Cor. 15.51–7).

1 Thessalonians 4.17 is the key text for the idea of the heavenly Rapture, which became increasingly popular, as will be seen, among certain evangelical groups. The context and language for this chapter's account of the Parousia or Second Coming of Christ has so far resembled that of a state visit by the ruling dignitary, when the city officials form a reception committee. Here the emphasis changes, however, as the welcoming committee are lifted bodily into the air when the visiting Lord takes the initiative: 'We who are alive, who are left, will be caught up in the clouds together with them [the dead who have been resurrected] to meet the Lord in the air; and so we will be with the Lord forever.' So the welcoming committee of survivors, greeting the return of their Lord, will not wait for him on the ground, but will be empowered to meet him halfway, on the mezzanine floor as it were.

There is, however, a widespread problem about the Parousia or return of Christ: when will it happen? (see Acts 1.6–7). Paul gently reminds the Thessalonians that his preaching had included an answer (1 Thess. 5.1–2). There is a nice irony here, for the Thessalonians know precisely ('very well') that the day of the Lord is essentially imprecise. A strong element of surprise – and unpleasant shock – is integral to the event, on analogy with the traumatic experience of being burgled in the night (compare 5.2 with Mark 13.32–7 and Rev. 3.3; 16.15). The day of the Lord has held the potential of shock since the days of Amos' prophecy (Amos 5.18: 'it is darkness and not light'). However, Paul can also reassure his watchful churches: 'as you wait for the revealing of our Lord Jesus Christ … he will also strengthen you to the end, so that you may be blameless on the day of our Lord Jesus Christ' (1 Cor. 1.7–8).

The contrast between light and darkness, day and night, is one that Paul uses again in Romans 13.11–14. In 1 Thessalonians 5.4–5 the Christian group is defined by these means, in contrast to outsiders. And in 5.8 Paul uses the metaphor of the soldier's armour, modelled on that of the Roman soldier. It is divine armour, depicted on the basis of the Old Testament image of God as a mighty warrior. As the armour of theological virtues it is God's gift for the protection of the solidarity of the group.

2 THESSALONIANS 2.1–12[8]

Time has moved on for Thessalonica: the second letter reflects a later and radically changed situation, although much of the language and themes echo the first letter. The question of Christ's Second Coming is still a critical issue. However, the argument of this section reveals two distinct ways of understanding the last things, with a vital difference concerning the timing of these events.

Some of the Thessalonians are regarded by the author of this letter as distinctly unorthodox. Perhaps because they have suffered greatly (see 1.4), they believe that the End has already come ('the day of the Lord is already here' – 2.2). According to the writer of this letter, working within the perspective charted by Paul in 1 Corinthians 15 and by the Gospel tradition of the Little Apocalypse in Mark 13, it cannot already be the End time, because other events must happen first – and they have not happened yet. What is still to happen is charted in 2.3–12.

As can also be seen in the book of Revelation, the apocalyptic expectation includes several personifications of evil powers, in various shapes and sizes. The height of blasphemy in these evil days to come will be an attempt to supplant the ultimate power of God himself: 'he takes his seat in the temple of God' (2 Thess. 2.4). This is the equivalent of the 'desolating sacrilege' of Mark 13.14, which uses that traditional apocalyptic symbol from Daniel 9.27 to denote interference with the very throne of God in Jerusalem. There had not been anything comparable, in the Thessalonians' experience, with the premeditated assaults on the Temple by Antiochus Epiphanes or the Emperor Caligula. For the Thessalonians, God himself remained the 'restraining' factor (2 Thess. 2.7), effectively stage-managing this cosmic drama, just as Mark 13.20 shows God to be still in absolute control of the timetable of the last things.

The dramatic climax to the eschatological timetable will come when 'the lawless one will be revealed' (2 Thess. 2.8). Whatever experience the Thessalonians have of the 'mystery of lawlessness', this climax had not yet been reached. The traditional designation for the maximum of evil is the 'Antichrist' (the opponent of Christ), but this term for personal evil is only found in the New Testament in the letters of John (see 1 John 2.18, 22; 4.3; 2 John 7). The language of 2 Thessalonians is closer to that of Revelation 12–13, with the collaboration between beast, false prophet and Satan. Ultimately the 'lawless one' will be exterminated at the ultimate confrontation with his opponent, in the victorious manifestation of Christ. This climax is comparable to the vision of Christ as the divine warrior in Revelation 19.11–20. The language of 2 Thessalonians gives the impression of a rigid predestination to salvation or wrath in the distinction between 'those who are perishing' (2.10) and 'the first fruits for salvation' (2.13).

THE BOOK OF REVELATION – THE 'PROPHETIC APOCALYPSE'?

David Aune proposed to regard Revelation as a 'prophetic apocalypse' that combines apocalyptic traditions within a prophetic framework. He regarded the introductory letter features (chapters 1–3) as an artificial framework, belonging to a late revision (although other scholars, such as Karrer, would not agree with this assessment[9]). Aune claimed that the merging of forms is

> an attempt to give a new lease of life to apocalyptic traditions that could not and did not retain their vitality in early Christianity because of their indissoluble association with nationalistic myths connected with the royal ideology of ancient Israel'.[10]

He summarised their different sociological functions and perspectives as follows: apocalyptic thought was the product of an oppressed minority who clearly distinguished between the righteous and the wicked in terms of their eschatological rewards and punishments; prophetic thought, however, assumed that:

a) the wicked could repent and change their ways, and
b) the righteous need admonition, censure and exhortation to remain faithful and/or repent.

Revelation has the formal characteristics of traditional apocalyptic, without either its nationalistic world view or its theological boundaries. Aune proposed a theory of composition, assuming that John was a Jewish apocalypticist with a lengthy career and responsibility for both authorship and editing. His was a layered composition, which includes material that can be dated to the 60s and the 90s. The two major editions, subject to subsequent stages of revision, are:

1) 1.7a–12; 4.1–22.5, dated to the mid-60s
2) 1.1–6; 1.12b–3.22; 22.6–21, dated to the mid-90s.

The Apocalypse of John certainly contains much traditional material, as the cross-references previously indicated have made clear. While it is important to give full weight to the wider context of historical and futuristic expectation described in these visions (traditionally ascribed to the reign of the Roman Emperor Domitian at the end of the first century CE and perhaps more subtly allocated, as has been seen, by David Aune), the special interest of this present volume encourages a focus on chapter 20 of Revelation. The key passage is Revelation 20.1–10, which describes how Satan is imprisoned and later released; between these two events is the thousand-year reign of Christ and his saints. This is the text that set the programme for a wide range of literal expectations about the millennial Kingdom, as well as the much larger sociological phenomenon of the millenarian sects.

A thousand years is a long span of time in human terms, but it is conceived in the Apocalypse as only an interim period within which Satan is imprisoned, and those who share in the resurrection of Christ will fulfil a priestly ministry (see 20.6). The Millennium is then an earthly triumph and vindication for the deaths of the Christian martyrs as well as of Christ himself. Some interpretations of this text, for example within the traditional doctrines of mainstream churches, have concentrated not on the literal duration of a thousand years, but rather have preferred a symbolic understanding of this as the time of the Church (between Christ's resurrection and the Last Judgement).

Apparent inconsistencies between the visions of the End in the concluding chapters of Revelation have suggested to critics the possibilities of speculative rearrangement of the contents. Different readings provide the basis for alternative theories about the time scheme for the key events of the coming of Christ and the Millennium. Those who follow the existing sequence of events in Revelation see the Second Coming (19.11–16) as preceding the Millennium; these final events will be established by divine cataclysm. Those who prefer to place the emphasis on the Last Judgement (20.11–15) as the reason for the Second Coming see the Millennium as coming first; the earthly reign of the Christian saints is both the climax, and the natural outcome, of the constant activity of the Church in the world.

Christians seem to have taken over the structure of the Jewish dream in chapter 7 of the book of Daniel, that is a dream of two ages (the present age and the age to come) that fall before and after the advent of a 'son of man', when the saints receive the Kingdom (see Dan. 7.18). The Millennium therefore faces both ways: it is a divine vindication demonstrated on earth and an earthly anticipation of life in heaven. In Daniel's vision the Kingdom of the Saints appears as God's final word, not an interim event. But, in the Apocalypse, God is seen as equally involved in the trial of humanity, the just sentencing, the new opportunity offered in the resurrection for the Millennium and the ultimate annihilation in 'the second death' of those rival powers who are hostile to God.

In his study of millennial expectations in the book of Revelation, J. Webb Mealy reflects theologically upon the different, and possibly inconsistent, aspects of this part of the Apocalypse. He considers the issues raised by the text with a modern sensitivity and a highly universalist interpretation, not always matched by interpreters in past centuries:

According to John, the millennium is the length of the just jail sentence that will be served by those who reject God in this life. And for him the last judgement is a picture of the gracious release granted to those who have served out that sentence ... The negative mystery is that those who have rejected God's grace in their mortal lives will never allow themselves to be reconciled to him, even though in his mercy they are granted the gift of resurrection itself ... The positive mystery is ... that God's patience towards the human race, his grace, and his willingness to give opportunity for repentance, never expire, come self-deception, come rebellion, come murder, come suicide. To the very end, and to the very final proof, enter them or not, the doors of his kingdom remain open (Rev. 21.25).[11]

IV

THE RETURN OF CHRIST

WHAT KIND OF EXPECTATION DOES THE BIBLE OFFER? QUESTIONS OF CLASSIFICATION

Maurice Wiles offers an admirable summary of the two contrasted expectations of the return of Christ:

The heavenly city is presented sometimes as a transformed world, sometimes as a place of escape from this doomed and irredeemable order.

The second coming of Christ is sometimes depicted as a coming to rule on this earth for a millennium, sometimes as a coming to snatch away the faithful to be with him on clouds of glory.

And so that hope functions for some as a spur to reforming zeal in relation to the social and political conditions of their times, and for others as a reason for accepting and tolerating these conditions as no more than secondary and transient realities.[1]

Martin Marty clarifies the principal distinction, in the technical terms of *postmillennial* and *premillennial* expectations:

Called 'postmillennial' because they taught that Christ would return and begin to rule *after* his agents and churches had won many converts and made the world attractive by reform.

Premillennialism saw the world *not* as getting better [in contrast to Enlightenment concepts of progress and the popular applications of Darwinian evolution] *nor* as producing the kingdom of God on earth. It was getting worse, and would do so until Christ came again for his thousand-year rule. Christians would do well to evangelize, to convert others quickly. There was little point in reforming social institutions.[2]

In important respects the distinction can be this simple: everything depends on when you locate the return or Second Coming of Christ. Do you conceive it as being before the Millennium happens (*premillennialist*) or as a consequence of the Millennium (*postmillennialist*)? Believers can be classified into two major categories, simply on the grounds of the decision they have made in the two related areas of chronology and psychology: which comes first, the Last Judgement or the return of Christ? And is one at heart an optimist or a pessimist? Real life and academic studies alike are rarely this simple, however. The system of labelling used by historians and the typology employed by sociologists can be overly simple or unnecessarily complicated. Classification may indeed be a good thing, in order to provide an overview of the subject. But when one studies an example of an individual believer, it may be preferable to let them speak for themselves, before consigning them to a single pigeon-hole.

Some historical scholars have chosen to distinguish between the meanings of the two words 'millennialism' and 'millenarianism' in ways that go beyond the derivation of the words and their popular functions, as defined by the *Oxford English Dictionary*. For such scholars the term 'millenarianism' applies to the premillennialist position, while 'millennialism' denotes the progressive optimism of the postmillennialist. There can also be a distinction of status between the two terms, such that serious philosophical thinkers are 'millennialists', while the representatives of popular culture and superstition are 'millenarians'. It rapidly becomes clear that such distinctions cannot be maintained across the whole range of historical examples, and it is better to agree with the dictionary and regard the two terms as virtually interchangeable.

It is probably much more important to maintain as a general principle the other distinction between 'pre-' and 'post-' versions of 'Millennialism', however. The motivation and rationale for these respective positions are bound to vary between the earliest and the most modern representatives. But the broadest reasons for making the distinction between these two types of millennialist positions are helpful in clarifying the analysis.

The *premillennialist* position operates with a quatrain of components: cataclysms – pessimism – doom – passivity. Such a believer, typically, would hold that the reign of Jesus Christ and the saints for a thousand years has not yet begun. When it is inaugurated, this will be a direct result of divine intervention; it will be accompanied by various cataclysmic happenings both in world affairs (affecting empires, governments and churches) and in the natural realm (such as earthquakes, floods and fire). Christ will become the physical ruler of this world until the final Armageddon, when Satan is at last unbound, the final conflict takes place, the righteous are raised from the dead and the Last Judgement occurs.

The corresponding position of the *postmillennialist* also works with a quatrain, only this time they are: reformism – optimism – progress – action. This believer also regards the Millennium as a future event, but instead of direct divine intervention it is the work of God's human agents, the current Christian community in particular, which brings to realisation the glorious future. The coming of the Millennium will not be accompanied by a series of cataclysmic events; instead it develops and evolves through human history. The case has been argued to show that the medieval use of apocalyptic concepts and utopian ideas itself became transformed into the modern, secular ideas of progress and evolution. So it could be claimed that 'the Enlightenment belief in progress was the spiritual heir of the prophetic vision of a perfect, future kingdom and thus had its roots in postmillennialism'.[3]

This comparison suggests, in the terms of modern theological debate about any doctrine as real or non-real, that for the premillennialist the Second Coming of Christ and his realisation of the Millennium are conceived in terms of realism. On the other hand, the postmillennialist employs the language of the Millennium in non-realist, that is, purely figurative terms. The basis of this belief is simply that humanity alone is ultimately going to fulfil the promise of the ancient prophecies.

Another way of classifying the varieties of millennialism is to employ the categories that sociologists use to distinguish between religious movements (such as churches, sects and cults). The criterion that is applied in such a classification is the attitude of the religious movement to wider society – in essence the nature of its response to the world. In this taxonomy there are seven categories, as proposed, for example, by Bryan Wilson:[4]

1. *Conversionist*: Humanity is corrupt, because the world is corrupt. God will change us as individuals as we undergo a conversion experience. This is a subjective attitude, but it is premised on a promise that God will change external reality at some future time.

2. *Revolutionist*: Only the destruction of the natural world and social order will be sufficient for salvation. This salvation is imminent; it is an objective change to be brought about by direct intervention of the divine.

3. *Introversionist*: The world is so evil that salvation is only attainable by the most complete withdrawal from the world, which God calls us to make. Those who belong to the withdrawn and purified community are the focus and source of salvation.

4. *Manipulationist*: Salvation is possible within the world and evil may be overcome if humanity learns the right means and improved techniques to deal with their problems. Salvation is a present possibility and God calls upon us to change our perceptions to this end.

5. *Thaumaturgical*: The individual is concerned with present ills and seeks supernatural help. God will grant special dispensations and work miracles to achieve salvation in this particular case. Salvation is brought about by oracles and miracles (or magic) and not by any wider change in the principles of life.

6. *Reformist*: Evil is an objective reality in the world, but God will give us insights into the ways in which the world and social organisation should be amended. Hearts that are open to the divine will receive special revelation as to these alterations. In

some ways this revelation may correspond to the rational principles of secular reformation.

7. *Utopian*: God calls upon us to reconstruct the world according to divinely given principles, establishing a new social organisation from which evil is eliminated. More radical than the reformist position, it differs from the revolutionary in that it is the result of human activity, although divinely inspired.

If we summarise these varieties of human orientation towards the world, it is possible to see how millenarian movements can correspond to the different categories. Accordingly, the way in which the Millennium is portrayed will differ radically. These seven types can be regrouped differently according to the emphasis placed on particular characteristics. For example, if we focus on the objectivity or subjectivity of our relationship to the world, then in the objective category the revolutionist holds that God will overturn this reality, the introversionist says that God calls upon us to abandon it, the reformist that God calls us to amend it, and the utopian that God calls us to reconstruct it. In the completely subjective category there are only the conversionists who believe that God will change us. But in the intermediate category of those who accommodate or work on the relationship, there are the manipulationists who say that God calls upon us to change our perceptions, and the thaumaturgists who hold that God will grant dispensations and work miracles.

Alternatively we might wish to draw attention to the extent to which the operative power is believed to come directly from God himself. Focusing the data in this way, we see that three positions – the revolutionist, thaumaturgical and conversionist – all place the greatest emphasis upon the autonomous operation of supernatural power. In these cases humanity needs do little but realise the fact and hold to it as the overriding belief.

THE LAST JUDGEMENT

The fear of a final judgement (the ultimate verdict on individuals and nations, delivered by the ultimate court of law in the presence of God himself) has been a frequent element in future expectation throughout the ages. The factor of surprise, the certainty that nobody knows the exact time when the end will come and the judgement will be delivered (and so it is difficult to make appropriate preparations for the event), only serves to intensify the element of fear. If one were to make comparisons on a human rather than a divine scale, it might be like the moment of dawning realisation that the personal situation was hopeless once the *Titanic* had struck the icebergs. Or perhaps it can be compared to the experience of participating for pleasure in an academic course, which one is enjoying hugely, until the moment when one is informed that everyone must sit an examination. Or it could be like the experience of an author who derives great pleasure in researching and writing a manuscript, until at the last moment when the book is almost complete he is informed for the first time that his manuscript is to be judged by other experts; he may have to make drastic changes because of their judgements, so the book is no longer solely his own work.

Recent discoveries in a cement quarry in Northamptonshire of 30 skeletons dating from the Roman period can help to illustrate some primary features of early Christian belief about the Last Judgement.[5] The burials were found together with the foundations of a wooden mausoleum, suggesting that some of the dead were of high status. They are dated between 300 and 360 CE, and therefore from the early period of Romano-British Christianity, shortly after the conversion of the Emperor Constantine in 312 CE. The skeletons are lying with their feet due east, so that on the Day of Judgement they will rise to face Jerusalem. Another potentially significant feature is the absence of any grave goods, since communities evolving from paganism to Christianity ceased to bury people with artefacts. Some of the skeletons are of children, who would not necessarily have received a formal burial in pagan times, but would have been included in the Christian expectation of the Resurrection.

When considering Christian iconography, what is at first sight an unexpected Biblical image in connection with the Last Judgement is that of Noah's Ark. However, upon closer consideration the combination of ideas of cataclysm and of means of salvation makes this image particularly appropriate for the purpose. Looking at the calm before the storm, this scenario can incorporate the ideas of paradisal bliss in the Garden of Eden. An early seventeenth-century panel, completed in the workshop of Jan Breughel the Elder, contains the following details and can be seen in the National Gallery in London:

> An improbable menagerie of paired creatures – including an awkward Magellan penguin … – roam harmoniously amid woodland glades. The guinea pig lies down with the leopard, the moorhen is at home with the monkey, and although spaniels yap at a pair of hissing swans … all is apparently at peace in this Eden.[6]

The most significant aspect of this description is the 'pairing' of the creatures, which anticipates the preservation of the species in the future Ark.

Noah's Ark can also be found as a typological symbol of the world's ending in the New Testament:

> For as the days of Noah were, so will be the coming of the Son of Man. For as in those days before the flood they were eating and drinking, marrying and giving in marriage, until the day Noah entered the ark, and they knew nothing until the flood came and swept them all away, so too will be the coming of the Son of Man. (Matt. 24.37–9)

> And if he did not spare the ancient world, even though he saved Noah, a herald of righteousness, with seven others, when he brought a flood on a world of the ungodly … (2 Pet. 2.5)

> by the word of God heavens existed long ago and an earth was formed out of water and by means of water, through which the world of that time was deluged with water and perished. But by the same word the present heavens and earth have been reserved for fire, being kept until the day of judgement and destruction of the godless. (2 Pet. 3.5–7)

> But the day of the Lord will come like a thief, and then the heavens will pass away with a loud noise, and the elements will be dissolved with fire, and the earth and everything that is done on it will be disclosed. (2 Pet. 3.10)

Noah is seen as a 'herald of righteousness' and a preacher of repentance.[7] In the words of *Apostolic Constitutions* (8.12.22) he is 'the end of the foregoing generations and the beginning of those that were to come'. The destructive flood and the Last Judgement are linked together by Irenaeus in the second century CE, using the symbolism of numbers that was then popular:[8] the number of the Beast of the Apocalypse is given as 666 (Rev. 13.18), which corresponds to the sum of the age of Noah at the time of the flood and the height and the width respectively of the golden statue in Daniel 3.1 (600 years + 60 cubits + 6 cubits = 666).

Although the surviving evidence may not tell the complete story, there is an abundance of indications in church art and music that the Middle Ages were preoccupied with ideas of the Last Judgement. Church authorities were concerned that the ordinary people, many lacking literacy, should be made aware of the realities of this expectation and thus prepare themselves. Many churches of this period, therefore, had prominent displays of what are known as Doom Paintings – frescoes on the chancel arch, for example – which demonstrated the contrast between the sinners, who are damned, and the righteous and the penitent who find salvation.[9]

Another 'visual aid', popular in the late Middle Ages in Europe, was the allegorical subject of the *Dance of Death* in which the figure of Death (often a skeleton) meets a variety of people and leads them all in a dance to the grave. This scene was painted on the churchyard wall of the old St Paul's Cathedral in London, for example, and could also be seen, before the recent fire, on the famous Kapellbrücke at Luzern in Switzerland.

In musical terms the most prominent example is the section of the Requiem Mass used in Western Christianity, known from its opening words as the *Dies Irae* (Day of Wrath). This Latin poem is attributed, not without some debate, to the Franciscan Thomas of Celano (the biographer of St Francis) who died in 1260 CE. The text is based on Zephaniah 1.14–16, which presents a vivid picture of a prophesied time of trouble and distress; this became associated in medieval exegesis with the apocalypse and Last Judgement. The actual phrase 'day of wrath' is found in Zephaniah 1.15.

The first printed missal containing the *Dies Irae* in the sequence for Requiem Masses is that from Venice in 1493.[10] The work became one of the most renowned melodies of the repertoire of Gregorian chant. Many composers set the full text as part of their Requiem Mass: see the highly dramatic version in Verdi's *Requiem* (1874) and by contrast the excerpt in the *Libera Me* section of Faure's *Requiem* (1890). The *Dies Irae* appears in other contexts too through the centuries, but all associated with death and judgement. It is used in symphonies, such as Berlioz's *Symphonie Fantastique* (1830), and in Walter Scott's poem *The Lay of the Last Minstrel* (1805).

V

MILLENARIANS AMONG THE CHURCH FATHERS

What sort of person this upstart teacher is, his own actions and teaching show. This is the man who taught the dissolution of marriages, who laid down the law on fasting, who renamed Pepuza and Tymion, insignificant towns in Phrygia, as Jerusalem, in the hopes of persuading people in every district to gather there; who appointed agents to collect money, who contrived to make the gifts roll in under the name of 'offerings', and who has subsidized those who preach his message, in order that gluttony may provide an incentive for teaching it.[1]

THE CHALLENGE OF MONTANISM

An orthodox Christian writer named Apollonius wrote this denunciation of the early Christian prophetic movement that was flourishing in the region of Asia Minor known as Phrygia in the first decade of the third century CE; he sought to prove point by point the fraudulent nature of their prophecies. This movement came to be known as Montanism, from the name of one of its three founders. The movement had originated as early as the middle of the second century CE and its proponents were powerfully charismatic figures, engaged in radically prophetic activity to counter the widespread intellectualising influence of Gnosticism. There were varieties of gnostic movements, whose common characteristic was a theory of religious salvation dependent upon esoteric knowledge, a blend of magic, psychology and metaphysics. Montanism was driven by a kind of fundamentalist protestant zeal to rescue the faith of Christianity.

According to Apollonius' account, as documented in Eusebius' *History of the Church*, Montanus was the original organiser of the movement and was responsible for establishing its rules of conduct and church structure, together with his two female associates Prisca (Priscilla) and Maximilla.[2] But their personalities were less important than their focus on the Holy Spirit; their prophetic utterances were delivered in the first person, as the words of the Paraclete himself.

The more localised, regional nature of the movement is indicated by the belief that the New Jerusalem when it descended to this world, as prophesied in Revelation 21.2, would be set down on a hill in their part of Phrygia. Montanus designated two settlements, Pepouza and Tymion, as 'Jerusalem', wanting people from other places to assemble there. Pepouza became the administrative headquarters of Montanism, as well as being a centre of pilgrimage for those Montanists who lived outside the region.

This entry appears in William Hazlitt's *The Classical Gazeteer*:

PEPUZA – A town of Phrygia Pacatiana. Destroyed in the second century. The seat of the heretics called Cataphryges or Pepuziani.[3]

Apollonius stated that Tymion was a relatively insignificant hamlet in Phrygia. This may well be accurate, and not merely the outcome of polemical prejudice. However, from a bilingual inscription in Latin and Greek (only discovered in 1998), which details an imperial rescript from Septimius Severus, probably dated to 205 CE, it is known that Tymion in fact belonged to an imperial estate.[4] This inscription, together with a rock-cut monastery and evidence for an extensive ancient city due south of where the inscription was found, provided vital clues for the likely identification of this Montanist centre in Phrygia.

From the summit of a mountain (or high hill of 1141m) called Ömerçali, about five kilometres to the south, the view north toward the monastery proved revelatory:

I imagined Montanus and his prophetic associates standing, more than 18 centuries ago, where I was standing with my scholarly associates … We could see clearly now why Montanus had named [*both*] Pepouza and Tymion 'Jerusalem'. It was not, as earlier scholars had assumed, because they were geographically adjacent settlements at either side of the foot of a mountain, but because they marked the northern and southern limits of the geographic area where he expected the 'New Jerusalem' to descend out of heaven ... Topographically, this vast agricultural tableland, which in Montanus' day was an imperial estate, was the ideal 'landing place' for the New Jerusalem. It was flat enough, level enough, and large enough to accommodate the dimensions of the New Jerusalem as described in Revelation 21.[5]

Archaeological evidence for the spread of Montanism is provided by epitaphs of a distinctive kind. As Sir William Calder described them, they are 'the monuments of a sect which looked on profession [the open declaration of Christian affiliation] as a duty not to be evaded, and martyrdom as a prize to be coveted'.[6] On such tombstones the expression *Miles Christi* ('soldier of Christ') becomes almost a technical term. The basic insights of Montanism can be said to derive from the Christian Apocalypse (see especially the letter to Philadelphia (Rev. 3.7–13) on which Calder concentrated). The descent of the New Jerusalem, the prophecy literally understood as applying to Pepouza, to the east of Philadelphia, was a foundational belief of Montanism, as has been noted.

Montanist controversies affected central Phrygia between 157 and 200 CE. Probably Montanus himself appeared in 157, and the prophetesses Priscilla and Maximilla then or a little later. Early sources[7] suggest that Montanus had been a priest of the goddess Cybele before converting to Christianity, bringing with him some ecstatic elements of the orgiastic Phrygian cult. From the middle of the third century there is evidence of Montanist communities in northern Phrygia, while central Phrygia had become orthodox again (from the evidence of inscriptions). Epiphanius[8] suggested that the church of Thyatira (see Rev. 2.18–29) had lapsed into Montanism, but was again orthodox in his own day. By the fourth century, in the north of the region, the heresy of Novatianism was strongly represented. Novatianism, named after its leader Novatian, was a schismatic movement in Christianity, following the Decian persecution (249–50 CE), and was a rigorist reaction against those who had compromised with paganism during the persecution. Adolf von Harnack[9] observed that those communities that earlier were Montanist appeared as Novatianist by the fourth century.

Another key figure for the Montanist movement was Tertullian, the most eminent of their converts among the Western Church Fathers. He went over to Montanism at an early stage in the third century and became its great expositor. However, the amount he actually quoted from the prophetic books of Montanus is only some 20 sentences. To penetrate behind Tertullian's advocacy and apologetic to the original Montanism represents a major task of reconstruction. Tertullian was a soldier's son, but as a Montanist he condemned the idea of a Christian serving in the army of the empire. The only military service that a Christian could undertake, according to Tertullian, was the *militia Christi*, being a soldier of Christ.[10]

Montanism had begun in the second century, as a movement emphasising prophecy and continuing inspiration within the Christian community. In this climate of thought there was no possibility of accepting that the first-century gospels could constitute any final and complete form of revelation. Montanus and his two female acolytes in this remote area of Phrygia claimed that here and now they were in fact receiving messages which were to be regarded as the ultimate communication of Christian prophecy. Montanus spoke with a proclaimed authority, regarding himself as Father, Son and Spirit – the Christian Trinity in person. Montanism thus illustrated for the remainder of the church the real dangers in allowing any claims of direct and private revelations, or of access to the personal presence of God. There was obviously a direct clash with those forms of church authority that were seeking to establish themselves in the second century. The emphasis on prophecy in Montanism stressed the impact of the future in revolutionary terms.

In 375 CE Epiphanius declared that 'prophecy was a gift which should continue in the whole Church to the end of time'.[11] However, much depends on the mode by which prophecy is recognised and transmitted. Ignatius' letter to the church in Philadelphia (written between 110 and 118 CE) had referred to a dispute there on the relationship of Old Testament prophecy to New Testament revelation. There are no anachronistic references there to later Montanism. *The*

Martyrdom of Polycarp[12] applies the term 'Phrygian' to a certain Quintus, who challenged for martyrdom and subsequently turned coward. As this text was written *c*.156 CE, this may be the earliest allusion to Montanism and its challenging of fate; certainly Montanists were subsequently referred to regularly as 'the Phrygians'.

Montanism clearly was not officially recognised by the Great Church, which had contested the inspiration of this movement and signalled thereby the ending of the age of newly inspired revelation, and of miracles, which had lasted since the time of the Apostles. The Church therefore effectively limited authentic revelation to the first century of Christianity. No authoritative church establishment and larger hierarchy could afford to remain open-ended to the vagaries of the future; the concept of a final received revelation thus became embodied in the canon of the New Testament texts, which was in the process of definition by the end of the second century. At this time also the rational arguments of the Church Father Irenaeus stiffened the anti-Montanist reactions of other Christians (Irenaeus was also eloquent in his opposition to Gnosticism).

However, Irenaeus' efforts did not diminish the widespread millenarian hopes among Christians, which were based either on intense emotional expectations in the face of religious persecution, or on an interpretation of the book of Revelation which was less literal than that of the Montanist. Another of the leading Church Fathers (and equally an opponent of Gnosticism), Hippolytus, wrote a substantial commentary on the book of Daniel in an effort to discourage the fervent apocalyptic expectations of the world's end. One incident that provoked this response was a bishop leading his flock out into the desert, in the expectation of meeting their returning Lord Jesus.

* * *

Montanism as a movement was destroyed at Pepouza by John of Ephesus in 550 CE. What remained was the orthodox Christian tradition from Byzantium, as can be seen in the development of the rock-cut monastery on the site, with its Byzantine dome and ornamentation. An orthodox bishop of Pepouza named Theophylactus, and an abbot of a monastery very near Pepouza, Euthymius, both attended the second council of Nicaea in 787 CE. Another bishop of Pepouza, named Nikolaos, was listed as attending the church council in Constantinople in 879 CE.

Christian Apologetics

Theophilus of Antioch was a Christian apologist of the second century; the only work of his that survives is entitled *Ad Autolycum*, written in three books *c*.180 CE.[13] In this he attacked pagan idolatry and emperor worship, contrasting Christian morality with the immorality of paganism, and stressing the superiority of the Christian idea of God and the doctrine of creation. He supplied a detailed allegorical interpretation of the account of creation in Genesis, and he included a sketch of world chronology, and of the history of Israel, to demonstrate the historical priority of Moses and the prophets as compared with any of the Greek philosophers. Another of his works, *The History*, has been lost.

According to the influential interpretation by J. Danielou,[14] Theophilus' historical scheme was based on the typology of the days of creation (six days followed by the Sabbath as recorded at the start of Genesis, regarded as the cosmic week). In this he would have anticipated Hippolytus and other early Church Fathers. The outline of the scheme is as follows:

Creation	
(History of Israel)	
Nativity of Jesus	5500 years later
End of the World ˙	6000 years
Earthly Messianic Kingdom	6000–7000 years
Heavenly Jerusalem installed	7000 years

Various conceptions of the Millennium or messianic Kingdom were current at this time and subsequently. Cerinthus is accused of speaking of a time of pleasure, passion and debauchery, 'a thousand years given up to wedding festivities' (according to Eusebius' *Church History* 3.28.2). Alternatively this was to be the time for the total destruction of the world, and a return to primitive silence, within which God alone would be glorified. Theophilus, with his typological interpretation of Genesis, is said to have envisaged the eschatological Sabbath rest of God, at the end of the world, with peace, abundance and eternal blessing (*Autol.* 1.14) and nature restored to its original harmony (*Autol.* 2.17).

Among the earlier writers of the Church Fathers, a belief in the millennial Kingdom was held by the authors of the Epistle of Barnabas, the Shepherd of Hermas, and the second Epistle of Clement, as well as by Papias of Hierapolis, Justin Martyr, Irenaeus, Hippolytus, and probably Julius Africanus. Papias is one of the key early figures, working in the first half of the second century, regarded as a link back to the first generations of Christians (according to Irenaeus, Papias had listened to the apostle John). The only doctrinal position definitely attributed to Papias was the 'unwritten tradition' that 'there will be a millennium following the resurrection of the dead, when the kingdom of Christ is to be established physically on this earth' (*H.E.* 3.39). Eusebius was disparaging about Papias, because of his belief in the Millennium:

> I suppose he got those ideas through a misunderstanding of the apostolic accounts, not perceiving that the things said by them were spoken mystically in figures. For he appears to have been of a very limited understanding as one can see from his discourses. (*H.E.* 3.39)

The materialistic nature of these expectations is illustrated by the famous parable which is told:

> The days will come when vines shall grow, each having ten thousand branches, and in each branch ten thousand twigs, and in each twig ten thousand shoots, and in every one of the shoots ten thousand grapes, and every grape when pressed will give five and twenty measures of wine.[15]

Justin Martyr demonstrated the belief in the millennial Kingdom in a more exact form, in the first explicit link that is known to John's Revelation.[16] The Lord Jesus Christ was to return to Jerusalem, which would be rebuilt; there he would eat and drink with his disciples. The Christian communities would gather to him in the first resurrection and live there in happiness alongside the patriarchs and prophets. Justin did not regard this belief as an essential part of the Christian faith; he acknowledges that many worthy Christians do not hold it. But he comments that many who reject the belief also reject the concept of the resurrection of the dead, which by contrast is an essential element of the faith. For those with the more comprehensive belief in Christ, the Kingdom at Jerusalem would last for a thousand years, to be followed by the second resurrection and the Last Judgement. To support these beliefs Justin quotes the prophet Isaiah (65.17–25) and the apostle John (actually Rev. 20.4–6); he uses also imagery from the prophet Micah (4.1–7), describing the renewal of heaven and this earth. All believers would inherit eternal and imperishable blessings, recognising the truth in the words of Jesus and his prophets.

On the basis of Justin's acknowledgment that not all Christians subscribe to these millenarian views, Jaroslav Pelikan comments that 'It would seem that very early in the post-apostolic era millenarianism was regarded as a mark neither of orthodoxy nor of heresy, but as one permissible opinion among others within the range of permissible opinions.'[17]

In the formative years of the Christian tradition a variety of viewpoints was possible, especially if the topic did not at all times appear to be of central and essential importance. Those early Christians who are readily labelled 'Gnostic', particularly those linked with Marcion in the middle of the second century, would have rejected millenarianism on two grounds: first, that such an idea originated from the God of the Jews and should therefore be abandoned along with the Old Testament by strong Christians within the tradition of the apostle Paul; and second, that the only possible concept of resurrection was not physical but spiritual – a spiritual resurrection that is to be partially anticipated in this world, and perfected hereafter.

The Roman presbyter Gaius, attacking Cerinthus' millenarian beliefs, opposed the idea of a physical Kingdom of Christ to come on earth, which he said is in 'enmity towards the Scriptures of God'.[18] Similarly, Origen condemns millenarian views as most absurd; he recounted the literal exegesis offered on the promises concerning the Kingdom of Christ, but concluded that such literalism was 'unworthy of the divine promises'.[19] Conversely, to interpret such passages 'in accordance with the understanding of the apostles' meant that such passages concerned the soul, not the body, and so the promised Kingdom was a purely spiritual one. For Origen to be found engaging in such fierce polemic in the first half of the third century would suggest that millenarianism had not disappeared at that time and that it was still arousing significant debate. In support of this we can observe that in the late third century Methodius, although he attacked literalistic exegesis of the Bible, also seemed to advocate an essentially millenarian view of the Kingdom, or at least retained millenarian terminology.[20] And Commodianus simply took such ideas for granted.[21]

The most outspoken of attacks on such millenarian views was made by Dionysius of Alexandria, in his treatise *On the Promises*. He sought to dispose of the Biblical basis for the Millennium by denying the apostolic authorship of the book of Revelation. He may well have been provoked to this reaction by a bishop of Arsinoe called Nepos, who had campaigned against the allegorical interpretation of Revelation, insisting that it must be read literally. Dionysius' work was widely influential in the church and arguably might even have excised Revelation from the canon of the New Testament. The strongly spiritual tendencies of Alexandrian theology made materialistic beliefs almost impossible to hold; in this part of Christendom it was only in the Coptic monastic tradition of Egypt and Ethiopia that such literalistic readings of the Apocalypse continued to circulate.

By the middle of the fourth century such millenarian views had come to be considered heretical. A conclusive act was that of Augustine of Hippo, in his later work on *The City of God*, where he taught that the Millennium was the present reign of Christ – that it had begun with Christ's own resurrection and was destined to last for a thousand years thereafter: 'Even now the Church is the kingdom of Christ ... even now his saints reign with him'.[22] As an interesting comparison one should note that at an earlier stage of Augustine's religious life he had thought in terms of a physical 'first resurrection' of the saints, to be followed by a millennial rest on earth, the delights of which were to be the spiritual enjoyment of the presence of the Lord. Jaroslav Pelikan comments:

> Augustine set the standard for most catholic exegesis in the West when he surrendered the millenarian interpretation of Revelation 20, to which he had held earlier, in favor of the view that the thousand years of that text referred to the history of the church.[23]

* * *

Charles Hill has claimed that 'millenarianism was never the dominant form of Christian eschatology even in the second and third centuries'. But the counterbalance is the fact (which he admits) that 'it was advocated by a number of very notable [and highly influential] Christian writers, including Justin, Irenaeus, Tertullian, Victorinus, and Lactantius, and was accepted early on by Augustine'. It is a matter of some debate whether 'the exegetical efforts of Jerome, Tyconius and Augustine combined to send Christian millenarianism virtually underground by the early fifth century'.[24] Certainly what seemed to Graeco-Roman cultural understanding a more mature eschatological outlook had turned attention away from the Jewish precedents of the messianic Kingdom towards a more spiritual conception.

VI

APOCALYPSE THEN:
THE YEAR 1000

S ir John Tavener, a modern composer who has a range of intensely religious concerns, recalls:

> I pointed out that at the time of the first millennium, AD 1000, churches were full of all-night chanting, and said what a pity it was that modern Western music is so bereft of this.[1]

The modern reader, influenced perhaps by the events surrounding the year 2000, would recognise the end of the first Millennium as a similar milestone. The correspondences are by no means exact, but it is likely that a population brought up in a strongly religious tradition within Christendom would have felt the reverberations as increasingly violent, the closer the approach of the key date of the year 'M' (in Roman numerals). Most people would have relied on readings from the Bible to provide assistance in recognising the nearness of the world's end and its likely aftermath. The apocalyptic chapters of the gospels (Matt. 24; Mark 13; Luke 21) offered, in the teaching of Jesus to his disciples, a scenario of warfare, famine, earthquake and pestilence.

It is important to qualify straightaway the use of the word 'reading', to avoid modern assumptions about widespread literacy. Historically, unless one knew Latin, and belonged to the educated and professional classes, one's knowledge of the Bible depended upon hearing the preachings and teachings of the Church, and upon a familiarity with the living tradition of the Bible in the form of wall paintings and other artistic representations in church buildings. The 'pearls' of the Biblical text were not directly accessible to ordinary people, but only indirectly as a result of the Church's decision to retain Scripture within its own doctrinal control. Nevertheless, the wall paintings that have survived the centuries show the dominant emphasis at that time to have been on apocalyptic themes and the Last Judgement.

The Biblical tradition also contained an apparently precise reference to the temporary liberation of Satan from his chains, after a time interval of one thousand years. The coincidence with the current calendar would not escape those who had any contact with the ecclesiastical and monastic use of *Anno Domini* dating. This does not mean everybody, for it is claimed that a general consciousness of the AD system of dating is a phenomenon of the late, rather than the early, medieval period. It may also be true that those who recognised the date would not necessarily know what to make of the eschatological implications. However, some assistance in this respect was provided by a common element of Christian teaching, which saw the world as currently living in the sixth age of cosmic history (up to six thousand years from the time of the Creation). This current age was thought to last from the birth of Christ until the advent of the Antichrist. If the exact duration of this age was supposed to be known only to God (see for example Matt 24.36) then it was perhaps too great a coincidence to overlook that the end of this sixth age could happen after 999 or 1000 years.

Around the latter part of the tenth century it is claimed that something approaching an epidemic of terror, concerning the end of the world, seized Christendom. Such claims are contested by some historians:

> It is quite paradoxical to search for evidence of elation or panic around the time of the end of the first millennium. Present historical opinion holds that the stories told about such phenomena were largely retrospective: that is to say, they were attributed to the year 1000 by later historians, on no very good evidence. Certainly the visual evidence for such concerns, collected by … Richard Gameson, in no way supports the view of an apocalyptic mentality on the eve of the year AD 1000.[2]

The claims for an apocalyptic mentality at this time may indeed have been exaggerated, but they are not as lacking in substance as such critical comments suggest. Even the critics have to agree that, at least very soon after this, there was a growing consciousness of the significance of such a passing of one thousand years in historical time. The popularity of the legend of the 'True Cross', for example, shows a disposition to celebrate the anniversary as represented in a millennial interval of time. The result was, effectively, a religious revival with the founding of new churches and monastic institutions, and an upsurge in Christian self-expression in liturgy, art and ideas.

Preachers appeared in France, Germany and Italy, proclaiming that the period of one thousand years, inaugurated by the Incarnation of Jesus Christ and foretold in the book of Revelation as the lifespan of this world's duration, was shortly to expire. Accordingly the Son of Man, interpreted as the glorified figure of Jesus, was about to return on the clouds of heaven, to carry out the Last Judgement. The Church may have done its best to calm such fears and condemn such outspoken preaching, but the panic nevertheless seems to have spread rapidly. The scenario is written up by a nineteenth-century chronicler as follows (possibly with some heightening of the drama):

The scene of the last judgement was expected to be at Jerusalem. In the year 999, the number of pilgrims proceeding eastward, to await the coming of the Lord in that city, was so great that they were compared to a desolating army. Most of them sold their goods and possessions before they quitted Europe, and lived upon the proceeds in the Holy Land. Buildings of every sort were suffered to fall into ruins. It was thought useless to repair them, when the end of the world was so near. Many noble edifices were deliberately pulled down. Even churches, usually so well maintained, shared the general neglect. Knights, citizens and serfs, travelled eastwards in company, taking with them their wives and children, singing psalms as they went, and looking with fearful eyes upon the sky, which they expected each minute to open, to let the Son of God descend in his glory.

During the thousandth year the number of pilgrims increased. Most of them were smitten with terror as with a plague. Every phenomenon of nature filled them with alarm. A thunder-storm sent them all upon their knees in mid march. It was the opinion that thunder was the voice of God, announcing the Day of Judgement. Numbers expected the earth to open and give up its dead at the sound. Every meteor in the sky seen at Jerusalem brought the whole Christian population into the streets to weep and pray. The pilgrims on the road were in the same alarm:

Lorsque, pendant la nuit, une globe de lumière
S'échappa quelquefois de la voûte de cieux,
Et traça dans sa chûte un long sillon de feux,
La troupe suspendit sa marche solitaire

Fanatic preachers kept up the flame of terror. Every shooting star furnished occasion for a sermon, in which the sublimity of the approaching judgement was the principal topic.[3]

Academic historians are in disagreement as to how widely the end of the first Millennium was seen as a significant turning-point in Christendom. And if it was, did the significance attach itself to the exact year AD 1000, presumably as representing that span of time since the birth of Christ, or should one rather focus on the year 1033, as a thousand years after the passion and death of Christ? Indeed, there are numerous English wills composed in the decade before 1000, but no single Anglo-Saxon will or charter[4] mentions any forthcoming Apocalypse; instead the general assumption is that the world would continue as before, with business as usual. Perhaps lawyers cannot afford to assume anything apart from the continuing pattern of life?

One must also notice, however, the five-volume history of his own times written by the Burgundian monk Ralph Glaber in the 1030s. His work is very conscious of just these millenarian questions, claiming that his abbot, William of Volpiano, told him to write his history on that theme. Christendom was encountering for the first time the reality of a thousand-year period of its history now about to end, and was understandably anxious: Is this the prophesied Millennium? Will its end mean a surge of Satanic activity, in the short time the Devil has at his disposal? Will this even entail the end of the world? Or will there be another Millennium to take its place? In this light Glaber supplies data relating to the periods around the years 1000 and 1033. There are also some sermons of the period, not focused exclusively on the key dates, but full of millennial foreboding, such as that by Archbishop Wulfstan of York. In addition there was the controversy in Rome surrounding the new Pope, Sylvester II, regarded by his enemies as the representative of the Devil and the Antichrist. Ralph Glaber reveals a remarkably wide view, developed as a result of his travels between ten different monasteries. He describes the portent that is now identified as Halley's comet, which appeared in 989 CE:

> It appeared in the month of September, not long after nightfall, and remained visible for nearly three months. It shone so brightly that its light seemed to fill the greater part of the sky, then it vanished at cock's crow. But whether it is a new star which God launches into space, or whether He merely increases the normal brightness of another star, only He can decide ... What appears established with the greatest degree of certainty is that this phenomenon in the sky never appears to men without being the sure sign of some mysterious and terrible event. And indeed, a fire soon consumed the church of St Michael the Archangel, built on a promontory in the ocean [Mont St Michel off the Brittany coast] which had always been the object of special veneration throughout the whole world.
>
> In the seventh year from the millennium ... almost all the cities of Italy and Gaul were devastated by violent conflagrations, and Rome itself largely razed by fire ... As one [people] gave out a terrible scream and turned to rush to confess to the Prince of the Apostles.
>
> All this accords with the prophecy of St John, who said that the devil would be freed after a thousand years.[5]*

In Glaber's view, the recorded disasters of the years before the end of the Millennium are succeeded by a more positive outcome. In church terms this is an expression of relief and celebration:

> Just before the third year after the millennium, throughout the whole world, but especially in Italy and Gaul, men began to reconstruct churches, although for the most part the existing ones were properly built and not in the least unworthy. But it seemed as though each Christian community were aiming to surpass all others in the splendour of construction. It was as if the whole world were shaking itself free, shrugging off the burden of the past, and cladding itself everywhere in a white mantle of churches.[6]*

---

* By permission of Oxford University Press.

The story seems to have repeated itself 30 years later, as the end of the Millennium was recalculated in terms of the death, rather than the birth, of Christ:

> After the many prodigies which had broken upon the world before, after and around the millennium of the Lord Christ, there were plenty of able men of penetrating intellect who foretold others, just as great, at the approach of the millennium of the Lord's Passion, and such wonders were soon manifest.

> It was believed that the order of the seasons and the elements ... had fallen into perpetual chaos, and with it had come the end of mankind ... It could portend nothing other than the advent of the accursed Anti-Christ who, according to divine testimony, is expected to appear at the end of the world.[7]*

Such fears were again succeeded by a period of intense relief:

> At the millennial anniversary of the Passion of the Lord, the clouds cleared in obedience to Divine mercy and goodness, and the smiling sky began to shine and flow gentle breezes ... At that point, in the region of Aquitaine, bishops, abbots and other men devoted to holy religion, first began to gather councils of the whole people ... When the news of these assemblies was heard, the entire populace joyfully came, unanimously prepared to follow whatever should be commanded them by the pastors of the church. A voice descending from Heaven could not have done more, for everyone was still under the effect of the previous calamity and feared the future loss of abundance.

> [Miracles] aroused such enthusiasm that the bishops raised their staffs towards heaven and all present stretched their palms to God, shouting with one voice, 'Peace! Peace!'[8]*

This popular movement, known as the Peace of God, certainly bears testimony to the characteristics of millennial fervour,[9] although there is also the suspicion that some of the emotion may have been orchestrated by the church to protect its position against acquisitive noblemen.

Archbishop Wulfstan of York (1002–23) had exploited millennial fears in a sermon composed in 1014 (*Sermo Lupi*), written in the con-

---

* By permission of Oxford University Press.

text of the most critical stages of King Aethelred's ineffective measures of resistance against the Danish invaders. Wulfstan served the English king, while being active in designing and preparing legislation for the Danish king's court. The Viking menace had of course been the consistent reality during this millennial period. The massacre of Danes in England on St Brice's Day, 1002, symbolised the strength of anti-Danish feeling among the English. Wulfstan sought to convince his listeners that present calamities were in fact punishment for their sins, and their repentance was therefore necessary; at the same time the invaders were plausibly excused by being coloured with the apocalyptic trappings of the Antichrist, for the Danish wars were readily identifiable with the prophecies of Matthew 24.7:

> Dear Friends, recognise the truth. This world is in haste and is drawing ever closer to its end, and it always happens that the longer it lasts, the worse it becomes. And so it must ever be, for the coming of the Anti-Christ grows ever more evil because of the sins of the people, and then truly it will be grim and terrible, widely in the world.
>
> The devil has deceived this people too much, and there has been little faith among men, though they speak fair words, and too many crimes have gone unchecked in the land ... The laws of the people have deteriorated altogether too often since Edgar died; and holy places are everywhere open to attack, and the houses of God are completely deprived of ancient rites, and stripped of all that is fitting; and religious orders have now for a long time been greatly despised; and widows are forced to marry unrighteously; and too many are reduced to poverty; and poor men are wretchedly deceived, most cruelly cheated and, wholly innocent, sold out of this land far and wide into the possession of foreigners; and through cruel injustice, children in the cradle are enslaved for petty theft widely within this nation; and the rights of freemen suppressed and the rights of slaves curtailed, and the rights of charity neglected; and, to speak most briefly, God's laws are hated and His commandments despised.[10]*

The text of Revelation 20.3 had particularly associated the unloosing of the Devil with the end of the period of one thousand years. In Rome there was a new Pope in 999, Gerbert of Aurillac, who had chosen the title of Sylvester II. His opponents envied and mistrusted

---

* By permission of Oxford University Press.

him for a variety of reasons. He wielded considerable political power and influence, through his association with the Ottonian kings who had sought to recreate the empire of Charlemagne.[11] He was the first ever French Pope, and it was said that he must have sold his soul in order to gain the throne. He was an intellectual, who was in a position to encourage innovative ideas; he had a fondness for scientific and mathematical instruments (especially the abacus) and an interest in astronomy; he had built himself a planetarium and written a treatise on the astrolabe. His enemies were convinced that the Antichrist had come to power in Christendom, exactly as prophesied. When he died just three years later, this seemed like proof of his identity, since the Devil was so eager to reclaim his own.

* * *

The academic evaluation of this Millennium year has ranged between 'the terrors of the year 1000', associated with apocalyptic expectation, and the dismissive 'a year like any other'. The latter position is likely to be unduly sceptical, even when proper allowance is made for the exaggeration of contemporary special interests and the enthusiasm of later romantic description. The evidence from Glaber, Wulfstan and the Ottonian kings is diverse and compelling. It is important not to impose modern millenarian perspectives on this period, but rather to observe the experiences of those who faced this crisis for the first time, the crisis of sensing the nearness of the end of a thousand-year span. Inevitably this expectation was informed by Biblical prophecies, and it resulted in a pattern of terror and hope, fear and relief, and a surge of religious fervour – features that are now taken to characterise millenarian movements.

Richard Landes in particular has argued for the recognition of important social implications at this time. He writes about:

> The powerful ambiguity of apocalyptic beliefs and the constructive as well as destructive impact they can have … their ability to generate new (voluntary) communities which survive the disappointment of a prophecy that failed.

[In France at] this millennial cusp, we find evidence of fundamental changes in values and family structures throughout the social strata, of enormous social and economic activity – new markets, burgeoning cities, bringing forested land under the plough. In a paradox characteristic of apocalyptic beliefs, the soil and society of a chaotic French 'kingdom' at the turn of the millennium produced a culture that would be the creative leader of medieval Europe.[12]

* * *

We noted at the opening of this chapter how John Tavener compared the year 2000 unfavourably with the year 1000, in terms of 'all-night chanting'. An interesting footnote to such a comparison, between the beginnings of the second and third millennia, is provided by a recently published book by Victoria Clark. Part travel book, part historical narrative, *The Far-Farers* is an experiment in 'mining the dawning eleventh century for parallels with this dawning twenty-first'[13]. The author retraces the journey from Iceland to Jerusalem of Thorvald the Viking, the son of early Norwegian settlers in Iceland. Thorvald converted to Christianity in the late tenth century and began to preach the gospel. He was outlawed for a crime and so embarked on a pilgrimage of penance to Jerusalem; on the way he was received by the Byzantine emperor. By comparison Victoria Clark's own modern travels are less satisfying, and almost inconclusive: 'Here in Jerusalem at long last, I was nevertheless being denied any grand sense of culmination, any satisfying feeling of fulfilment.'[14]

VII

JOACHIM OF FIORE
(C.1135–1202 CE)

I n Western and Central Europe from the eleventh to the sixteenth
centuries there is widespread evidence for messianic movements
among the dispossessed and refugee elements of both rural and
urban poor. These movements have been studied, for example, in Norman Cohn's classic work *The Pursuit of the Millennium*. He wrote:

> Revolutionary millenarianism drew its strength from a population
> living on the margin of society – peasants without land or with too
> little land even for subsistence; journeymen and unskilled workers
> living under the continuous threat of unemployment; beggars and
> vagabonds – in fact from the amorphous mass of people who were
> not simply poor but who could find no assured and recognized place
> in society at all. These people lacked the material and emotional
> support afforded by traditional social groups; their kinship-groups
> had disintegrated and they were not effectively organized in village
> communities or in guilds; for them there existed no regular,
> institutionalized methods of voicing their grievances or pressing their
> claims. Instead they waited for a *propheta* [a messianic or prophetic
> figure] to bind them together in a group of their own.[1]

The name Cohn gave to this phenomenon was 'revolutionary millenarianism and mystical anarchism'.

A figure who operated in the twelfth century on a much more
elevated intellectual plane than that described was Joachim of Fiore
(*Gioacchino de Fiore* in Italian), otherwise known as Joachim of Flora.
Dante was to honour Joachim as a 'prophet', one of the spirits who

contributed most to the enlightenment of the Church,[2] in Canto XII.141 of *Paradiso*. Joachim was born *c*.1135 in the village of Celico, near Cosenza, in Calabria (then part of the Kingdom of Sicily) and he died on 30 March 1202. His father was an influential notary named Mauro, but his mother died when he was only seven years old. Joachim was educated at Cosenza, and became a clerk in the courts and then himself a notary. In 1166–7 he worked for the archbishop of Palermo, Etienne du Perche, during the reign of Roger II, king of the Two Sicilies. A pilgrimage to the Holy Land *c*.1169 proved to be a turning point for Joachim. In a visionary experience in the Church of Holy Sepulchre in Jerusalem an angel opened the text of the Apocalypse in front of him and sought to explain its meaning, at that stage apparently unsuccessfully.

Joachim returned from Jerusalem, converted to the spiritual life and became a hermit for several years. He joined the Cistercian abbey of Sambucina, near Luzzi in Calabria, as a lay brother. He was ordained priest and applied himself to the study of Biblical texts, especially the book of Revelation. In 1177 he was made abbot of the monastery of Corazzo, very much against his will. When relieved of administrative responsibilities by the Pope, he devoted himself to writing, keeping (it is said) three scribes busy day and night with his dictation. When Joachim retired, still with papal approval, he founded the abbey of San Giovanni (St John) in the mountains of Calabria at Fiore (now Jure Vetere), as a stricter branch of the Cistercian order (*Ordo Florensis*).

There is a story, possibly apocryphal, of an encounter between Joachim and the English king Richard I, when the king asked for an explanation of chapter 12 of the Apocalypse:

> [Joachim] could offer Richard the Lionheart little comfort when the English King, *en route* to the Third Crusade, summoned him down from his mountain retreat and asked for a glimpse of the future. 'What black tidings lie beneath that cowl' a contemporary is supposed to have exclaimed.[3]

The influence of Joachim's ideas proved to be very extensive, throughout Europe, and lasted from the thirteenth to the sixteenth or seventeenth centuries; these ideas were mingled within the millennialist tradition, and had a particular impact upon the thought of the Franciscans. Joachim's apocalyptic views, advocating a return to poverty and simplicity, fuelled the Franciscan protest against the wealth and privileges of the church, as a result of which the Franciscans were persecuted in 1318 under Pope John XXI and their doctrine of Poverty was condemned in 1323.

Joachim himself, however, did not start from a marginalised and revolutionist position; instead he believed that the Christian Church had within its social and ecclesiastical base the potential to fulfil the required conditions for the apocalyptic time that was assuredly coming. Joachim saw this world as the theatre of all God's activity. And so, as an organised thinker, the abbot mapped out a schematic vision as to how this eschatological expectation would be fulfilled. He incorporated the traditional features of warfare and the ultimate victory over the Antichrist, with its sequel in the Last Judgement.

The basis of his work was an evaluation of the book of Revelation, as a description of the seven periods in the history of the Church (an historical exegesis and application of the text often referred to as 'world-historical' or 'church-historical'). The particular focus is on the seven-headed beast of Revelation 17.9–10:

> the seven heads are seven mountains on which the woman is seated; also, they are seven kings, of whom five have fallen, one is living, and the other has not yet come.

The text is taken to represent six ages of suffering for the Church, followed by a Sabbath (which is the Millennium), and then a climactic eighth period, which is that of final consummation and eternal rest. The original source of this scheme of world ages probably lies in the Biblical account of the six days of Creation followed by a seventh day of rest. Similar schemes had been developed by the early Church Fathers,[4] notably by Augustine of Hippo. Augustine's divisions of history into ages had been intended to identify the relationships between universal and sacred history, to mark out the turning points in sacred history as fixed points in universal history.[5] Augustine's predecessors, in the use of the six-fold scheme of ages, had borne in mind the text from 2 Peter 3.8 (see also Ps. 90.4) : 'with the Lord one day is like a thousand years, and a thousand years are like one day'. However, although Augustine was fond of number symbolism, he repeatedly dissociated himself from the idea that each world age would therefore necessarily last for one thousand years.

A visual impression of the medieval understanding of the ages of the world and of man can be glimpsed in the stained glass of the fourth typological window in the north choir aisle of Canterbury Cathedral. An underlying principle is the significance of the number six (as Augustine and other commentators understood it) based on the six water jars of stone at the marriage feast at Cana, according to John's Gospel (2.6). The window demonstrates the connection by illustrating the Cana story between two other windows depicting (on the left) the ages of the world and (on the right) the ages of man. In the window on the left the ages of the world (in Biblical sacred history) are represented by the seated figures of Adam, Noah, Abraham, David, Jechoniah (see Matt. 1.11–12) and Christ. The ages of the 'typical' human being are seen in the right-hand window as: infancy (a baby); childhood (a boy with ball and stick); adolescence (a youth in red holding a sceptre); a young man in his prime (bearded with a sword); maturity (an older bearded man with a wallet and a loaf); and old age (an old man with a crutch). The Latin inscription on this window is translated: 'By working the first of his signs [at Cana] God turned the water of vices into the wine of good morals.' A comparison could be made with the speech of Jaques ('All the world's a stage…') in Shakespeare's *As You Like It*.[6] There is little problem in moving between six and seven ages, given the seven days of the week composed of six days of creation and the Sabbath rest.

An interesting comparison can be made between Joachim and Otto, the twelfth-century bishop of Friesing. Otto was claimed to be the outstanding historian of his century. *The Two Cities* was his master work,[7] spanning in time from Adam and Eve to the coming of the last days – which he believed had actually begun. In form and philosophy it stands as a landmark in medieval historiography. As brother of the Emperor, Otto had an insider's view on the significant events of his day, including the Investiture Controversy and the Second Crusade.

To come back to Joachim, the first four periods in his scheme of ages are the times of strife for the various orders within the Church against their opponents. These are:

1) The apostles against the Jews, in Revelation 2–3.

2) The martyrs against the Romans (from Nero to Diocletian) in Revelation 4–7.

3) The doctors of the Church against the Arian rulers of Constantinople (Vandals, Goths and Longobards) in Revelation 8–11.

4) The 'virgins' against the Saracens (the Muslims as enemies of monasticism) in Revelation 12–14.

The fifth period is that of a conflict between the Church in general and Babylon, representing the degenerate Holy Roman Empire – a period that Joachim depicts in terms of events contemporary to himself. It is followed by the sixth period, the time of Antichrist, in which Babylon will come to judgement. After this the Church will be renewed for the Millennium by a return to the poverty and simplicity of apostolic times, as a result of the influence of the new orders of monks and friars devoted to the contemplative life (*novi viri spirituales*). It is not surprising that such a confrontational and adversarial interpretation was turned subsequently against the papacy itself, first by certain Franciscans, notably Peter John Oliva in his work *Postilla super Apocalypsim*, and subsequently by various sectarian and reforming movements. The tradition of this interpretation was inherited by Martin Luther and is reflected in the Lutheran exegesis of the Bible in the sixteenth and seventeenth centuries.

The initial force of Joachim's interpretation of the book of Revelation lay in its prophetic statement of an eschatological message rooted in his own times. He was able to establish a cumulative effect from the individual conflicts of the first five periods by reapplying a theory of Recapitulation,[8] first initiated by the Church Father Irenaeus in the second century CE. Each of these conflicts is taken up into the total conflict confronted by the Church. Joachim suggested that the years following 1200 would see the start of a transition to a new age, but he himself never assigned a specific date to this happening.

Joachim also saw this historical process in theological terms, such that the Christian doctrine of the Trinity provided the overall structure for the action, with each of the persons of the Trinity – Father, Son and Holy Spirit – belonging in different epochs of the history of the world. Again, the three-fold scheme, whether this is based on the Trinity or on the pattern of ages that can be suggested by Luke's Gospel and the Acts of the Apostles (the times respectively of Israel, Jesus, and the Spirit and the Church), was an available resource for analysing the world periods (just like the six days of Creation), having been used extensively before Joachim (for example by Augustine of Hippo). In Joachim's scheme, the time of God the Father began with Creation and extended over the period of the Old Covenant or Testament, represented by the Hebrew Bible; and the time of God the Son was represented in the New Covenant or Testament, beginning with the Incarnation but continuing until the end of the twelfth century. From the accomplishment of these two stages or states of time (Joachim's preferred term was *status*) there would follow the third and last state, the eternal reign of God the Holy Spirit.

A modern reader is likely to raise questions about the selection of these interpretative patterns of six or seven world ages and a Trinitarian theological scheme of three. How can these coexist, particularly when three into seven does not go without remainder? At least a partial solution is offered by the original sources in the book of Revelation itself, where patterns of the week and of threes are both employed (see Rev. 6.1, 8.6 and 9.12 for examples). It is rightly observed that Revelation's patterns have a mystical effect when superimposed – rather like a kaleidoscope.

The late Marjorie Reeves, the historian from St Anne's College, Oxford, who researched the thinking of Abbot Joachim, interpreting a series of strange diagrams to be found in the manuscripts of his *Liber Figurarum* with the claim that they depicted this grand theory of providential history, stemming from certain key passages in Scripture with a prophetic character. Dr Reeves saw the *figurae* as:

the work of an artist and a mystic who endeavoured to express the mysteries of the Trinity and the patterns of history in strange and rich visual forms ... It is as if each happening had a vertical point of reference, a 'thread' in the hand of God who combined threads into patterns on the inner side of history, whereas we look only for the horizontal connections and the pattern of visible cause and effect spun out along the time span.[9]

Marjorie Reeves went on to substantiate and explore the implications of this in a succession of publications, of which the climax was *The Influence of Prophecy in the Later Middle Ages* (1969). Her work was readily accepted by specialists in the period, but the wider claims about the influence of this outlook and philosophical tradition of apocalyptic prophecy upon mainstream mediaeval theology took longer to become accepted. Beryl Smalley admitted, in the preface to the third edition of her classic work *The Study of the Bible in the Middle Ages*, that:

I dismissed Joachim of Fiore and Joachism as 'an attack of senile dementia' in the spiritual exposition. The outflow of books and papers on the subject has made my metaphor look silly. I must change it and say that the spiritual exposition in its old age produced a thriving child, though not one that I should care to adopt.[10]

The culmination of the historical process in the third *status* of God the Holy Spirit was seen as bringing about what Marjorie Reeves described as 'a new quality of life rather than a third set of institutions, a quasi-mystical state rather than a new age'.[11] This was to be a state essentially of contemplation, not action, building on the mystical language of St John in the book of Revelation, rather than developing the papal power structures of the see of St Peter. With the coming of the Eternal Evangel the true Spirit of Christ's teaching would prevail, and the Church would be spiritualised and reformed.

In Revelation 14 we find this angel flying midway between heaven and earth, with an 'eternal gospel' (14.6) to proclaim to everyone on earth, a gospel that turns out to be judgement and injunction rather than obvious good news. From the outset this image had proved to be something of a puzzle, as fascinating as it was hard to interpret. The major role of structural importance it played in the understanding of the ages of history in the work of Joachim was a solution worthy of the puzzle. What is also remarkable is the extensive influence of this interpretation in Western thought long after the twelfth century.[12] Joachim had provided a prototype for the idea that there may be an arcane and mysterious wisdom, passed on from generation to generation, as the key to the future. This thought fascinated many in modern times, and it is suggested that the doctrine of the Three Ages has a direct echo in the philosophies of history of Saint-Simon (scientific society), Hegel (the age of the actualised Spirit) and Marx (the society of full communism), as well as in Hitler's Third Reich. It spread more widely still in works of literature, including, for example, those of Lessing, Schiller, George Sand, George Eliot,[13] W.B. Yeats and D.H. Lawrence. Both Yeats and Lawrence studied Joachim intently and used him in their 'apocalyptic' writings.

W.B. Yeats wrote in his 1921 poem, 'The Second Coming':

Things fall apart; the centre cannot hold;
Mere anarchy is loosed upon the world …
Surely the Second Coming is at hand …
And what rough beast, its hour come round at last,
Slouches towards Bethlehem to be born?

On 30 April 1930, Yeats was staying at a hotel at Portofina Vetta, overlooking the bay of Genoa, where he made a note in his diary of a subject for another poem:

Describe Byzantium as it is in the system towards the end of the first Christian millennium. A walking mummy. Flames in the street corners where the soul is purified, birds of hammered gold singing in the golden trees, in the harbour dolphins, offering their backs to the wailing dead that they may carry them to Paradise.[14]

It has been seen already that Joachim had developed his own thinking as to what this mystical concept in Revelation might entail, within that complex series of *figurae*, which formed a detailed depiction of human life through the stages of history, as represented in the overall Trinitarian structure of thought. A church in Paris, La Sainte Chapelle du Palais, was wholly built and completed between 1240 and its consecration on St Mark's day, 25 April 1248, as a project by Louis IX, both in fulfilment of a personal vow and equally in anticipation of the world's end, expected 12 years later in 1260 CE.[15] The church was designed as a shrine for the relics acquired by Louis during the Crusades, but its real jewels are the stained glass windows that encapsulate the Biblical interpretation of the thirteenth century, particularly as represented in the mysticism and prophecies of Joachim of Fiore.[16]

Joachim's ideas were subsequently associated also with heretical movements, especially some in southern France. A provincial synod at Arles in 1263 CE condemned Joachite teaching and ordered his works to be burned. His writings had also been condemned by the Fourth Lateran Council in 1215, for what was regarded as a tendency to speak of three gods, rather than to affirm the integrity of the Trinity. The year 1260 began to assume, among Joachite followers, the critical point when the third age would dawn (the Biblical basis for this speculation is in references to 1,260 in Rev. 11.3 and 12.6). The preparations for this event produced the strongly ascetic and anticlerical movement of the *disciplinati* or Flagellants (who practised penitential self-flagellation). Thousands participated in such penitence, and 1260 became known as the Year of the Flagellants. It was when the prophecies subsequently failed to be fulfilled that Joachim's mystical historicism lost its influence. Katie Grant, the novelist and historian, writes:

> I think of the year 1260 when people also knew, with absolute certainty, that the world was doomed, through sin rather than environmental carelessness. Encouraged by their leaders, they beat themselves in hysterical preparation. The year dawned, waxed and waned. And what happened? Absolutely nothing at all.[17]

* * *

Gary Dickson assesses the legacy of Joachim as follows:

> The presupposition of Joachite philosophy is a providential Christian philosophy of history in which scripture, both Testaments brought into concordance with one another, allows the prophet–exegete to project the biblical vision forward toward the divinely ordained millenarian future for mankind. If Joachim's vision of the future is an ultimately optimistic, joyous one under the sway of contemplative Christians, in the foreground lies the imminent persecutions of Antichrist, bringing terrible affliction of all kinds before that blissful future dawns.[18]

Some of Joachim's followers, particularly the Flagellants, construed the 'terrible affliction' within the following century in terms of the Bubonic Plague of the Black Death,[19] and responded to it with their ritual response of self-flagellation. In the next chapter we turn to a consideration of ideas associated with plague.

VIII

THE BLACK DEATH AND OTHER PLAGUES

It is difficult to describe the atmosphere of rural England at this moment [during the foot and mouth outbreak in March 2001]. I find myself thinking that the countryside must have been rather like this during an outbreak of plague. Arrested, still, holding its breath, wondering what next.[1]

A small crowd was at the centre of the village, gathered around the preacher. He was warning them of hellfire...

'Step by step we are going down the road to ruination. Today the plague walks the streets of London as freely as a favoured guest. Not a home is safe against it, not a person can be sure he will escape. Not a family in the city but loses one or two. And it is not only London — every village across the land must be wary of strangers, and fearful of sickly people. It is coming, it is coming to all of us — and there is only one escape: repentance and turning to Our Lord.'

'Why is it come to us?' the preacher asked. 'Why should it strike us down? Let us look at where it starts. It comes from London: the centre of wealth, the centre of the court.'[2]

PLAGUES

The incidence of plague strikes terror into the population, comparable to fears about anthrax in the war on terrorism. Highly contagious plagues such as the bubonic plague could sweep through Europe, as they did from the mid-fourteenth century periodically until the eighteenth century. Daniel Defoe wrote a classic account in *A Journal of the Plague Year* relating to the London plague of 1665:

> Nothing but the immediate finger of God, nothing but omnipotent power, could have done it. The contagion despised all medicine; death raged in every corner; and had it gone on as it did then, a few weeks more would have cleared the town of all, and everything that had a soul. Men everywhere began to despair; every heart failed them for fear; people were made desperate through the anguish of their souls, and the terrors of death sat in the very faces and countenances of the people.[3]

The extract at the head of this chapter comes from Philippa Gregory's novel about the gardening family, the Tradescants, and refers to the same period. At these times desperate remedies were sought, and people resorted to magical charms to protect themselves. One such even had the letters of the word 'ABRACADABRA' arranged in a triangular form. Another favoured remedy was to take a live chicken and press its rump against your plague sores, to absorb the badness; when the poor bird fell dead you replaced it with another and another, until one survived and you could be sure that the illness had abated.

The Derbyshire village of Eyam provides a particularly vivid recollection of this time of plague. A London tailor by the name of George Viccars had fled north from the plague and arrived in Eyam with a parcel of cloth for the village tailor, Alexander Hadfield. He opened the parcel because it was damp, and tried to dry it off next to the fire. It is thought that the parcel also contained some fleas that were carriers of the plague. The tailor's assistant was the first to die five days later, but many others rapidly became ill. The vicar of the parish, William Mompesson, took the brave decision to isolate the community from the surrounding world and limit the spread of infection. Bread, flour and other staple supplies were to be left at local landmarks (the boundary stone and the village well) to be collected by the villagers, and paid for by coins disinfected with vinegar.

The vicar's wife, Catherine Mompesson, could have left the village before it was quarantined, but she stayed to nurse the sick and in turn was buried by her husband. When she was taking an evening stroll with her husband, she commented on how sweet the evening air smelled. This normally innocent remark struck a chill in the vicar's bones, for he knew that a cloying, sugary smell in the nostrils was one of the first symptoms of the disease.

The vicar was an able organiser, planning the larger strategies of food distribution and safe burial of the dead. To reduce the risk of infection he held services in the open air, so that family groups could stand well apart from each other. The tradition of this open-air service, in the natural hollow (called Cucklet Delph) where Mompesson preached to his dwindling congregation, is perpetuated to the present, on the last Sunday in August each year, whereupon the present rector's wife lays a symbolic wreath of red flowers on Catherine Mompesson's grave. When the plague was over, it was found that 317 villagers had died and only 33 survived. As a result of their brave decision, however, the illness did not spread further.

This children's rhyme and dancing game is thought by some to have originated at this time of plague (although alternative origins have been proposed). According to the theory, its popular language now veils the description of the deadly symptoms:

Ring a-ring o' roses
A pocket full of posies
Tish-u, Tish-u
We all fall down.

THE GREAT FIRE OF LONDON

Coupled with the experience of the plague in London, and redoubling its apocalyptic lessons, comes the event of the following year, the dramatic fire that destroyed the medieval city of London. What gave special credence to this as an event of judgement in the divine plan of things as prophesied in the Bible was the numerical 'coincidence' of the year 1666, which contained within its digits the number of the Antichrist (666), as in Revelation 13.18. The circumstances of the Great Fire are well documented by the two famous diarists of the period, Samuel Pepys and John Evelyn. Here is a brief extract from

Pepys' diary for 2 September 1666, describing the perspective from an alehouse at Bankside:

> and there stayed until it was dark almost and saw the fire grow; and as it grow darker, appeared more and more, and in Corners and upon steeples and between churches and houses, as far as we could see up the hill of the City, in a most horrid malicious bloody flame, not like the fine flame of an ordinary fire … We stayed till, it being darkish, we saw the fire as only one entire arch of fire from this to the other side of the bridge, and in a bow up the hill, for an arch of above a mile long. It made me weep to see it. The churches, houses, and all on fire and flaming at once, and a horrid noise the flames made, and the cracking of houses at their ruine…[4]

It is surprising to discover how little was done to halt the spread of the flames: partly this would be due to the inexorable advance of the fire, and the fascination with the spectacle, but there was also an air of fatalism, induced by previous and widespread prophecies of the destruction of the city of London.

THE BLACK DEATH

'The Black Death' specifically refers to the great epidemic of plague that ravaged Europe in the fourteenth century, killing between one third and one half of the population. In 1100 the population of Europe had been about 48 million; in 1347, the year of the outbreak of the Black Death, the figure was 75 million, of which an estimated 25 million died, thus reducing the population to its level of 250 years earlier. The Black Death has been widely identified as a form of bubonic plague, caused by the bacteria *Yersinia* or *Pasteurella pestis*, transmitted by fleas borne by migrating Asian black rats, who are the principal vectors.

However, recent research by scientists at Pennsylvania State University has cast some doubt on this precise identification.[5] To judge from English church records, kept by bishops, of the rate of replacement of priests in 1349 and 1350, there was a rate of infection and death (a 45-fold greater risk of death than in normal times) incompatible with modern forms of bubonic plague. Plague does not normally spread directly from person to person, and the transmission by fleas on rats is apparently too slow, and the disease is not sufficiently virulent, to explain the effects of the Black Death. Boccaccio, describing the plague in Florence in the fourteenth century, had observed that the disease struck with such speed that victims often 'ate lunch with their friends and dinner with their ancestors in paradise'.[6] Another discrepancy is that there do not appear to be reports of dead rats in the streets in the 1300s, as are common in recent epidemics caused by bubonic plague in India (Surat in 1994, for example), the Far East, Africa and South America. Research has not yet identified an alternative culprit for the Black Death: possibilities include haemorrhagic fever similar to the Ebola or Marburg virus, anthrax, or a cousin of the bubonic plague organism that has subsequently become extinct.

Contemporary descriptions from the fourteenth century may be insufficiently specific for modern diagnosis. The recorded symptoms of the Black Death include high burning fevers, fetid breath, coughing, vomiting of blood and foul body odour. Other familiar indicators were red bruising or haemorrhaging of the skin, with blood vessels breaking to cause internal bleeding, and the swelling of the lymph nodes or 'buboes' in the armpits, neck and groin. Many of these are features of bubonic plague, but they appear in other diseases as well. The Black Death spread quickly along major routes of communication, such as roads and rivers, defying the natural barriers that might have prevented the transmission of a rat-borne illness. As for the name 'Black Death', it seems that this was not commonly used in England until the early nineteenth century. The name was apt enough because the red patches under the skin quickly turned black, and mortality could be as high as 90 per cent of victims.

Victims of the Black Death were recognised most readily by the swellings, which they referred to as caused by the arrows or darts of God. Within three or four days they would be dead. The epidemic originated in and spread from the Far East and in a span of 18 months nearly half the population of England died. With death tolls this high and a disease this horrible it is easy to understand the fear, panic and disbelief expressed in writings of the time. It is possible that people would not have noticed the incidence of dead rats (if they had been the carriers) or connected flea bites with the black spots of dead flesh that appeared at the site of contagion. There was widespread belief that the plague could be passed by breath, touch or even by sight alone. Everyone was caught off guard, even royalty, the affluent and the clergy. Nobody – even doctors with their astrological methods – had any idea how to cure it. With no explanation of its source, it was natural to believe that so ferocious and decimating an epidemic could only be sent as a punishment from God.

Signs, symbolic happenings and strange occurrences that accompanied the plague augmented the superstitious sense of it having a religious cause. Contemporary writings show how these events were linked with the visions of plague and punishment in the Christian Apocalypse, the book of Revelation. Popular belief pointed to God as the cause, and so God became the only cure. The Catholic Church ordered prayers, processions, fasts and pilgrimages; saints Sebastian and Roch were quickly acknowledged as the patron saints of the plague. Sebastian had been a Roman martyr in the third-century persecution of Diocletian, perhaps chosen as protection against the plague for his courage in the face of a death by arrows. Roch was a hermit and pilgrim of the fourteenth century who himself caught and survived the plague and was believed to have cured other sufferers by a miracle.

After the plague had passed, several accounts depicted its onslaught in apocalyptic terms, or are reminiscent of the miracles performed by Moses against the Egyptians (see Exodus chapters 7–11):

> In the East, in Cathay, which is the greatest country in the world, horrible and terrifying signs appeared. Serpents and toads fell in a thick rain, entered dwellings and devoured numberless people, injecting them with poison and gnawing them with their teeth. In the South, in the Indies, earthquakes cast down whole towns, and cities were consumed by fire from heaven. The hot fumes of the fire burnt up infinite numbers of people, and in some places it rained blood, and stones fell from the sky.[7]

A similar, if more structured, account comes from an anonymous cleric's chronicle of the plague in Avignon:

On the first day it rained frogs, snakes, lizards, scorpions and many other similar poisonous animals. On the second day thunder was heard, and thunderbolts and lightning flashes mixed with hailstones of incredible size fell to the earth, killing almost all the people, from the greatest to the least. On the third day fire, accompanied by stinking smoke, descended from heaven and consumed all the remaining men and animals, and burnt all the cities and settlements in the region.[8]

In such a recollection of the Exodus sequence, the Black Death replaces the assault on the firstborn as the climax of this God-given judgement. The Exodus events had already been linked with apocalyptic happenings in the book of Revelation (especially the final plague sequence of chapter 16). Such occurrences foster the fear of the End; they may provide a chance for repentance, but they certainly heighten the scale of the climactic event. In the popular memory this is something as colossal as Noah's flood, representing the ultimate judgement of God upon the sinfulness of the earth.

Some writers use descriptions of actual flooding, with consequent damage and death. One in particular uses the image of the Flood, and other Biblical disasters, to put the Black Death into perspective, or rather out of any perspective:

The plagues in the days of Pharaoh, David, Ezekiel and Pope Gregory now seemed nothing by comparison, for this plague encircled the whole globe. In the days of Noah, God did not destroy all living souls and it was possible for the human race to recover.[9]

Such a comparison illustrates the overriding sense of hopelessness felt during the plague; it was truly believed that this plague was going to be the end of the world, on a scale of devastation not conceived since Biblical times. During the plague in Ireland John Clynn writes in utter despair, just before he himself dies from the plague: 'I leave parchment for continuing the work, in case anyone should still be alive in the future, and any son of Adam can escape this pestilence and continue the work thus begun.'[10]

The awesome and furious power of God could have been seen as particularly directed to the clergy, either as a warning, or in judgement, because the public's faith in the clergy was slipping on account of their corruption. In 1348 a gigantic column of fire was seen as hovering above the palace of the Pope at Avignon. A ball of fire appeared over Paris, bloody rain fell in Burgundy and in Bologna a giant cross of blood appeared in the sky and hung there for a day until it fell into the ocean. The plague was associated not only with the terrifying nature of God, but also with the hateful practices of demons and evil spirits. These interpretations were not necessarily contradictory, if God is seen as using the malevolent demons to wreak havoc upon, and so to punish, mankind.

The havoc caused by demons was a popular theme during the time of the Black Death. In one description of Messina:

> Just as all the people were entering the city a black dog appeared in their midst, carrying a naked sword in its paw. It rushed raging into the church, and broke and smashed all the silver vessels, lamps and candlesticks on the altar.[11]

There is blatant prejudice against Messina in this account, for the inhabitants had attempted to borrow a statue of St Agatha from the neighbouring town of Catania in order to purify their city from the plague.

There were reported sightings of Plague Virgins: ghostly women who walked slowly through towns, touching the doors and windows, or sweeping dust onto front steps, in order to spread the plague. The pestilence was also disguised as a wandering blind woman, or a black man riding on a black horse. Just before the Black Death arrived in Yorkshire, Thomas Burton reports the sighting of a human monster (most likely a Siamese twin):

> And shortly before this time there was a certain human monster in England, divided from the navel upwards, and both masculine and feminine, and joined in the lower part ... They died, aged about 18, at Kingston-upon-Hull a short time before the pestilence began.[12]

The phenomena before and during the Black Death were linked to the signs prophesied in the book of Revelation. Accordingly there was a universal belief that the End was at hand, since the plague was identified with the fourth apocalyptic rider, the one mounted on the pale horse signifying Death and Hades (Rev. 6.8). The Church was fervent in its preaching and prayers, imploring God to stop, through all agencies within reach:

> At this time a child lying swaddled in its cradle at Cremona is said to have addressed its mother by name, and to have related that it had seen the Holy Virgin Mary beseeching her Son that he would not destroy the world; hereafter the child spake never a word till the rightful time had come.[13]

The Black Death was easily placed within the chronology of the Last Days. The preceding earthquakes and wars, and the horrors of the plague itself, were seen as the destruction following the un-leashing of Gog and Magog (Rev. 20.8). The theological justifica-tion for this was seen in the essentially corrupt and sinful nature of the people. At this time workers and servants had been demanding higher wages or better treatment, not least because many were dying from the plague and replacements were hard to find. Such work-ers' protests arguably anticipated the later Peasants' Revolt, but at this earlier time such action was regarded as sinful and dangerous, a sure indication that the demons and Satan himself were directing the people. As the chronicle from the cathedral priory at Rochester states:

> No workman or labourer was prepared to take orders from anyone, whether equal, inferior or superior; but all those who served did so with ill will and a malicious spirit. It is therefore much to be feared that Gog and Magog have returned from hell to encourage such things and to cherish those who have been corrupted.[14]

A wealth of such apocalyptic symbolism is brought together in the famous prophecy about the Cedar of Lebanon. In a Cistercian monastery at Tripoli it was claimed that a hand appeared out of thin air and wrote this prophetic message on the cloth that was covering the sacraments:

The lofty cedar of Lebanon shall be set ablaze, and Tripoli destroyed and Acre taken, and a borderer will conquer the world. Within 15 years there will be one faith and one God. The bark of Peter will be tossed in mighty waves, but will escape and have dominion at the end of the day. There will be many battles and great slaughter, fierce hunger and mortality, and political upheaval; the eastern beast and the western lion will subjugate the whole world by their power; and for 15 years there will be peace and an abundance of crops. Then all the faithful will pass to the Holy Land over the parted waters, and the city of Jerusalem will be glorified and the Holy Sepulchre honoured by all. In this tranquillity there will be heard news of Antichrist. Be watchful.[15]

Rumours abounded that Antichrist was already living in the world, and had a terrifying or impressive appearance. He was supposedly ten years old in 1349, and was amazingly intelligent and skilled, such that none could equal him. The Antichrist would slay his adversary, a good strong boy raised as a Christian in the Far East, and would assume total power after the deaths of the current Pope and his successor.[16] During the Black Death popular fear was so great that terror of the End Time dominated thinking and writing. Utter hopelessness pervaded the attitudes both at the time and in retrospect. It seems that, even if such symbolic events could not be irrefutably proved to have happened, people needed such reports and devoured them as avidly as celebrity gossip in the modern media. The serious point is that such fulfilment of apocalyptic expectations gave a justification for the Plague. The Church declared that it was God's punishment for their sins, and these happenings supplied a physical and concrete corroboration of the message. It was a curious comfort to pass the ultimate responsibility to God. People's fear and anger and pain thus could find an outlet in pleading with the Almighty or cursing their fate.

Even when the crisis seemed to be past, the recollection of such emotions could serve as a solemn warning to others. In the ambulatory of St Leonard's church at Hythe in Kent, there is a spectacle to arouse the curiosity of the modern visitor, and to provide historical evidence of the use of the church as a charnel-house. An extensive ossuary collection of medieval skulls and bones was assembled there before 1500; it may well be related to the Black Death, designed to serve as a memorial of the religious lessons of human mortality.

The circumstances of warfare, especially in the heat of battle, could seem at least as apocalyptic as the sufferings of plague. International warfare was a fact of life and death throughout much of the period considered in this chapter – as, for example, in the Hundred Years' War. The novelist Bernard Cornwell researched the background of his *Harlequin* trilogy with great care. One illustration, of the hero's reflections in battle, can indicate the apocalyptic view:

> The day of judgement, Thomas thought, would feel like this, as men and women waited for the heavens to break and the angels to descend and for the graves to open so that the virtuous dead could rise into the sky. His father, he remembered, had always wanted to be buried facing the west, but on the eastern edge of the graveyard, so that when he rose from the dead he would be looking at his parishioners as they came from the earth. 'They will need my guidance,' Father Ralph had said, and Thomas had made sure it had been done as he wished. Hookton's parishioners, buried so that if they sat up they would look eastwards towards the glory of Christ's second coming, would find their priest in front of them, offering them reassurance.[17]

Perhaps one should mention, in the sharpest of contrasts to the 'sombre melancholy',[18] grief and pessimism that characterised the waning of the Middle Ages – and this was a pessimism induced by a whole raft of problems, including war, sickness, plague and economic depression – that there is an instance of theological optimism in the writings of Julian of Norwich (c.1342–c.1413). She asserts that in God's plan all shall be well, while not therefore denying the adversarial power of sin:

> I may make all things well, and I can make all things well, and I shall make all things well, and I will make all things well, and you will see yourself that every kind of thing shall be well.[19]

SPECIALIST BIBLIOGRAPHY

Champion, Justin, *London's Dreaded Visitation: The Social Geography of the Great Plague 1665*, Historical Geography Research Monograph 31 (London, 1995).

Deaux, George, *The Black Death* (London: Hamish Hamilton, 1969).

Defoe, Daniel, *A Journal of the Plague Year* (London: J.M. Dent, 1957).

Horrox, Rosemary, *The Black Death* (Manchester: MUP, 1994).

Nohl, Johannes, *The Black Death* (London: George Allen and Unwin, 1926).

Ziegler, Philip, *The Black Death* (Harmondsworth: Penguin, 1969).

IX

APOCALYPSE AND CIVIL WAR (1500 CE AND AFTER)

The diverse activities of Savonarola, Michelangelo, Botticelli, Columbus and Dürer, together with the reading of the works of Dante, all provide cumulative evidence for the contemporary significance in apocalyptic terms of the year 1500 CE. The theme of political disturbance and revolution is there from the outset, particularly in late fifteenth-century Florence. A compilation of these details is followed here by an assessment of the evidence for sixteenth-century millennialism (including the geographical presuppositions identifiable in the work of Mercator). It is also important to examine the later evolution of such ideas, both in the politics of Oliver Cromwell and also in the activities of the Fifth Monarchy Men, Levellers, Diggers, Ranters and Muggletonians.

GIROLAMO SAVONAROLA (1452–98)

Savonarola was an Italian – a fervent ascetic – and a zealous reformer and outspoken preacher, who entered the Dominican Order at Bologna in 1474. When he moved to Florence in 1482 he gained notoriety by his passionate denunciation both of the immorality of the Florentines in general and of the clergy in particular. As he preached, with a tongue of flame, upon apocalypse and the rebirth of grace, he could be seen as part of a movement for 'new learning' and *rinnovazione* in Italy. Savonarola made effective use of apocalyptic language in prophesying the future of the Church. As the Prior of San Marco in 1491 he laid down political reform for the city in his treatise *Rule and Government of the City of Florence*; he accurately predicted the end of Lorenzo de' Medici (the 'Magnificent') and the exile of Lorenzo's son Piero; and he supported Charles VIII of France as the instrument of God for the reform of the Church (during the king's Italian campaign of 1494–5). Savonarola became the moral dictator of Florence for several months, following the defeat and expulsion of the Medicis in 1494.

He ruled by instilling spiritual fear into the people of Florence, foretelling a great disaster that would be the consequence of offending God. The republic of Florence was to be a Christian commonwealth, with God as sole ruler and the gospel as the law. Savonarola, in his puritanical beliefs, encouraged many of the citizens to gather in the public square and to discard their costliest ornaments and paintings, together with their profane books, to be made into a huge 'bonfire of the vanities'.[1]

Savonarola made enemies as a result of these political and religious activities, rather like the prophet Jeremiah speaking in support of Babylon. He had disobeyed a papal summons to Rome to explain his prophecies, and he disregarded the subsequent excommunication by Pope Alexander VI. Among his enemies were other religious orders, particularly the Franciscans; one of them proposed an ordeal by fire between himself and Savonarola, to test the validity of the prophecies. The trial by ordeal did not happen, but the citizens imprisoned Savonarola and had him tortured. The marketplace of Florence, the Piazza della Signoria, was the scene of his execution by hanging, as a schismatic and heretic, in 1498, although many of his writings actually represented an orthodox Catholicism. The Medici returned to Florence after his death, the French armies invaded Italy again in 1498, and Cesare Borgia also threatened Florence: such events were readily seen as the troubles heralding the last days, while the Devil was loose upon the earth.

MICHELANGELO
(MICHELANGIOLO BUONARROTI, 1475–1564)

The famous artist of the Italian Renaissance was born on 6 March 1475 at Caprese in Tuscany, the second of five sons. His career in art had begun in 1488 as a pupil of two Florentine painters, but he was attracted to sculpture and studied under Bertoldo (a disciple of Donatello) who introduced him to the circle of Lorenzo the Magnificent and the traditions of the Medici. At court he was in contact with many brilliant thinkers, artists and writers of his day; he himself studied anatomy (with the assistance of the local priest), wrote poetry and developed an interest in architecture.

Michelangelo came under the influence of Savonarola, whom he had first heard preach in 1492, the year in which his first patron Lorenzo died. The monk's sermons and example had a lifelong effect on Michelangelo, but he was also deeply affected by the loss of Lorenzo. In these two conflicting associations he first felt within himself the major tension between the classic ideal of sensuous beauty, and the religious asceticism represented by Savonarola; for a significant part of his career this remained an ongoing conflict. It could be said that the *Pietà* completed in Rome in 1501 represented the harmonisation of classic beauty and Christian austerity.

Probably best known are his frescoes on the ceiling of the Sistine Chapel in the Vatican (1508–12) representing the preparation for the gospel, in the Old Testament sequence from Creation through the Hebrew prophets and the Gentile Sybils.

The Sistine ceiling is the Renaissance at its most optimistic … His history of the universe reflects the celebratory sermons the pope [Julius II] liked to hear, the humanist theology that said it was important to praise God's creation. It perfectly expresses the Renaissance belief that human beings are special.[2]

Michelangelo's later work, the fresco *Last Judgement*, painted over the altar on the east wall of the Sistine Chapel from 1534 to 1541 at the request of Pope Paul III, is a very different concept, the antithesis of Renaissance optimism. But here too he brings his own personal perspectives to the work; this time it is a religious vision formed from the ascetic influence of Savonarola on Michelangelo, not the classical influence of Lorenzo de' Medici. This is a 'personal hell – a painted inferno – modelled on that in the great poem by his Florentine literary hero, Dante'.[3] As a symbol of Dante's influence, the figure of Charon can be seen at the bottom of the fresco; he is presented as in Dante's description, standing in his boat with an oar raised to strike.

In classical myth Charon had been the ferryman to take the dead across Acheron; here he is herding the damned into Hell. The theme of Last Judgement (changed from Pope Julius II's original request for a depiction of Resurrection) was thought appropriate for Rome at that time as it was recovering from a number of murderous attacks on the city, and also on the papacy, with resulting famine, poverty and plague.

This fresco depicts the last day of the world, with Christ returning to the earth to pronounce judgement, with a powerful energy even suggesting revenge. Michelangelo places Christ centrally, towards the top of the painting, and the circular movement of the whole picture revolves around him. Rather than the grotesque tortures of earlier medieval depictions, Michelangelo's account of the torments of Hell is dominated by the torment of personal remorse. One man holds a hand to his face as he is dragged down to Hell by devils; he offers no resistance, but his anguished face shows that he recognises his fate. Beneath him is one of the golden trumpets belonging to the seven angels of the Apocalypse who have heralded the Day of Judgement (see Rev. 8). The large figures of the saints each carry the instruments of their martyrdom. One of them, Bartholomew, holds his own skin as a symbol that he was flayed to death. On this flayed skin Michelangelo has included his own self-portrait.

Alessandro Filipepi Botticelli (1444/5–1510)

Sandro Botticelli's fame today rests on his large-scale pictures of mythological subjects, deployed as elaborate allegories (for example *Primavera* (1481–2) and also *The Birth of Venus* (1484–5)). His work was rediscovered by the Pre-Raphaelites in modern times. It is not true (as Vasari claimed) that Botticelli never painted again after the Dominican preacher Savonarola was hanged and burned on 28 May 1498. Botticelli's brother Simone was certainly a follower of Savonarola, and it is possible that other members of the family were as well; Simone was still using Sandro's studio for clandestine meetings of disciples and sympathisers (known as the *Piagnone* or 'snivellers') as late as November 1499. Botticelli's own style of painting had effectively changed under the influence of the preaching of Savonarola, becoming harsher, more linear and prone to exaggerated, even distorted figures.

The *Annunciation* of 1493 shows the transition, moving away from the classical goddess image of the Madonna, to an angular 'sweet melancholy' more akin to the image of Mary Magdalene. Most dramatically of all, the *Mystic Crucifixion* (a damaged work now in the Fogg Art Museum at Cambridge, MA) is said to be a reflection of one of Savonarola's apocalyptic sermons, depicting both the fate of Rome suffering violent destruction, and also Jerusalem (here Florence) as the brilliant focus of salvation.

The only picture that was signed and dated by Botticelli is the companion work *Mystic Nativity* (in the National Gallery, London). The date is highly significant, at 1500 CE, when the Second Coming of Christ was expected. The painting represents the Nativity (or first coming) of Christ in ways that heighten its significance for Botticelli's own time. The date is found inscribed within a text in Greek, on a gold band across the top of the picture:

> I Alessandro painted this picture at the end of the year 1500, during Italy's troubles, in the half time after the time [the half millennium], which fulfilled the 11th chapter [of the Revelation] of St John, in the second woe of the Apocalypse when the Devil is set loose for 3½ years; afterwards he will be chained, as in the 12th [chapter] and we shall see clearly [ ]⁴ as in this picture.

On other scrolls held by angels in the sky are inscribed a litany to the Virgin Mary (with words written by Savonarola), and on the scrolls held by the angels in the foreground are the words of Luke 2.14 (*Gloria in altissimis Deo, et in terra pax hominibus bonae voluntatis*).

The *Mystic Nativity* shows angels and men celebrating Jesus' birth. Mary kneels in adoration before her son, watched by the ox and the donkey at the manger; Joseph sleeps nearby. Shepherds and Magi with their angel escort hurry to worship at the inner shrine of the stable. In the foreground three human figures embrace angels: the men are thought to represent Savonarola and the two other friars (Silvestro and Domenico) who shared his martyrdom. Seven demons flee from the scene to the underworld. The mysterious symbolism of the picture succeeds in combining the twin themes of Christ's birth and his Second Coming (when he will be victorious over the Devil and his demons).

As has been seen already, these were dangerous times in Florence (where Botticelli lived and worked), when one could be denounced for political reasons. Botticelli himself was anonymously accused of sodomy in 1502. He was known to be profoundly neurotic by temperament and affected by millennialism; he may well have expected that the Second Coming of Christ would coincide with the year 1500.

DANTE ALIGHIERI (1265–1321)

The following details provide some relevant clues from what is known of Dante's biography. He was born in Florence, the son of a lawyer, on 14 May 1265, and was educated by the Dominicans. Beatrice, his early love (encapsulated in the mysterious figure in the *Divina Commedia*), was probably the daughter of a Florentine citizen, Portinari. In 1301 Dante became involved with the anti-papal faction in Florence; the city was split between two parties, and, because his faction was defeated, Dante was tried for corruption, was exiled and had his property confiscated. So he became a wanderer between the cities of Italy. He induced the Emperor Henry VII to besiege Florence when he visited Italy in 1310. However, Henry died, Dante's optimism for a return to Florence was short-lived, and the city renewed its sentence against him. In 1317 he settled in Ravenna. His political philosophy favoured a universal monarchy, where all temporal power was vested; in his view its authority was independent of the Pope, but seen in parallel with the Pope's supreme spiritual authority. This was in accordance with the two-fold destiny of humanity: temporal happiness in this world, and eternal blessedness in the world to come.

In the mid-fourteenth century, Dante's *Divine Comedy* had been read, copied and illustrated throughout Italy. As the half-millennium (1500) approached, Dante's account of the afterlife seemed especially worthy of study. Between 1499 and 1502 Luca Signorelli painted the Chapel of the Madonna di San Brizio in Orvieto Cathedral with scenes of the Last Judgement, the elect, the damned and the deeds of the Antichrist. Below these stupendous scenes are portraits of the most important authors: Empedocles, Lucan, Ovid, Horace, Virgil and Dante – the last two are surrounded by scenes from their respective works, *The Aeneid* and *The Divine Comedy*. Dante takes his place alongside the writers of the ancient world as an authority on the afterlife. Signorelli's frescoes were painted as a timely reminder to all of the consequences of abandoning Christianity's precepts. Today, Signorelli's paintings are used as cover illustrations for Mark Musa's translation of Dante in the Penguin Classics series.

ALBRECHT DÜRER (1471–1528)

The artist Albrecht Dürer was born in Nuremberg and also died there. He was the son of a goldsmith and the godson of one of Germany's leading publishers at the time. By this association he recognised the potential for an artist of mass production: Dürer's lasting reputation is based on his engravings, originals made both in wood and copper, which were reproduced many times. An series of woodcuts called *Apocalypse* was published by Dürer in 1498 (as the end of the world was thought to be approaching).

This was a pioneering work, notable for the fact that Dürer produced and published the whole book of the series, not only making the blocks for the illustrations but also cutting the text. The image *Four Horsemen of the Apocalypse* is the best known of the series, but Dürer's whole work became definitive as a representation of the visions of John in the book of Revelation, and was reproduced frequently during the sixteenth century. The scholar Erasmus, a contemporary of Dürer, declared that the artist 'even depicts what cannot be depicted: fire, rays of light, thunderstorms, sheet lightning … characters and emotions … the whole mind of man as it shines forth … and almost the very voice'.[5]

As a friend to leading humanists, Dürer had championed the power of the human word in his prints. One such depicted the Son of Man, with flaming eyes, stars and a sword-hilt to his lips (*St John Beholding the Seven Golden Candlesticks* from the *Apocalypse* series).

When Albrecht Dürer inscribes the date 1500 on the self-portrait where he represents himself in the image of Christ, it seems certain that he is acknowledging the mythic importance of the lapse of one and a half millennia since the Incarnation. His self-image gains in spiritual profundity from the association with this significant date.[6]

MILLENNIALISM IN SIXTEENTH-CENTURY SOCIETY

Immediately prior to the start of the sixteenth century many were affected by Millennialism; there was an air of expectancy that an apocalyptic event would occur at the turn of the century. There was much debate as to who would be saved and who would not. Because of the Church's dominant position in society at that time, people naturally turned to the Church for aid. The Catholic Church was thus able to impose a traditional form of capitalism upon society by playing on the fears of the populace. Society was pre-industrial, the economy had a traditional agrarian base, and the movement of labour was frowned upon. Indeed, such movement was considered unbiblical, in accordance with 1 Corinthians 7.20 ('Everyone should remain in the state in which he was called'). The movement of produce and goods around the country was slow and difficult, and over-production could lead to waste or profligacy. What was required was a sufficiency for everyday needs at a reasonable level, after which the need to produce declined.

The issue of 'The state in which he was called' set the terms for the next stage of the debate. If it is accepted that 'many are called, but few are chosen' (Matt. 22.14), then people would query who was doing the calling – and how did people know whether or not they were of the Chosen? Such questioning of the Church represented the beginnings of change, at the end of which was the Reformation, the coming into being of Churches that were non-Catholic and were more dependent upon an interaction with society. Martin Luther is naturally seen as a leading light of the Reformation, but in many respects he still operated within traditional perspectives of religious calling; for example, Luther condemned the Peasants' War of 1524–5 in southern Germany, which had been precipitated by economic hardships.

Johann Stöffler was a mathematician in Tübingen who predicted a universal flood for the year 1524, in his *Almanack* of 1499. The satirical poet Sebastian Brant, author of *Das Narrenschiff* (1494 – *The Ship of Fools*), was nearing his death and in 1520 wrote his last poem in a mood of acute pessimism:

> Such confusion will arise everywhere, such horrible happenings,
> as though the whole world were to be destroyed.
> May God help holy Christianity!

Arks were built in Germany and France against the flood, and the wet summer of 1520 was followed by a famine. The war that erupted in 1521 between the Habsburgs and the French crown led to massive tax demands by the Habsburg administration, from the need to finance its army. In 1522 taxes were at three times their 1470 levels. The war crippled trade and led to recession. In 1525 revolution finally engulfed Germany:

> Castles and monasteries [were] put to the torch … For two weeks in April, Cologne burned. By the summer of 1525, copies of 'Twelve Articles' listing the grievances of the Upper Swabian peasants were circulating in Antwerp. Already printed in 25 editions, as many as 25,000 copies of the Articles were distributed through the Holy Roman Empire. Having reserved his judgement earlier, Luther now condemned the rebels. By the end of the year, 100,000 peasants had been slaughtered.[7]

Gerard Mercator in his *Chronologia* of 1569 himself predicted the end of the world ages. The key date as a starting point for these calculations was the year 1517, when Martin Luther made his public criticism of Indulgences. To this date was added the period of 71 years that the population of Judah spent in their Babylonian captivity. The result was the year 1588, to be dated as the time of the Apocalypse. As a prelude to this time of the End, the year 1576 was seen as the beginning of a ten-year cycle, following the prophecy of Hosea (10.12), in which the 'fallow ground' must be broken up.

Mercator's time of the End was not depicted with any of the traditional images of Antichrist, deluge, or all-consuming ball of fire; rather it followed the predictions of Hosea's reign of righteousness (8.4–7,14; 10.2; 14.4,7). This use of Old Testament prophecy by Mercator compares with his citing of Micah's lament (6.3: 'O my people, what have I done to you? In what have I wearied you? Answer me!') on his very first map, that of the Holy Land. In Mercator's mind mathematics was applied to theology, and the Scriptures thus verified as historical fact.

CHRISTOPHER COLUMBUS
(1451–1506)

The Byzantine calendar of the emperor Constantine VII Porphyrogenitus (in 950 CE) measured the years from the *Annus Mundi* or *Cosmogenesis* (the Creation of the Universe), which in our terms would work out as 1 September, 5509 BCE. The benefit of this calendar was, as the emperor expressed the wish, that 'hereby may the imperial power be exercised with due rhythm and order; may the empire thus represent the harmony and motion of the Universe as it comes from the Creator'.[8] The other aspect of this calendar was that it had a built-in End of Time, with a Day of Judgement on the Eighth Day, the Millennium or Era. This ending, according to the Greek Patriarch of Constantinople, Gennadios II Scholarios, who died 20 years before it happened, was calculated to be AM 7000, or 1492 CE. When the time came many of the Orthodox seemed to have underplayed it, although the Day of Judgement was depicted even more vividly in their churches in the ensuing years. However, the year 1492 CE was the year when, on 27 October, Christopher Columbus discovered America (actually Cuba).

Columbus was an Italian navigator and explorer, who in 1478 settled in Portugal, and from there made four journeys to the New World (in 1492 to San Salvador Island, Cuba and Haiti; from 1493 to 1496 to Guadaloupe, Montserrat, Antigua, Puerto Rico and

Jamaica; in 1498 to Trinidad and the mainland of South America; and from 1502 to 1504 to Honduras and Nicaragua). The commercial intention of his voyages was ultimately to find a westerly route through to the kingdoms of the East, to India and Asia, and thence round the world. As he wrote in his journal, 'Gold is most excellent … he who possesses it may do what he will in the world, and may so attain as to bring souls to Paradise.'[9] Unfortunately there was no room on the globe, as he had drawn it, for another ocean, the Pacific, because he thought the earth was much smaller than it is. And so as he sailed along the coast of Darien in 1502 he was deceived into thinking that Cuba, which lay behind him, was actually part of China, and he expected at any moment to round the Malayan peninsula, to see the cape where Singapore now stands and to draw closer to the river Ganges.

Columbus saw in his expeditions to the lands of the west the confirmation of Biblical prophecies that Joachim of Fiore[10] and others had interpreted, the principal effect of which was to indicate the imminence of the end of the world:

> Millenarianism of the kind advocated by [Joachim of] Fiore, hermetic philosophy, Jewish Messianism, prophetic movements, Holy Wars waged internally and externally for the victory over the Antichrist, the omnipresent power of the Inquisition, disputes within universities and palaces. This is the world that Christopher Columbus inhabited.[11]

His voyages were also made in the hope that he might discover the earthly Paradise described in Genesis 2; Columbus was actually confident that he had succeeded in this aim, as he described the mouth of the river Orinoco in Venezuela: 'I confirm that this river flows out of the Earthly Paradise and from an infinite country … it is my firm conviction that there in the place which I indicated lies the Earthly Paradise.'[12] Columbus's journals indicate his strong sense of a vocation to reveal the new heaven and the new earth; he regarded this not as some kind of revelation from heaven, but rather the discovery of what was actually hidden on earth: 'Of the New Heaven and earth which our Lord made, as St John writes in the Apocalypse, after he had spoken it by the mouth of Isaiah, he made me the messenger thereof and showed me where to go.'[13]

OLIVER CROMWELL (1599–1658) AND
CONTEMPORARY MILLENNIAL MOVEMENTS

Oliver Cromwell was born at Huntingdon, north-west of Cambridge, the son of a small landowner. He entered parliament in 1629 and became active in the events leading to the English Civil War. He was a member of the special commission that put the reigning king (Charles I) on trial, and condemned him to death; following Charles' execution in 1649, Cromwell declared Britain a republican Commonwealth. He forcibly expelled the corrupt 'Rump Parliament' and in its place summoned a convention (the 'Barebones Parliament'), which was soon dissolved for being too radical. Under an Instrument of Government drawn up by the leaders of the army, Cromwell was declared Lord Protector in 1653. After a period of military dictatorship, his last parliament offered him the crown, which he refused, so as not to betray the prevailing republicanism.

Among historians, no one can really decide if Cromwell was a millenarian or not, but such attitudes certainly influenced his politics. This was the intellectual climate when people

> were convinced of the special nature of the times through which they were living, and persuaded by the millenarian writings of contemporary English and German divines that the sufferings of Continental protestants were a period of trial which would eventually end in triumph ... They were inspired by biblical promises of the restoration of human perfection at the end of time, and by the belief that contemporary wars and disasters were signs that human history was coming to its conclusion.[14]

B.S. Capp summarises in similar terms the factors leading to the Fifth Monarchy movement:

> The tension produced by the Reformation thus combined with nationalism, Protestant literalism, Calvinist elitism and perhaps Lollard tradition to produce widespread apocalyptic and millenarian

beliefs. The civil war, breaking out in 1642, soon came to be seen as the decisive apocalyptic or millenarian struggle intensifying earlier excitement.[15]

Similarly, as Simon Schama writes specifically of the English scene:

For the hottest Protestants, free to speak their minds in the void left by bishopless England, the only proper successor to King Charles was King Jesus. Prophecies abounded that a new millennium was at hand, and that the destruction of Antichrist and the coming of the Last Days were imminent. Combing through the books of Daniel and Revelations, the most fervent declared that the Four Monarchies – of Egypt, Persia, Greece and Rome – would now be succeeded by a Fifth: the reign of the godly, the visible saints. To those gripped by this ecstatic fervour, the execution of the king had not just been a political act but a sign from God that he had indeed chosen England as his appointed instrument for a universal redemption. And the freshly sanctified country would look like no other realm, for its mighty would be laid low and its humble raised up.[16]

As Schama says, the basis of this 'fifth monarchy' view is to be found in the Old Testament book of Daniel: the four beasts of Daniel 7 are the four empires of the ancient world; the fourth (the Roman) had been usurped by the papacy (identified as Antichrist: the beast of Rev. 11–20). The fifth monarchy is that of Christ, exercised on his behalf by his saints for a period of one thousand years, until Christ will return in person to pronounce the Last Judgement. A classic exposition like that by Mary Cary in 1651, *The Little Horn's Downfall* and *A New and More Exact Map or Description of New Jerusalem's Glory when Jesus Christ and his saints with him shall regn on earth a thousand years and possess all kingdoms* indicates the way in which the Apocalypse succeeded Daniel in providing resources to outline the Kingdom of God on earth.

The Fifth Monarchy Men were extreme Millenarians, in movements that arose in 1649 and spread out from London (under the leadership of Christopher Feake and John Simpson) and also from Wales (led by Vavasor Powell and Morgan Llwyd).[17] It has been maintained that the Fifth Monarchist movement can be traced back to the Anabaptists, who emerged as a consequence of the revolutionary activities of Thomas Müntzer early in the previous century. A dramatic account of Thomas Müntzer's progress as pastor, apocalyptic mystic and revolutionary during the early Reformation period is given by Hans-Jürgen Goertz.[18] From Müntzer's first appointment to Zwickau in 1520, to his bitter end at Frankenhausen in 1525, his theology remained consistent and stable: to manifest the Kingdom of God through 'a full and final reformation in the near future', which would engage humanity both spiritually and temporally. Theological texts with provocative doctrines, such as *Imitatio Christi* – which emphasised the necessity of suffering, in the spirit of mystic piety – were not by any means Müntzer's sole source of inspiration; his experiences through working with miners, peasants and artisans augmented his views toward an open encouragement of revolution. His forced confession, followed by his execution, are portrayed by Goertz as the witness and example of a martyr who is attempting to continue the spirit of his reform both through the experience of suffering and in his utter subjection to the will of God.

The Fifth Monarchy Men of the seventeenth century differed from orthodox puritans, although holding similar views, because they applied Scripture very literally to current events, especially the regicide. They set an early and precise date for the destruction of Antichrist, and were confident that they themselves were the saints; their task was then to overturn the government and erect the promised Kingdom by their own efforts. Militants led uprisings in 1657 and again in 1661. They accused Cromwell in that he 'tooke the Crowne off from the heade of Christ, and put it upon his owne'.[19]

If we try to assess Cromwell's personal disposition, temperament and psychology, Schama's comments are helpful once again:

> Throughout his life as a public figure, Cromwell believed himself to be no more than the weak and imperfect instrument through which an almighty Providence worked its will on the history of Britain. Often he sounded like the stammering Moses, drafted by an insistent Almighty into business he would rather leave to someone else. But there was, as he wrote to Oliver St John in 1648, no shirking the call: 'The Lord spake thus unto me with a strong hand and instructed me.' Cromwell, then, believed he worked for God. Real dictators believe

they are God ... Psalm 110 was much on his mind and his lips: 'The
Lord shall send the rod of thy strength out of Zion: rule thou in the
midst of thine enemies.'[20]

Within the political situation there were those, like the Levellers,
who demanded the most radical of reform solutions. The Levellers
were a party originally of mutineers, some ten troops from the par-
liamentarian 'New Model Army', who were essentially republicans,
calling for a freeholder democracy. But Cromwell, who was not un-
sympathetic to their cause, had been compelled to execute the three
ringleaders, after a court martial, in the churchyard at Burford in
Oxfordshire on 17 May 1649. Although the original spark for the
mutiny in Salisbury had been arrears in military pay, and the sol-
diers' desire to return home rather than fight in Ireland, many were
influenced by Cromwell's failure to recall the General Council of the
Army and endorse a draft document, 'The Agreement of the People'.
A system of political equality, rather than economic equality, was in
mind. The Agreement stated that parliament should not have power
to 'level men's estates, destroy property, or make all things common'.
Although some enthusiasts, calling themselves 'True Levellers', did
talk of turning the world upside down.

Another group, called 'The Diggers', was already practising com-
munal living in Surrey. This was the most radical movement of the
day, with an aspiration for 'making the earth a common treasury'. The
Diggers were certainly influenced by apocalyptic ideas, most notably
the scheme of three ages expounded by Joachim of Fiore,[21] and they
believed that the Age of the Spirit was now dawning. However, they
were not Christians in any recognisable sense. It was the spirit not the
letter of religion that mattered to them. Their leader Gerrard Winstanley preferred the word 'Reason' to 'God' and described Christ as
'the spreading power of light', present in creation, so that those who
recognised it could become Sons of God.[22]

'The Ranters' was the name given to an anarchic movement that
emerged in 1648, to the horror of orthodox puritans. They were never an organised sect; their writings are so diverse that it is disputed
whether they ever really constituted a single movement. Their belief
was expressed in an immanent deity who is present in all his creatures.

Human beings who are attuned to the godhead would be free of sin and could indulge in dancing, drink, smoking, swearing and the sharing of sexual partners.

The Muggletonians, or 'believers in the third commission', were followers of Ludowicke Muggleton (1609–98) and his cousin John Reeve (1608–58). In 1651–2 the two of them received revelations, for which Reeve was the messenger and Muggleton the spokesman. Their message affirmed Jesus but denied the doctrine of the Trinity; they claimed that they themselves were the Two Witnesses of Revelation 11, and held that Elijah had governed heaven during the time of Christ's Incarnation. Muggleton was convicted for blasphemy in 1653–4 and again in 1677. The Muggletonians engaged in controversies with the Quakers, in particular William Penn (who wrote *New Witnesses Proved Old Heretics* against them in 1672).

A variety of secular and religious goals were ultimately on a collision course during these years. The historian Jacqueline Eales wrote on preaching in Kent in the 1640s and explained how Royalist preachers, like the minister of Goudhurst, faced being shot by parliament's troopers during the English Civil War.[23] The Baptist churches were involved in radical action, stimulated by messianic and millenarian expectations; they with others were part of the Nominated Assembly (an extraordinary parliament with a millenarian inspiration, convened after the collapse in 1653 of the republican 'Rump Parliament'). The 'Seekers', as their contemporaries called them, adopted a hyper-radical position, waiting for a new beginning of the Church; the mood of expectancy in the 1640s and 1650s encouraged the thought of new and miraculous revelations. Of course, it could be said that such thinking was the result of disappointment (that the execution of Charles I had been a negative achievement rather than the establishment of Christ's Kingdom) just as much as the product of messianic expectation. Of the most intense religious motivation,

> Barebone's was the closest that Britain … ever came to a theocracy: a legislature of Christian mullahs, and it was not very close at all. For all Cromwell's holy thunder about the imminent reign of the righteous, the crackpot frenzy of their matter and manner put him off the saints in a hurry.[24]

One of the Biblical themes that attracted particular attention and detailed exposition in the sixteenth and seventeenth centuries was the Temple of Jerusalem. Originally built by King Solomon, it had been restored after the Babylonian Exile, and then splendidly rebuilt by Herod, client king of Rome. The Temple had also featured in Old Testament prophecy, particularly in the extended visions of the prophet Ezekiel. In the terms of Christian prophecy the corresponding expectation was of the New Jerusalem, descending from heaven to take the place of the historical site. It was in these terms of the book of Revelation that the rebuilding of the Temple and the restoration of Jerusalem were seen as essential preconditions for the Millennium, when Christ would come to reign on earth for a thousand years. The Puritan William Prynne (1600–69) declared, for example, that at this time 'the holy Temple [would be] restored at Jerusalem; the holy utensils prepared'.[25] Scriptural accounts include the dimensions of the building; the decoding of these details fascinated Biblical interpreters, and indeed inspired developments more widely in the science of architecture. The most holy place in the Jerusalem temple was designed as a perfect cube, and so this was also a structural requirement of the New Jerusalem.

The narratives of the Bible were understood historically and literally within the Protestantism of this period. Exposition was frequently concerned with questions of Biblical chronology and geography; how could one reconcile with the Biblical account more recent knowledge about countries or peoples such as the Americas or the Chinese? Georg Horn, a history professor from Leiden, was among many writing on these newer discoveries who saw no reason to modify the accepted narrative derived from Scripture. His work of 1666, *Arca Noae sive historia imperiorum et regnorum*, has a title page showing Noah's Ark tossing on stormy seas. In the skies above the ark four animals (lion, bear, leopard and eagle) are depicted fighting for dominion over the globe. These represent the four beasts of the Old Testament vision in Daniel 7; the eagle may reflect the later modification of the apocalyptic tradition in 2 Esdras 11–12, to include the eagle of the Roman Empire, but it is more likely to be an upgrading or modernisation to represent the Imperial Habsburg eagle. These creatures, in whichever form, symbolise the four great empires that will have ruled the world, before the coming of the Kingdom of the Saints. Providence has ordered the rise and fall of nations; ultimately it will bring about the downfall of contemporary tyrannies (which, for Horn, included the papacy) and the establishment on earth of millennial harmony.

* * *

All the radical movements of this period shared the belief that history was moving towards its end, in ways that had been prophesied and elaborately anticipated. This shared conviction that they were now living in an age that was 'somehow the climax of human history, the era for which all previous events had been a mere preparation'[26] is explicable simply because the Civil War and the execution of a reigning monarch were events unparalleled in English history.

The English scientist and mathematician Sir Isaac Newton (1642–1727) can supply a tailpiece to this story. Here was a scientist guided by religious fervour, taking the Bible seriously and wishing to identify God's activity in the world. Newton

> spent endless hours studying the floor plan of the lost Temple of King Solomon in Jerusalem (teaching himself Hebrew in the process, the better to scan original texts) in the belief that it held mathematical clues to the dates of the Second Coming of Christ and the end of the world.[27]

In a paper Newton wrote in the early 1700s, which has been largely lost to sight until it recently was placed on public exhibition at the Israel National Library in Jerusalem, he developed clues from the book of Daniel to claim that the world would be safe from destruction until at least 2060 CE: 'It may end later, but I see no reason for its ending sooner.' This statement supports the value of Scripture, but opposes the widespread use of text for apocalyptic predictions:

> This I mention not to assert when the time of the end shall be, but to put a stop to the rash conjectures of fanciful men who are frequently predicting the time of the end, and by doing so bring the sacred prophecies into discredit, as often as their predictions fail.

X

EDWARD IRVING (1792–1834 CE) AND THE CATHOLIC APOSTOLIC MOVEMENT

E dward Irving was born in 1792, in Annan, Dumfriesshire, the son of a tanner. As a boy he loved popular sport and swimming, but also had a reputation for physical violence. He was educated at the University of Edinburgh and subsequently became a schoolmaster (at Kirkcaldy Academy), and a licensed preacher. For years he was to experience frustration as merely a probationer for the ministry. In 1819 he was appointed as assistant to the Scottish theologian, preacher and reformer Thomas Chalmers (1780–1847), at St John's church in Glasgow, where Chalmers was conducting a social experiment to support the poor out of the free-will giving of the church. Chalmers and Irving presented quite a contrast in style, attitudes and churchmanship.

Three years later Irving moved to the Caledonian Church in Hatton Garden, London, where he was to enjoy great success as a preacher. But he also stirred up controversy, for example with a three-and-a-half hour sermon preached in 1824 for the London Missionary Society on the theme of the 'ideal missionary' (someone like St Paul, without worldly commitments and support); it was also tactless to dedicate the sermon to the semi-heretical Samuel Taylor Coleridge. As a result of his studies of the book of Revelation he began to announce that the Second Coming of Christ was imminent. His work *Argument for Judgement to Come* was published in 1823, and regarded by many as naive. However, Irving's initial troubles with the Church of Scotland were not on these grounds. In 1828 he was first charged with heresy for maintaining the sinfulness of Christ's nature, based on his personal conviction that Christ must have suffered and been tempted. He then published *The Orthodox and Catholic Doctrine of our Lord's Human Nature* in 1830; this became the basis of the heresy charge on which the London Presbytery of the Church convicted him in 1830, and the reason for his ejection in 1832 from the new church in Regent's Square to which he had moved. He was finally deposed in 1833.

Irving, as a minister of the Church of Scotland, worked primarily with a fashionable middle-class congregation in London. From 1825 onwards he had become engrossed in studying, in ever greater detail, the prophecies of the book of Revelation, as they were applicable to the years following the French Revolution. At this time there had been an upsurge of both literary and artistic interest in the themes of Romantic millenarianism. Irving himself preached that the climactic seventh bowl (Rev. 16.17) was shortly to be poured. The Irvingites are a good example of an involvement, within the popular millenarian revival, that was recognisably more middle-class and intellectual. They 'rapidly developed gifts of prophesyings, glossolalia, spiritual healing, automatic writing and telepathy'.[1] When Irving was expelled from the Church of Scotland, the majority of his congregation remained loyal to him. His followers continued to meet at the Owenite socialist headquarters (clearly this group was no longer acceptable in the eyes of the middle-class world!), before they formed themselves into a new communion called the Catholic Apostolic Church, widely known as the Irvingites.

The Catholic Apostolic Church had its derivation from a series of meetings that had been held in 1826 at Albury Park, the home of the London banker and Tory politician Henry Drummond (1786–1860). Irving himself established a congregation meeting in Newman Street in 1833, the first time the name 'Holy Catholic Apostolic Church' was used. Irving was not actually its leader, for he was not regarded as possessing apostolic gifts; again, his probationer's frustration must have reasserted itself. The Church developed its own hierarchy under the names of apostles, prophets, evangelists and pastors, as well as deacons whose responsibility was to superintend material needs:

There are those alive who can remember the feeling of trepidation with which surviving members of the Irvingite Church watched the declining years of the last survivor of these 12 'Apostles' within the life-time of whom Edward Irving, the founder of the community, had prophesied the visible return of Christ. And when the last of these did die, and the Lord did not return, that community received a grievous shock.[2]

The celebrated New Testament scholar B.H. Streeter was discussing this phenomenon as an analogy to the apparent belief, among some early Christians (as reflected in John's Gospel, see 21.22–3), that the Parousia would take place before the death of the last of the original believers. The last Irvingite Apostle actually died on 3 February 1901, at the age of 96. The Catholic Apostolic [Irvingite] Church[3] subsequently admitted that it had made a mistake, but the nature of this mistake was carefully defined.

A letter to the *Church Times* in June 1993 from Mr Robin Davies claimed:

> The Catholic Apostolics saw themselves as a movement within the Universal Church calling on all Christians to prepare for the Second Coming – as all who recite the Nicene Creed do, at least in theory. In anticipation they produced a liturgy[4] which has received much praise from liturgists. Their corporate life emphasised sound biblical teaching (including tithing) and discipline. That Our Lord did not return as expected was seen as caused by their failure to prepare the Church adequately. The 'time of silence' is one of humility, not embarrassment, and it is in this spirit that members continue in prayer and piety to wait for Our Lord to show his purposes more clearly.

A reference made by Dr Edward Norman in a previous issue of the *Church Times* to the Irvingites – 'It is difficult to see the Catholic Apostolic Church as anything other than a refuelling stop on the road to Waco'[5] – is rejected by this correspondent as bizarre because 'they did not stockpile arms'.

The Catholic Apostolic Church came into existence officially in 1835, the year after Irving's death. Father Flegg's book (see note 5) suggests that Irving's lasting influence was comparatively slight. It is argued by him (not entirely convincingly) that they were a church, not a sect, because they were led by educated people of the professional classes. The magnificent church building of cathedral-like proportions, best known now as the Church of Christ the King, in London's Gordon Square, was opened on Christmas Eve 1853, as the Central Church of the Catholic Apostolic movement. Its hierarchy was complex, with as many as 64 clergy and officials associated with the building. The 'Apostles' were bankers, landowners and professional men. Some of the 'Angels' (the equivalent of bishops) were renegade clergymen from the Anglican church. The building in Gordon Square still retains its original fittings and there is said to be a storeroom in the vaults full of elaborate vestments for the Apostles, Angels and Christ himself.

The Apostles had been brought together by the banker Henry Drummond at a series of conferences held at Albury Park in Surrey. There were 12 Apostles, each charged with the task of proclaiming the new revelation to a particular area of Europe, during the course of a mission lasting 1,260 days. This mission started early in 1838, seeking meetings with the Pope, monarchs and other church leaders. Mostly their requests were refused, and William Dow, Apostle to Russia, who requested an interview with the Tsar, was served with a deportation order. By the middle of the nineteenth century the church had grown to around six thousand members and 30 places of worship. The church in Gordon Square represented the new-found confidence of the movement.

The leadership of the movement sustained it throughout the nineteenth century, but because of its expectations it was at risk in the longer term: 'Precisely because the end is perceived to be imminent, it is not necessary to make adequate structural or organisational provision for the future.'[6] Some of the Catholic Apostolic movement expected the Second Coming to happen in 1900, and were shaken when it did not take place. When the last of the Apostles died in 1901, there could be no more ordinations. The last priest apparently died in 1971.

In 1871 the Reverend Charles Maurice Davies compiled a series of reports for the *Daily Telegraph* on the variety of alternative beliefs to be found in London; he was sharp in his comments about the Irvingites of Bloomsbury: 'singular for their spirit voices and three-hour rituals, for which they adopted every colour of robe – black tippets, puce tippets, short surplices, coloured stoles'. Gavin Maxwell (1914–69), the Scottish writer, traveller and conservationist, who was brought up in the church, also reminisced about the wearisome experience of services with seemingly endless sermons and depressing hymns, conducted by frail elderly men.

* * *

The year of Irving's birth (1792) was of course the year that the effects of the French Revolution began to set Europe ablaze. In Sheridan Gilley's words, 'The French Revolution, and a new kind of social and political unrest, reawakened the Protestant apocalyptic mentality, with a new attention to the letter of the scriptural text, which proved that the last days had come.'[7] The events of 1792 and 1793, with the Revolution's ultimate attack on the Roman Catholic Church, marked the end of the period when the papal Antichrist would persecute the saints of God. This was the death-knell of the Scarlet Woman of Revelation 17. The time of the Beast/Harlot/Antichrist's domination was calculated as 1,260 days, standing for 1,260 years (equal to the three-and-a-half times or the 42 months of Daniel and Revelation). Subtracting 1,260 years from the date of 1792 produces the date of 533 CE, the time when the universal jurisdiction of the Pope had been recognised by the Pandects (the digest of the Roman law) of the Emperor Justinian. So from the Protestant perspective this was the timescale of the papal authority, which began from Justinian and faced its end at the Revolution.

These calendrical calculations, for Irving and some of his Protestant contemporaries, only arrived at the year of Irving's birth, however significant that might be. It should also be noted that scientific historians would regularly date the watershed of the French Revolution to 1789, not 1792. As described in the balanced assessment by Alec R. Vidler:

The French Revolution was a great dividing-line in the political history of Europe, the sign of the downfall of the *ancien régime*, a sort of atomic bomb of which the fallout is still at work. It was a beginning as well as an end: the beginning of a still continuing series of attempts to build new structures to take the place of the system that had collapsed.[8]

However, the book of Daniel (12:11–12), provided a further set of possibilities for Irving and his contemporaries in calendrical calculation, by mentioning not only 1,260 days, but also 1,290 and 1,335 days (or years). These provided for an additional period of up to 75 years, and it seemed attractive to subdivide this into two eras of 30 and then 45 years. While the end could come finally in 1867, in the meantime 1823 was a highly significant date. Between 1792/3 and 1823, the first five bowls containing the woes described in Revelation 16 had been poured out on the apostates of humankind. So now in 1823 the sixth bowl of divine wrath is being poured, containing suffering of the kind that the current political and industrial revolutions were causing. And Edward Irving had just moved to take up his ministry at the Caledonian Chapel in Hatton Garden.

Irving's own absorption in the study of the apocalyptic can be dated to his reading of the work by a Chilean Jesuit, Manuel de Lacunza Y Diaz, *The Coming of the Messiah in Glory and Majesty*. Lacunza had become a recluse in Italy after 1767 when his order was disbanded. His work was published under the pseudonym Juan Josafat Ben-Ezra, a converted Jew. It was translated from the Spanish by Irving himself, who had only just begun to learn the language.[9]

Irving preached a three-hour sermon in 1825 to the Continental Society, in which his pessimistic philosophy, coloured by his exegesis of Revelation and his reflection on the Second Coming of Christ, is clearly represented. He spoke of a premillennial event in catastrophic circumstances that only Christ's return would be able to redeem. In Sheridan Gilley's words, Irving

interpreted prophecy as a sanction for … crusades against Roman Catholicism and liberal Protestantism. Irving spoke of the assurance in prophetic Scripture of the end of the 1260-year-old Babylon of

Rome, the 'Little Horn' of Daniel, in 1792; of the time of trial and tribulation which was to last for 75 years following; of the ravages of radicalism and revolution in politics, and of liberalism and rationalism in religion, sometimes uniting with Rome, as in the campaign in Britain to emancipate the Roman Catholics; of the existing churches as increasingly under these influences, both apostate and fallen; of the restoration of the Jews to Palestine; and of Christ returning in 1867 to a darkened and unconverted world.[10]

Irving converted his sermon into a two-volume work, published in Glasgow in 1826.

Another factor in Irving's prophetic pessimism was related to his view of the suffering vulnerability in the nature of Christ. He related Christ's suffering to his own, in a sequence of a broken love affair, an unhappy marriage with a wife who was unwell, and the early deaths of most of their children. His infant son died in October 1825. Irving wrote of this:

And why should I not speak of thee, my Edward! seeing it was in the season of thy sickness and death the Lord did reveal in me the knowledge and hope and desire of His Son from heaven? Glorious exchange! He took my son to His own more fatherly bosom, and revealed in my bosom the same expectation and faith of His own eternal Son! Dear season of my life, ever to be remembered, when I knew the sweetness and fruitfulness of such joy and sorrow.[11]

Edward Irving's ministry was comparatively brief; his chief work had been done in the years between 1822 and the date of his death from consumption in 1834, at the age of 42. He had been consecrated as a Catholic Apostolic Angel by John Cardale, a solicitor proclaimed as the first of the Apostles. Ernest Sandeen commented on Irving:

If early nineteenth-century millenarianism had produced a hero, he would have been Edward Irving. Instead Irving came to the end of his life in 1834 as an outcast among the millenarian party, his very name transformed into a term of reproach among evangelicals and decent citizens.[12]

However, it will be realised that Irving's espousal of premillennialism – which of course included the idea of the Rapture,[13] as well as the revival of interest in the Biblical basis for a view of the Second Coming of Christ that had been born out of desperation with the state of the world – left a legacy that was rapidly inherited, especially in America. The next chapter continues this story with a discussion of the Millerites.

XI

ACROSS THE POND

This chapter investigates the Millerites in America, beginning with the calendrical calculations of William Miller (1782–1849) and continuing the story with the Seventh Day Adventists and the Jehovah's Witnesses. When the New York farmer, William Miller, predicted that the world would end on 22 October 1844, and that Christ would then return to reign for a thousand years, he was believed by a million followers. Even after their immediate hopes had been dashed by what became known as the 'Great Disappointment', many of these believers remained faithful to their new church, maintaining their expectation that the Second Coming of Christ was imminent. The Millerites were thus the original nucleus of the Seventh Day Adventist and Adventist Christian Churches, which are still vigorous today.

THE MILLERITES

William Miller was born in Pittsfield, Massachusetts. He experienced a religious conversion to the Baptist church during the evangelical revivals of 1815–16. He was a farmer and devoted himself not only to farming but also to the study of the Bible. His principal preoccupation was with elaborate mathematical calculations about the date of Christ's Second Coming, based on the book of Daniel. For example, the 2,300 days of Daniel 8.14 were to be interpreted by substituting years for days (the 'year for a day' principle goes back at least to Joachim of Fiore, see Chapter VII).

Miller was ordained as a Baptist minister, and lectured at churches and conducted revival missions. In Massachusetts he met another Baptist preacher, Joshua V. Himes, who took over the management of what had become a millennial campaign. As a result, William Miller's predictions formed the basis for a mass movement, known to outsiders as the Millerites, while those inside the movement preferred the name 'Adventist'. David L. Rowe reckons that 'these Millerites represent the most significant "end of the world" movement in American history … This was a mass movement, focusing on ideas and expectations that were deeply rooted in early nineteenth-century American culture.'[1] The one unifying factor of the movement was the belief in an imminent Second Coming of Christ and the end of the present world.

According to the Millerites, the letters to the seven churches in Revelation 2–3 were to be understood as a chronological record of stages in church history. This kind of interpretation goes back to the Puritan Thomas Brightman (1557–1607). As church history had continued, so the dates of some of these ages had to be adjusted, but Miller was still convinced that such a historicist interpretation of the churches was 'one of the greatest evidences we have of the truth of the divine inspiration of revelation, and this evidence fixes the authenticity of the Scriptures beyond a reasonable doubt'.[2] Miller understood that he himself was living in 'Laodicea' (Rev. 3.14–22), the last period of Christian history, which he dated as 1798 to 1843–4, that is, the end of time.

In the 1830s the Millerites began to proclaim that the Apocalypse would happen in 1843, and they attracted tens of thousands of converts:

At this dread moment, look! The clouds have burst asunder; the heavens appear; the great white throne is in sight! Amazement fills the Universe with awe! He comes! He comes! Behold the Saviour comes![3]

Sometime in 1843 Jesus would return to earth, God would judge the living and the dead, and he would shatter the earth and create the New Jerusalem out of its ashes. The faithful who were still living would rise to meet Jesus in the air and the unfaithful would be sent to eternal punishment in the flames of hell.[4]

There was no exact agreement on the date when this would happen. The prophecies were derived from the Jewish scripture, and so allowance had to be made for the fact that the Jewish calendar was lunar rather than solar. The span of 1843 was therefore set between 21 March 1843 (the first calculated option) and 21 March 1844. The message of the movement attracted tens of thousands of followers – apprehension about the End reaching fever-pitch when a spectacular comet appeared in the sky. The combination of religious fervour and the scientific prediction of astronomy was a potent mixture. Previously a French mathematician had calculated that Biela's comet, last seen in 1826, would return and cut across the orbit of the earth on 29 October 1832. Panic had been widespread in Europe, until the significant but missing detail emerged that the earth would be about 49 million miles away from the crossing-point at the time. Similarly with Miller's predictions, there was a corresponding anticlimax of relief or disappointment when the latest of his deadlines passed uneventfully a year later.

The date was then revised to precisely 22 October 1844 by Samuel S. Snow of New Hampshire, and this calculation subsequently received a public endorsement from William Miller himself, two weeks before the event. In readiness for this day many left their occupations and homes, wearing white ascension robes in anticipation of the 'Rapture of the Saints':

> On 22 October 1844 thousands of Americans in the North and Midwest spent the day looking for Jesus to appear in the clouds of heaven. Most had only recently heard the warning to prepare for the end of all things, but some had been getting ready for this great day since the early 1830s.[5]

A belief in the Second Coming of Christ, based on the Bible and interpreted in Christian doctrine, is a fairly conventional Christian view of this period. Two aspects are distinctive about the Millerites, however: first, they were premillennialists (in contrast to the postmillennialism stemming from Jonathan Edwards, discussed below), and second, they could accept that insights of this kind could come from the scientific calculations of an ordinary farmer studying the Biblical text. No charismatic personality, with personal revelations and visionary experience, was required.

By contrast Jonathan Edwards, born in East Windsor, Connecticut, and educated at Yale, had succeeded his grandfather Solomon Stoddard as minister of the Congregationalist Church in Northampton, Massachusetts, in 1729. In Northampton Edwards was renowned for his powerful preaching in the hard-line Calvinist tradition; a typical sermon was that of 1741 – 'Sinners in the Hands of an Angry God'. Nevertheless he helped inspire what is known as the 'Great Awakening', from a much more optimistic perspective than would be seen later with the Millerites. He is regarded as the greatest theologian of American Puritanism. His work heralded a revivalism that was to become a continuing thread in American religious life, and is equally related to renewal movements in Britain. Edwards not only invited people like George Whitefield to come and be involved, he also set up a circle of correspondence and prayer involving people in England and Scotland and through them people around the world.

Edwards had a view of history as being divided into three stages: from creation to the birth of Christ; the life and death of Christ; and from Christ's death to the final consummation. He believed that Christian history would be divided into seven epochs, and that the last three were relatively imminent. At the Millennium all could be 'brought into the church of Christ and it looks as if they would generally be true Christians'[6]. Thus there was an imperative to preach and engage in mission to fit in with the evolution of history, and a postmillennial perspective on the climax for the world.

Back with the premillennialists, as a result of what became known candidly as 'The Great Disappointment', when their latest prophecy also failed in October 1844, the Millerite movement largely dispersed. Miller himself recanted, but was expelled from the Baptist church, and then formed a small Adventist church, keeping alive his vision of the Millennium until he himself died in 1849. His remaining followers continued to meet and formally organised the Seventh Day Adventist Church in the year 1863, the name being first adopted in 1861.

DISPENSATIONALISM

Premillennialism had been discredited temporarily in the world at large because of the non-event of 1844, but it would rebound in popularity by the 1870s in the form of a movement known as Dispensationalism, which in turn contributed to the development of Fundamentalism as well as Christian Zionism in the twentieth century.[7] Dispensationalism divides sacred history into various periods (known as 'dispensations'), during each of which God orders his relations with human beings in a different way. It distinguishes therefore between Israel and the Church, arguing that God has here two peoples with two destinies. This is to be contrasted with the alternative Biblical theme of Covenant theology, in which the Church is seen as a development from, and essentially a replacement of, Israel. The dispensationalist movement believed in a Rapture of the Saints prior to the Tribulation and that a millennial reign of Christ would be seen in Jerusalem (see 1 Thess. 4.17 and Rev. 20. 1–3). Dispensationalism began in the USA as a late nineteenth-century phenomenon, and is usually associated with the work and influence of John Nelson Darby and the Plymouth Brethren from Britain.

John Nelson Darby (1800–82) was born in London of an established Anglo-Irish family, educated at Westminster School and then at Trinity College, Dublin. He abandoned the study of law and was ordained in the Church of England. He rapidly renounced his ordination, declaring that the Christian Church was 'in ruins'. He then became the principal founder of the Plymouth Brethren in 1830, gathering together others who shared his convictions about premillennialism and a literal interpretation of the Bible. Ten years later he founded an exclusive sect of the Brethren, which was often referred to as the 'Darbyites'. He travelled widely, especially in the USA, preaching his doctrine of seven 'dispensations'.

The basic building blocks for Darby's system have already been seen in previous centuries of Christian history. However, unique to him was his emphasis on the pre-Tribulation Rapture and his perspective on the distinctions between the dispensations of Israel and the Church. This underlined the importance of the conversion of the Jews and their restoration to their homeland (not least for the practical reason that this would facilitate the Second Coming of Christ). Darby's ideas spread widely through his own efforts and those of other ardent evangelists. Notable among them was Cyrus Ingersoll Scofield, who incorporated Darby's ideas in the annotations of the *Scofield Reference Bible* of 1909. They were popularised further by Hal Lindsey's 1970 novel *The Late Great Planet Earth* and by the recent Left Behind series of novels written by Tim LaHaye and Larry Jenkins, as well as by the missions conducted by the Revd Billy Graham.

CHRISTIAN ZIONISM

William Blackstone, American financier, evangelical Christian and follower of Darby, presented a petition, supported by more than four hundred others, to President Benjamin Harrison in 1891, calling on America to facilitate the restoration of the Jews: 'Why not give Palestine back to them again? According to God's distribution of nations it is their home, an inalienable possession from which they were expelled by force.' Cyrus Scofield also identified Biblical support for the return of the Jews to Jerusalem and the Holy Land. A likely consequence was the destruction of Islamic holy places and the rebuilding of the Jerusalem Temple, thus marking the end of the 'dispensation' of the Church with its Rapture, at the point when the Antichrist would arise.

The term 'Christian Zionism' is defined in Wikipedia as:

> a belief among some Christians that the return of the Jews to the Holy Land, and the establishment of the State of Israel in 1948, is in accordance with Biblical prophecy ... This belief is primarily ... associated with Christian Dispensationalism, mainly in English-speaking countries outside Europe ... Many Christian Zionists believe that the people of Israel remain part of the chosen people of God, [with] the added effect of turning Christian Zionists into supporters of Jewish Zionism.[8]

A leaflet distributed by Christian Friends of Israel states:

We believe the Lord Jesus is both Messiah of Israel and Savior of the world; however our stand alongside Israel is not conditional upon her acceptance of our belief. The Bible teaches that Israel (people, land, nation) has a Divinely ordained and glorious future, and that God has neither rejected nor replaced His Jewish people.[9]

Contemporary Christian Zionism is not an insignificant or archaic movement. Indeed, in a letter from the Archbishops of Canterbury and York written to Tony Blair on 25 June 2004, critical of government policies in Iraq and the Middle East, there was a guarded reference to the growing influence of the Christian Zionist movement in the USA:

Within the wider Christian community we also have theological work to do to counter those interpretations of Scripture, from outside the mainstream of the tradition, which appear to have become increasingly influential in fostering an uncritical and one-sided approach to the future of the Holy Land.[10]

THE SEVENTH DAY ADVENTISTS

Out of the ruins of Millerite expectation came new churches, before the end of the nineteenth century – notably the Seventh Day Adventists and the Jehovah's Witnesses – who would keep the Millerite hope alive. The Adventists worldwide, in a complex doctrinal apologetic known as the 'Investigative Judgement', hold to the belief that the year 1844 saw the beginning of a pivotal era, a point of transition in the heavenly sanctuary ('the beginning of the end'), and therefore as a result the Millennium must be near. They remain premillennialists, like the Millerites, and combine this with a belief in themselves as the 'Remnant Church'. It is their conviction that they are called to proclaim the messages of the three angels in Revelation 14.6–12 to the rest of the world at the end of time:

The prophecy to the last stage of the church of Jesus Christ given in AD 96, looks forward nearly eighteen hundred years, to 1873, and describes, with minute exactness, the condition of things among us, [and] utters a terrific warning of utter rejection without zealous repentance.[11]

[the letter to Laodicea in Revelation 3 was] 'designed to arouse the people of God, to discover to them their backsliding, and lead to zealous repentance, that they might be favored with the presence of Jesus and fitted for the loud cry of the third angel.' [This last phrase is a euphemism for the Second Coming.][12]

Ellen (Harmon) White held that Christ had in fact come, to cleanse the sanctuary of heaven, thus initiating the Final Judgement. But this would be happening quietly, with the evildoers being annihilated rather than damned eternally. Her followers observed their Sabbath after the Jewish pattern from sunset on Friday to sunset on Saturday. The name of the movement 'Seventh Day' derived from this weekly observance. They practise a believers' baptism and have a distinctive belief in the sleep of the soul following death. The Adventists 'crossed the pond' and reached England as early as 1878, with a mission to Southampton.

Currently the calculated total of these premillennialists ('Millerites after the movement', as Harold Bloom calls them [13]) is about ten million. The number has fallen substantially in the USA, but the Adventists are now established in 205 nations and their growth, doubling every decade, is concentrated in the developing world.

JEHOVAH'S WITNESSES

Charles Taze Russell was born in Alleghenny, Pennsylvania, in 1852, the son of Presbyterian parents of Scottish–Irish descent. He had business training and at the tender age of 11 he was a partner with his father in a thriving store for haberdashery and men's clothing. It was not long before Charles was running a number of stores. In 1870 he and a few friends formed a small study group of Bible Students (an early name of their preference) and together they discovered basic scriptural truths that became the basis of a new outreach – 'proclaiming the Lord's return'. In July 1879 Charles Russell began publishing a regular journal, *Zion's Watch Tower and Herald of Christ's Presence*, the first issue of which had a print run of 6,000 copies. By 1914 the print run had expanded to 50,000 copies and by 2002 *The Watch Tower* claimed an average print run of over 24 million.

Russell had reworked several of the doctrines of the Millerites and their date calculations. He engaged in some powerful preaching, claiming that the end of the world was close at hand. Between 1889 and 1904 he wrote a series of books entitled *The Millennial Dawn*. It was reckoned that in the period up to 1914 the Jews would return to Palestine; this migration had already begun when the prophecy was made. There would also be a gradual overthrow of the secular leadership of Gentile nations. The climax was to come in 1914, when the saints would receive glorification and God would begin direct rule over the earth. This would be a year of testing, as *The Watch Tower* declared on 1 November 1914:

> Let us remember that we are in a testing season … If there is any reason that would lead any to let go of the Lord and His Truth, and to cease sacrificing for the Lord's Cause, then it is not merely the love of God in the heart which has prompted interest in the Lord, but something else: probably a hoping that the time was short; the consecration was only for a certain time. If so, now is a good time to let go.[14]

These were harsh words, but clearly this was a very difficult time for the Bible Students, as they analysed their motivation.

When this prophecy of God's direct rule was overtaken by the start of the First World War in 1914, it was not seen as the failure of the prophecy but as dramatic evidence of its truth. The war was interpreted as the apocalypse, the definitive signal that God had indeed taken control over human events. The end was predicted to come in 1918, but Russell himself died first in 1916. There were obvious problems posed in 1918, when the war came to a close, but the Advent did not arrive. Russell's followers reinterpreted the scheme to mean that Christ would have begun a period of 'invisible rule' in 1914 and that this would soon end. Russell's adherents had split into different groups on a number of occasions, but the main body of followers became known as Jehovah's Witnesses.

In the 1990s the Jehovah's Witnesses claimed a worldwide membership of over 5.5 million in more than two hundred countries. In the USA, the country of the movement's birth, the membership is less than a quarter of the total, at approximately one million. The movement as a whole is organised as a theocracy, under the direct rule of Jehovah through Christ, and their government is claimed to be modelled on that of first-century Christianity. They have a president and a governing body of 17 members, with direct control over the whole organisation. Jehovah's Witnesses are Bible-believing followers of Christ, but they reject some of the mainstream Christian beliefs, such as the doctrine of the Trinity, the Incarnation of Christ and traditional ideas of heaven and hell. The Bible is regarded as the infallible source of truth, such that every detail is true. They oppose the medical practice of blood transfusion because of warnings in the Bible against the drinking of blood. They do not celebrate birthdays, Christmas and Easter because these are seen as having pagan origins. They refuse to undertake military service, to vote, or to give allegiance to any country or flag. There is currently much controversy within the movement about the questions of blood transfusion and of pacifism, however.

Central to their belief is the expectation of the imminent end to the world, with a mighty battle and the destruction of all apart from Jehovah's Witnesses. This will be followed by a Millennium, during which Satan will test the saved, to discover whether they are still faithful to Jehovah. Those who survive this testing will inherit everlasting life, mostly here on earth, but for an elite numbering 144,000 this will be with Jehovah in Heaven. Jehovah's Witnesses believe that they are called by God to prepare people for this imminent future; to this end their main activities are door-to-door visiting and the publication and distribution of a mass of literature. An image from Charles Taze Russell, dating from 1889, concerning the studying of Scripture to see that the time is at hand, is to be found still on the Internet, along with teachings such as the following:

> A wonderful modern device, which serves well to illustrate the divine arrangement of time prophecy, is what is termed a Combination Time-Lock, used in some of the largest banks. Like other combination locks, the key or handle remains in the lock constantly. Certain peculiar movements of the handle, known only to one aware of the arrangement, are needful to open it … The Combination Time-Lock

adds the peculiar feature, that the doors when closed at night are so locked that they cannot be opened by any one until a fixed hour the next morning: and then, only in response to the use of the right combination upon which the clock has been set.

Thus our Heavenly Father has closed up and sealed many features of his plan during the night with his great Time-Lock, which was so set as to prevent their being opened until 'the time appointed' – in the morning of the great day of restitution… [cf. Rev. 3.7][15]

XII

JOANNA SOUTHCOTT
(1750–1814 CE)
AND HER FOLLOWERS

J oanna Southcott was an English prophetess in the late eighteenth
and early nineteenth century. She sealed up several of her prophecies in a box which, she insisted, was to be opened at a time of
national crisis, or at the latest in 100 years' time, by a gathering
of 24 bishops of the Church of England. The number 24 reflected the vision of the 24 elders mentioned in Revelation 4.4. She
died following a prophecy that she was giving birth to 'Shiloh'. Her
Box still remains unopened, although the fact of its existence became very well known (indeed, quite notorious) in the early years
of the twentieth century as a result of a publicity campaign and
national advertisements to persuade the bishops to open the Box.
The Box is still retained by the Panacea Society of Bedford, with
some active promotion of the prophecy to this day, and indeed
some funding by them for academic research into the Second Coming. There was, however, a cynical (and perhaps scurrilous) report
that claimed the Box was in fact opened in 1927, although in the
presence of only one bishop, when it was found to contain merely a night-cap, a book, a lottery ticket, a dicebox and some coins.
However, as Jane Shaw of New College, Oxford, declared:

> Joanna Southcott is interesting for much more than 'the Box'. She
> wrote hundreds of books and pamphlets about her prophecies, many
> of which were published in her lifetime. She attracted thousands of
> followers, including prominent Anglican clergymen, and captured
> the public imagination when she claimed in 1814, in her 60s,

that she would give birth to the second coming of Christ. This is all especially remarkable when we remember that she had little education and began life as a maidservant and upholsterer in Devon. She began to prophesy in the 1780s and 1790s, and was known as an accurate predictor of weather, wars and famines. She soon went on to bigger things, prophesying about political and national events in the wake of the French Revolution, and claiming her own identity as the Woman Clothed with the Sun (from Revelation [12]).[1]

In Joanna Southcott's own words:

Remember [the Spirit said] in what powerful manner thou wast visited by day and by night in 1792. And how the whole Bible broke in upon thee, as though Angels that were ministering Spirits were Sounding in thy Ears, that the End of all things was at hand.[2]

[I] dreamed I was on a high mountain, and saw the sky as bright as noon day sun, and two men come out of the clouds, with long robes of purple and scarlet, with crowns of gold on their heads and swords in the hands, standing in the sky. Two men came out with heavy horses, and spoke to those that stood on the clouds, and soon after rode away, like lightning in the air. Soon after, I saw the men on horseback coming out of the clouds, as fast as they could, till the whole skies was covered with men in armour and spears glittering in the air. I thought, I looked down, and saw the world in confusion, men in armour riding fast. This dream alarmed me; and I was meditating with what divine majesty and splendour our dear Redeemer was coming into the world. Once he came meek and lowly, persecuted by men; but now he will come, as a prince and a king, conquering and to conquer.[3]

Joanna Southcott was born on 25 April 1750 at Ottery St Mary in Devon. Her education was very basic; she was literate, but read little other than the Bible and the texts of her great-aunt Sarah's hymns. She had various employment in domestic service and as an upholsterer in Exeter, until, in her early forties, her prophetic gifts took over the whole of her life. In 1791 she claimed that she had received a divine command to join the Methodist Church, but the leadership of the Methodists were no more welcoming of her newly assumed public role than were the Anglicans. Indeed, the Exeter Methodist congregation she joined at Christmas 1791 gave her a distressing rebuff. She interpreted this as the act of the Spirit, however, testing her obedience, in a way parallel to that of Abraham when he was tested with the sacrifice of Isaac. She still held tenaciously to a belief in her role in the Established Church but the Anglican clergy returned her letters, writing to her in what she called 'Billingsgate language' that it was unacceptable to an academically trained hierarchy that an uneducated woman should be the channel of God's message. England's catastrophes could then be seen as God's punishment of the clergy's disbelief in her. The momentum towards a separate congregational movement, parallel to Methodism, became the inevitable consequence of these church reactions.

In the following year, 1792, came her announcement that she was chosen by God in relation to the Second Coming of Christ. In this connection she claimed to see visions of the coming Millennium and of Satan's destruction. She expected to see salvation in the last days, with the earth transformed, as a result of divine intervention that could happen at any moment. The 1812 picture of her, 'drawn and engraved from life' by William Sharp, also shows an open Bible in her hands; the text is open at the end of Isaiah, at the prophecy of new heavens and new earth. In the words of Frances Brown:

> Joanna Southcott was 42 years old and earning her living as a domestic servant in Exeter when she claimed that God had chosen her to announce the Second Coming. In normal times perhaps few would have taken her seriously. But this was 1792 and times were far from normal. The American War and the Revolution in France had shattered everyday certainties for many who, turning to their Bible for consolation and guidance, read in the prophetic book of Revelation that they must expect just such upheavals in the Last Days.[4]

The influence of international events can be corroborated, for example, by noticing the sermon of Joseph Priestley, published in 1794, on 'The Present State of Europe Compared with Ancient Prophecies'. Priestley interpreted the French Revolution as fulfilment of the prophecies in Revelation 11.13 and 17.16 of widespread destruction of cities and the handing over of power to the Beast. He stated it was 'highly probable that what has taken place in France will be done in other countries'. The result would be the 'sudden and most unexpected coming of Christ'. As W.H. Oliver commented in his study *Prophets and Millennialists*, 'in the later 18th and earlier 19th centuries the habit of looking at the world in a manner shaped by biblical prophecy was a normal and widespread activity'.[5]

Joseph Priestley had been a controversial figure, both as scientist and theologian, for some decades. He held a highly individualistic millenarian view that progress in society had to be aided by 'particular providence', namely the possibility of direct Divine intervention. Such dramatic changes in the fortunes of the world might well be accompanied by dramatic incidents and calamities, involving apparently random suffering. On the anniversary of the Gunpowder Plot, 5 November 1785, Priestley had preached a sermon, subsequently published as 'The Importance and Extent of Free Enquiry', in which he said:

> We are, as it were, laying gunpowder, grain by grain, under the old building of error and superstition, which a single spark may hereafter inflame, so as to produce an instantaneous explosion; in consequence of which that edifice, the erection of which has been the work of ages, may be overturned in a moment, and so effectually as that the same foundation can never be built upon again.

Many people – and not only the leaders of the Established Church – remained unconvinced of Joanna's status as a prophet. Indeed, a certain John Leach responded that there were a thousand more likely and worthy recipients for God's message whom he would have employed in preference to her. Even Joanna's family took a lot of convincing; her brother Joseph, sceptical of her prophecies and her mission, declared that God had never communicated so freely with womankind since the Incarnation of his Son, and would never do so again. In contrast Joanna could claim to be the only one who was awake, while the rest of humanity was fast asleep, judging their Bibles as in a dream. But a select few were more ready to respond: for example, William Sharp, a celebrated engraver and friend of William Blake, was convinced that the Millennium was at hand. He originally supported the prophet

Richard Brothers (1757–1824) from Newfoundland who was about to lead the Jews back to the Holy Land. Sharp had already prepared for his own journey to Jerusalem by ordering strong shoes and a coat with specially large pockets to hold shirts and cravats. Now he made the celebrated Box, to enclose Joanna's sealed prophecies until the time of proof.

While not necessarily appreciated by the modern feminist movements, Joanna had a clear sense of the Biblical mission of woman, to reverse the effect of Eve's gullibility in the Garden of Eden and to declare doom to the serpent who was the real villain, Satan himself. Joanna disputed with Satan: 'A woman's tongue no man can tame. It is better to dispute with a thousand men than with one woman.'[6] She identified Napoleon Bonaparte with the Great Beast of Revelation and declared herself the Bride of the Lamb and the Woman Clothed with the Sun (Rev. 12.5). This made her the third most important woman, after Eve and the Virgin Mary.

After the first announcement of 1792, the prophecies were renewed in a sequence of crises over the next 22 years. In London from 1802 the process began of 'sealing the faithful' – the 144,000 in accordance with Revelation 7.4. The Day of Judgement was announced on 25 July 1804. On Maundy Thursday 1806 came the act of boiling up the Bible in a pot, so that it should be fulfilled. The delay in the announced Second Coming raised serious questions and doubt. Joanna sought to explain this by analogy with a visit to the West Country: it all depended on which way round one made the circular tour as to when the Second Coming could be said to have occurred. Expectations of the final crisis built up in 1811 with the public awareness of the madness of their ruler, King George III. But the climax came with the announcement of the coming of Shiloh (according to the Authorised Version of Gen. 49.10): Joanna Southcott, at the age of 64, and never having been married, was to give birth to a boy child, to be named Shiloh. In her confinement she was attended by numerous doctors, most of whom confirmed her symptoms of pregnancy. She refused internal examination, leading some to suspect that disease of the uterus was the real cause of the symptoms, or that it was perhaps a confidence trick.

Strenuous efforts were made to obtain official support from church and state, by books and pamphlets, newspaper advertisements, letters of invitation and seeking to establish semi-public trials to prove Southcott's prophetic writings. Between 1801 and 1814 some 65 books and pamphlets had been published. Another aspect of her Spirit-inspired writing was the production of apparently coded texts, in almost illegible script. It was so illegible that everything she wrote had to be copied out again, and even then the printer levied a charge for the corrections. Her work was claimed to be the product of automatic handwriting, written at the Spirit's dictation. Subsequently examples of the script have been investigated by handwriting experts and cryptographers. A partial explanation of the unusual language lies in the recognition of regional dialect forms native to Devon. As Eric Poole, a lawyer and an expert in deciphering historical documents, once said to me, the spelling is regular and seems 'to reproduce, more or less phonetically, a West Country dialect'. The decipherment 'had to be done by methods similar to the breaking of a simple cryptogram'.

Popular response to Joanna's mission was uneven and patchy, occurring in particular social and geographical areas. Like many others, Joanna had moved from the relative security of a rural economy to the extreme uncertainties of life in the capital city when she travelled to London in 1801. But the response to her built up significant momentum: across the country her followers numbered tens of thousands, including both unsophisticated country folk and educated members of existing millennialist traditions. The poor of Exeter had certainly seen their economic hardships in a new light with Joanna's message of the Second Coming; one in 30 of the population had acknowledged this millennial belief within a single month. The message to the inhabitants of London was terrifying, built as it was on the fear of French invasion: 'nine parts of the inhabitants of London will perish, as the streets will be filled with dead Bodies, French as well as English'.[7]

Joanna offered a symbolic document (a 'seal' or inscribed paper bearing her signature) to all who themselves countersigned her prayer for the Coming of the Kingdom. In January 1803, for example, 58 humble people received a seal. By 1804 the number had grown to more than 8,000. Some Methodist preachers supported Joanna

Southcott and, when expelled from their churches, became powerful advocates of her cause. She resisted for years the setting up of independent worship communities, hoping to win over the Established Church to her support. However, in 1811 she moved in frustration to sanction such independent worship, while stressing the need to apply for legal permission to hold such assemblies.

Some of Bryan Wilson's categories have been employed to characterise the Southcottian movement as 'revolutionist', 'introversionist' and 'thaumaturgical':[8]

> [The] movement was, therefore, 'revolutionist', if not revolutionary, in that its followers did not see a role for themselves as implementers of the new dispensation. [this was to be entirely the result of divine intervention].

> There were significant 'introversionist' aspects in the movement, but, during her lifetime, Joanna's followers viewed themselves as members of a community which was separate from but still part of a sinful world, not one in withdrawal from [the world].

> Because of the pre-industrial culture from which many of the believers came, not surprisingly there was, additionally, a strong 'thaumaturgical' element in their world view. For example, they gained reassurance and emotional release through dreams and visions and, in addition, were given (or, in some instances, purchased) a 'seal' … which was interpreted by many to have magical properties, protecting the possessor against misfortune and, perhaps, guaranteeing long life and even immortality.[9]

Joanna died of a brain disease at the end of 1814, on 27 December, still a virgin at the age of 64. She had not given physical birth to any child, and her medical examiner Dr Reece had declared that the child was 'gone'. Some of her followers still believed that there would somehow be a physical birth, but that this had been delayed because of the bishops' unbelief; although others of her followers variously believed that some kind of spiritual birth had taken place, that Joanna had been mistaken over the physical nature of the birth but ultimately she had not been deceived. King Shiloh was to have a spiritual birth (William Sharp declared that 'on Christmas Day the Child was born') and having been 'snatched away' to heaven he would return to earth as a conquering prince (see Rev. 12.5; 19.11). Just in case, Joanna's body had been kept warm and a post mortem delayed, for four days at her specific instructions, to facilitate resuscitation of the mother and the child if that had been God's will. Her funeral was further delayed as her followers could not believe this turn of events and feared a popular reaction. Even then, some still awaited the miraculous birth as prophesied – but nothing happened.

Joanna's body was buried at St John's Wood in London. Her close friends and followers established the regular practice of meeting at Broadway Tower in the Cotswolds. This splendid vantage point on the ridge commands a view over several counties. It is also close to Rock Cottage in Blockley where John Smith, who became Joanna's nominal husband at the end, lived. This cottage subsequently became connected with the Southcottian mission; it was purchased by Alice Seymour in 1917, a lady who did much to revive the cause of Joanna Southcott in the twentieth century. The Panacea Society, based in Bedford, which is still the custodian of Joanna Southcott's Box, among other activities advertised on its website (*www.panacea-society. org*), offers grants for research into prophecy and the book of Revelation, the life of Joanna Southcott, the significance of her Box, and the beliefs of her followers.

Joanna's followers raised their voices in an optimistic hymn:

The glorious Flag of Liberty,
Which heads all Zion's host;
Jesus suffered death on Calvary,
To redeem the world that's lost;
And Shiloh, he shall reign the King
Of everlasting peace;
When Christ shall reign a thousand years,
All sorrow it shall cease.
God's Spirit now does strive again,
His standard is unfurl'd,
Joanna's children again shall bid
Defiance to the world![10]

One can imagine them singing this on the top of Broadway Tower.

XIII

J.J. JEZREEL: THE TRUMPETER
AND HIS TOWER

James Jezreel and the 'New and Latter House of Israel' formed a Southcottian sect that produced the 'Flying Roll', as God's final message to man. Of particular interest was their architectural project to build the New Jerusalem at Chatham in Kent (a building that was nearly completed but has now been demolished). A few scattered members of the group still survive in the present, and related groups in the USA advertise themselves on the Internet.

Until it was demolished in 1961, there stood for three-quarters of a century, at the top of Chatham Hill in Kent, a massive building known locally as Jezreel's Tower. It was not far short of a perfect cube, with the theoretical dimension of 144 feet, built as an assembly room and headquarters for the Southcottian sect called the New and Latter House of Israel. In the long history of millennial sects, this is a striking example of trying to force God's hand by a literal implementation of prophecy. It was a fanatical attempt to build the New Jerusalem on earth according to the blueprint of John's vision in Revelation 21.10–21.

Of course the builders of medieval cathedrals, like Abbot Suger of St Denis, had also been concerned to reflect in their buildings the symbolism of Revelation. So there were 12 bays with vaulting to represent the fact that the church of God is built upon the 12 apostles, for example. The book of Revelation expressed in visionary language truths that can be found elsewhere in the New Testament. So Revelation 21.14 ('And the wall of the city has twelve foundations, and on them are the twelve names of the twelve apostles of the Lamb') corresponds to the building metaphor to be found in Ephesians 2.19–22, where the apostles are designated as the foundation, and Christ himself is the cornerstone (or alternatively the keystone) of the building which is referred to as the 'household of God' or the Church.

Jezreel's Tower was planned to contain a number of quite remarkable features:

> Chief of these, perhaps, was the circular platform in the centre of the floor of the Assembly Room. It was to be 24 feet in diameter, and capable of being raised by hydraulic pressure to a height of 30 feet. It was to accommodate the choir, and the preachers, and it was to be made to rotate slowly so that each part of the congregation in the vast circular hall could be faced in turn.[1]

James Rowland White, who was born in approximately 1840, was a newly recruited private in the Sixteenth Regiment of Foot (the 'Bedfordshires') who were stationed at Chatham in Kent in 1875. He chose to join a small Southcottian sect which met in a private house on Chatham Hill, under the name of the 'New House of Israel' (which subsequently became the 'New and Latter House of Israel'). White rapidly asserted himself within the group, claiming the prophetic role of 'Messenger of the Lord' and calling himself James Jershom Jezreel. Jershom was based on the name Gershom in Exodus 18.2–3, and Jezreel was converted from a geographical to a personal name under the influence of the prophetic text of Hosea 1.2–5, 10–11 ('great shall be the day of Jezreel'). The selection of names was probably influenced by the alliteration with his own name, James. He signed his initials J.J.J. with a continuous line across the top, signifying the prophet's iron rod.

Jezreel claimed for himself the task of the sixth trumpeter (Rev. 9.13), delivering an apocalyptic warning, and claimed to follow his five predecessors, namely Richard Brothers, Joanna Southcott, George Turner, William Shaw and John Wroe. His new message was contained in the *Flying Roll* (see Jer. 36.2, 28; and Zech. 5.1–2: 'I see a flying scroll; its length is twenty cubits, and its width ten cubits'). Jezreel saw the Southcottian group as representing the Old Testament

'Remnant', identified as a third church after the Christian and the Jewish. According to his prophecies, the part of the 'Remnant' in England would be the first to be saved. They would be 'sealed' as constituents of the 144,000 of Israel (according to Rev. 7.4–8). The expected 'ingathering', or the time of the 'third watch' ('near dawn', as in Luke 12.37–38, when the 'little flock' or the slaves are ready and waiting for their master's return), was very near:

> Blow the Trumpet in this land of England first, and say 'England! The day of thy judgement is come: thou shalt be the first to be judged and the first to be redeemed. England! Thou art the land of Joseph, the granary of the Lord's corn, wine, honey and milk. All Israel shall be driven into this land; there shall 144,000 bones of the Virgin be gathered, when the Trumpet of War shall sound over the earth, but no foreign sword shall enter thy borders!'

> We proclaim to all the nations of the earth that the time is now come (the third watch) that the people of God shall no longer perish, but that the time has arrived when the last enemy death shall be destroyed.

> The people of God are called upon through this message of 'The Flying Roll' to stand for their lives, for they will now be as the children of the bridechamber, mourning when the bridegroom is taken away from them … and they will stand and not perish.[2]

Jezreel's calculations of the nearness of the world's end are based on the equation between one day and a thousand years according to 2 Peter 3.8. The date of God's creation of the world was taken as 4004 BCE (in accordance with the calculations of Archbishop Ussher). The six days of Creation as described in Genesis 1 were the equivalent of six thousand years, divided into three dispensations. The first two dispensations, totalling four thousand years, lasted from the fall of Adam to the crucifixion of Christ. Human beings are now within the third and final dispensation. The year 1875 represented the third watch of the 11th of 12 hours of the present dispensation.

However, ordinary life took a hand in 1876 when White (or Jezreel) found that his regiment was due to be posted to India. He went with the army but maintained contact with his community in

Chatham, sending them further instalments of his prophetic sermons in subsequent parts of the *Flying Roll*. His followers carefully preserved these messages and decided to publish them as *Extracts from the Flying Roll*. The first volume, containing the first long sermon of a projected series of 12, appeared on 1 January 1879.

Jezreel was released from his regiment in 1881, after six years of service, and returned from India on 4 November. Upon his return he married Clarissa Rogers, an ardent member of the original sect. She had already been to the USA on behalf of the group, and now they travelled back across the Atlantic together on a missionary tour of the USA and then subsequently of Australia. Earlier contacts with Southcottian groups in England had met with a rebuff (for example in Ashton-under-Lyne). On their wider missionary tours, when they were accepted it was on the basis of existing sectarian groups who were more favourably disposed; there was little success with the general public. So they returned to Gillingham in Kent, with plans to establish their headquarters there. Jezreel ran an 'International School' for boys and girls, the children of sect members, and he set up several shops that proved surprisingly profitable, as a result of local advertising.

Sufficient money had been raised from such business enterprises and donations that in 1884 the group embarked on the ambitious plan to build a tower as a headquarters on the top of Chatham Hill. Jezreel claimed to have been shown a possible site, following a revelatory dream.

> His main desire was that it should be a perfect cube, each side of which was to be 144 feet (the mystical number!) in length. After much argument the architects convinced him that this design was impracticable, both for technical reasons and on grounds of cost. In the end therefore Jezreel had to accept a modified version: each side was to be 126 feet 6 inches, and the height of the corners 120 feet.

> The structure was to be built of steel and concrete with yellow brick walls, and eight castellated towers of the same material. On each side of the outer walls emblems and symbols of the 'New and Latter House of Israel' were to be portayed in stone, standing out

in bold relief. Chief of these were the Trumpet and the Flying Roll, the Crossed Swords of the Spirit, and the Prince of Wales Feathers, signifying the Trinity.[3]

By January 1885, when Jezreel died, only the foundations and the basement of the project had been completed. Jezreel was buried in a simple ceremony in accordance with the rites of the Church of England. His wife Clarissa, who since their marriage had used the name Esther – and was often known as Queen Esther – now took over responsibility, securing for herself the leadership of the community and concentrating on completing the sanctuary of the building. The cornerstone of the building was officially laid on 19 September 1885, 'on behalf of the 144,000. Revelation vii.4'[4] by Mrs Emma Cave, a major benefactor.

The evangelical Church of England publication the *Record* printed a highly critical review on 11 December 1885 of the published *Extracts from the Flying Roll*:

> We deplore the appearance above the English horizon of this ill-omened organization (the 'New and Latter House of Israel'). The Flying Roll of Zechariah was a moral message with holy sanctions, instinct with eternal justice; this *Flying Roll* is a Gnostic lucubration, intellectually feeble, morally worthless.

* * *

In recent years there has still been some evidence of surviving groups, or individual members, of the New and Latter House of Israel. An advertisement in the *Daily Mail* in the 1970s offered copies of *The Flying Roll* for sale (30 pence for a hardback or 25 pence for a paperback edition) from an address in Newcastle-upon-Tyne. Ten years ago the *People's Friend* magazine had a half-page spread advertising extracts from the *The Flying Roll* that were obtainable from an address in Hailsham, Sussex.

My correspondent from Newcastle in 1977 wrote of their beliefs in these terms:

Immortality – Life without death – can be obtained by keeping Law and Gospel combined, as did Our Lord Jesus. This 6,000 years of evil will soon be up and will give place to God's glorious reign. Scriptures in the Old and New Testament all point to this time. Matthew 24 gives a picture of what the state of the world will be in these, the end of days. The *Flying Roll* points the way to perfection by overcoming evil. The belief in immortality pervades the Bible. Jesus never told us to prepare for Death, but said 'Keep my commandments and live'. But the time was too far off then to gain life. Now we are in the very hour when Life can be obtained.

J.J. Jezreel was inspired to write the *Flying Roll* to hand to the public who would either accept or reject its teachings. There has been over the years a worldwide acceptance of the truths in the *Flying Roll*. And today there are many believers in the British Isles, Canada, America, and other countries.[5]

It seems likely that the original followers of Jezreel, after disagreements between them on practical and doctrinal matters, will have gone their separate ways in fissiparous groupings just like the Southcott sectarians. There is the suggestion that the group based in Newcastle, who were responsible for much of the subsequent publication and dissemination of the *Flying Roll*, may in fact have been a purist community that rejected the attempts to build the temple and headquarters in the south-east at Gillingham, either as an illegitimate actualisation of the religious ideas, or as a building on a scale that was unrealistic for the needs of the movement. There was apparently a schism that took place over the issue of the tower.

However, there are certainly people with a concern for Jezreel's temple (and a knowledge of the plan to build it) elsewhere and especially in the USA. An organisation known as 'Mary's City of David', a schism from a group of Jezreelites in the USA, has excellent archives and is quite approachable.[6] The 'Israelite House of David', famous for a baseball team, share many identical beliefs. But they do not accept Mary Purnell (the Mary of 'Mary's City') as the seventh co-angel in their hierarchy, but James J. Jezreel is still in their listing.[7]

* * *

The final decades of Jezreel's Tower tell a story of decay, comparable with the dissolution of the Gillingham group. Several attempts were made from the early years of the twentieth century to acquire the site for commercial redevelopment. An inconclusive auction on 4 March 1913 had been advertised and featured in *The Times*:

> The structural monstrosity of which an illustration appeared in *The Times* advertising columns last Saturday, known as 'Jezreel's Temple' on Chatham Hill, Kent, is to come under the hammer of Messrs. Brackett and Son at Tokenhouse-yard on March 4.
>
> It was founded many years ago by an ex-soldier, who claiming to be a second Elijah, collected his adherents at the spot and began building a 'New and Latter House of Israel'. The career of the place has been chequered, but not stained by tragedies such as marked an earlier 'religious' movement in the same county, when a young army officer was killed near Faversham in dispersing the followers of a notorious impostor.[8]

The allusion in the last sentence is to Sir William Courtenay, also known as John Nichols Tom, who raised a small force of discontented farm labourers from the Kent countryside. There are numerous historical precedents for such peasants' revolts, coloured variously with religious ideas. A much earlier Kentish example is the Peasants' Revolt of 1381, led by Wat Tyler who marched his supporters out of Rochester and from Canterbury to Blackheath and then to London, demanding from King Richard II an end to serfdom, and the provision of a greater freedom of labour. Another instance is that of Thomas Müntzer who led a group of millenarian believers into a confrontation with the state in the Peasants' Revolt of Thuringia in 1525.[9]

Courtenay's labourers fought with the militia and were defeated at the battle of Bossenden Wood on the afternoon of Thursday 31 May 1838. Lieutenant Henry Boswell Bennett of the 45th Regiment was killed and is buried in the Precincts of Canterbury Cathedral. A special constable also died and another soldier was wounded. Courtenay and seven of his followers were killed in the brief course of the battle, and are buried in the churchyards at Hernhill and Boughton-under-Blean (Courtenay himself in an unmarked grave at Hernhill).

John Tom was born in Cornwall in 1799 and in a short life imaginatively assumed several different identities, including those of Count Moses Rothschild, and of Sir William Courtenay, ninth earl of Devon and third Viscount Courtenay of Powderham Castle near Exeter. In the latter role he campaigned for election to Parliament to represent Canterbury and East Kent. He failed in the attempt, ending up in jail and then in Maidstone Asylum. But four years later he re-emerged, in the care of a local farmer; he rapidly began to recruit a group of followers from among the oppressed and long-suffering agricultural workers and local farm labourers. He drew attention to social and economic inequalities, the imbalance of wealth and property on the one side, and the low wages, lack of work and harshness of the operation of the Poor Law on the other.

By 1838 Courtenay was raising the stakes on his own claims as leader of the revolt. He provides a climactic example for our study, as he functioned not merely as a prophetic leader but as the central protagonist in the End as prophesied in the book of Revelation. In P.G. Rogers' words:

> He was no mere earthly righter of wrongs. He was divine, the reincarnation of Jesus Christ, and his body was the temple of the Holy Ghost … He was particularly fond of invoking the Book of Revelation, and he used its apocalyptic statements to terrify … and to impress.[10]

When he rode into a village, as caricatured on his favourite charger, he would point to this light grey mare and declaim Revelation 6.2: '…there was a white horse! Its rider had a bow; a crown was given to him, and he came out conquering and to conquer' (see also Rev. 19.11–16).

XIV

An Anglican Israel at the End of Time: The Seventh Earl of Shaftesbury

Palestine, the Land of the Bible, exercised a powerful influence on the English Protestant mind. In Lord Curzon's words, the land of the Scriptures, the land also of the Crusades, was the 'holiest space of ground on the face of the globe', the land 'to which all our faces are turned when we are finally laid in our graves in the churchyard'.[1] A tendency towards Biblical mysticism was to be found among members of the ruling class of Victorian England. One such example is General Charles Gordon, the future martyr of Khartoum, who spent a year in Jerusalem studying the Bible and local topography, identifying the Garden (or Gordon's) tomb, from the shape of the hill like a human skull (Golgotha) in which it was found.

In 1875 the then Archbishop of York, Dr William Thomson, addressed the Palestine Exploration Fund (PEF) and declared, 'Our reason for turning to Palestine is that Palestine is our country. I have used that expression before and I refuse to adopt any other.' He explained that Palestine was his country because it had given him the 'laws by which I try to live' and was the source of the 'best knowledge I possess'.[2] By these two references he meant the Bible of the Hebrews and in particular its prophecies.

A widespread notion, similar to one held by contemporary American fundamentalist Christians, was the desirability – as the fulfilment of Biblical prophecy – of the 'restoration' of the Jews to Palestine from their worldwide dispersion or diaspora, a development that (it was presumed) would be followed by their conversion to the true (that is, Anglican) Christian faith. The consequence of this would be the Second Coming, or the return, of the Messiah as the leader of a thousand-year era of peace and justice on earth, before the end of the world. This chiliastic belief led to the establishment of missionary societies dedicated to the conversion of Jews in England and even in Palestine itself. Although the success rate of organisations such as the London Society for Promoting Christianity among the Jews (established 1808) was dismal, making only about six or seven converts a year even after 30 years, its members remained optimistically active throughout the nineteenth century.

The best known proponent of this movement was the seventh Earl of Shaftesbury, Anthony Ashley Cooper, politician, philanthropist and evangelical Christian, who based his life on a literal acceptance of the Bible. He is probably better known now for his campaigns for benevolent social legislation, such as the Ten Hours Bill, limiting the working hours of factory workers. The same evangelical Christianity that inspired his social campaigning at home led him to work equally hard for the conversion of the Jews, and he became president of the 'Jews' Society' in 1848. Although he saw little evidence that mass conversion had begun as he hoped, Shaftesbury had considerable success in influencing British foreign policy in line with his ideas. He persuaded Foreign Secretary Lord Palmerston to establish a British consulate in Jerusalem during 1838, charged with the protection of local Jewish interests and granting Palestinian Jews British citizenship. A few years later his lobbying bore fruit in the creation of an Anglican bishopric in Jerusalem, with a converted Jew, Dr Alexander (a professor of Hebrew and Arabic), as its first incumbent.

Lord Shaftesbury proclaimed himself as 'an Evangelical of the Evangelicals', dedicated to bring everyone else, especially the Jews, to share in one and the same salvation. He envisaged, in the words of Barbara Tuchman, 'an Anglican Israel restored by Protestant England, at one stroke confounding popery, fulfilling prophecy, redeeming mankind'. Tuchman also writes:

> For the Jews were the hinge. Without them there could be no Second Advent. They were the middle member of the Evangelical's unbreakable syllogism. Biblical prophecy = Israel converted and

restored = Second Advent. Of course, if rationalism, which cuts the prophetical connection between New Testament and Old, leaving only a historical connection, is allowed to crack the syllogism, the whole thing falls apart. Therefore rationalism must be held at bay. This Lord Shaftesbury understood well enough. 'God give me and mine grace,' he prayed, to stem 'the awful advance of saucy rationalism.'[3]

Shaftesbury told his biographer, Edwin Hodder, that belief in the Second Coming 'has always been a moving principle in my life, for I see everything going on in the world subordinate to this great event … Why do we not pray for it every time we hear a clock strike?' According to the prophecies of Scripture, the return of the Jews was indispensable to this great event, so Shaftesbury 'never had a shadow of doubt that the Jews *were* to return to their own land … It was his daily prayer, his daily hope. "Oh, pray for the peace of Jerusalem!" were the words engraven on the ring he always wore on his right hand.'[4]

Lord Shaftesbury worked in the context of an Evangelical Revival, a neo-puritanism among the people of property. The London Society for Promoting Christianity among the Jews (or the Jews' Society, as it became known) had been founded in 1808. It held demonstration sermons on Wednesdays and Sundays, setting out to prove that Jesus was the Jews' Messiah. Later missionaries conducted services in Hebrew on Mount Zion in Jerusalem. Success was limited, however. As a Jew was said to have told an English traveller, E. Warburton, when he visited Bishop Alexander's church in Jerusalem in 1844: 'The Hill of Zion is not a likely place for a Jew to forsake the faith of his fathers.' But hopes remained. Lewis Way, a wealthy barrister who supported the Jews' Society financially, came into the Society, so the story goes, after he had ridden from Exmouth to Exeter and admired a stand of oak trees en route; he was told that a former owner of the trees, Jane Parminter of A la Ronde near Exmouth, had given orders in her will that the trees should not be felled until such time as the Jews were restored to Palestine.

Critics of the Jews' Society held that the Jews would only be converted by miraculous divine intervention, comparable to the rescue of the Israelites from the power of Pharaoh in Egypt. But supporters argued that human activity to this end was justified, in support of the divine plan, not least as some degree of retribution for the Christian persecution of Jews. But the Society was really only interested in giving the Jews Christianity – which they did not want. Members of the Society, including Lord Shaftesbury, even opposed the Emancipation Bill, which would have permitted Jews to enter Parliament without taking the Christian form of oath. In the last resort Jews were regarded as some kind of passive agents of the Christian Millennium.

With a rational rather than a religious motivation, the Palestine Association had been founded in London in 1804, to promote exploration and researches in the Holy Land. However, because travel in the country was hazardous, it declined and merged with the Royal Geographic Society in 1834. Later it re-emerged in 1865 as the PEF in order to:

> obtain and disseminate information respecting ancient and modern Syria [i.e. Syria, Lebanon, Jordan and Israel] … and the ancient and modern inhabitants thereof … the History, Literature, Ethnology, Mineralogy, Numismatics, Topography, Geography, Geology, Zoology, Botany, Meteorology, Natural History and the manners and customs of the same countries.[5]

The Fund continues to support research in the land up to the present day. Although it was founded in the spirit of rationalist investigation, the original impulse still came from a group of evangelicals in Jerusalem (who had founded a Jerusalem Literary Society to study local antiquities). There were other paradoxes in the work of the PEF, not least the fact that the earliest geographical research on the land of the Bible was carried out by army officers (most notably Colonel Conder and Sir Charles Warren) appointed by the War Office.

Conder, after extensive mapping work, wrote on the prospects for the regeneration of Palestine by means of Jewish colonisation. He bluntly observed that 'there is not a mile of made road in the land from Dan to Beersheba'.[6] Although the practical problems were thereby revealed as enormous, the other effect of the PEF research was to show that Palestine had been habitable in the past, and that the land had supported a much larger population and a more advanced civilisation. Archaeologists revealed that the territory had been covered with settlements and had only reverted to nomads because it had not been cultivated in recent times.

In 1875, Shaftesbury became president of the PEF. In his first address to the organisation as its president he spoke with undiminished enthusiasm:

> Let us not delay to send out the best agents ... to search the length and breadth of Palestine, to survey the land, and if possible to go over every corner of it, drain it, measure it, and, if you will, prepare it for the return of its ancient possessors, for I must believe that the time cannot be far off before that great event will come to pass. ... I recollect speaking to Lord Aberdeen when he was prime minister, on the subject of the Holy Land; and he said to me, 'If the Holy Land should pass out of the hands of the Turks, into whose hands should it fall?' 'Why,' my reply was ready, 'not into the hands of other powers, but let it return into the hands of the Israelites.'[7]

Nearly 40 years after his first article on this subject in the *Quarterly Review* Lord Shaftesbury wrote again, in a classic statement of England's role in the revival of Palestine:

> Syria and Palestine will ere long become most important. The old time will come back ... the country wants capital and population. The Jew can give it both. And has not England a special interest in promoting such a restoration? ... She must preserve Syria to herself. Does not policy then – if that were all – exhort England to foster the nationality of the Jews and aid them, as opportunity may offer, to return as a leavening power to their old country? England is the great trading and maritime power of the world. To England, then, naturally belongs the role of favouring the settlement of the Jews in Palestine ... The nationality of the Jews exists; the spirit is there and has been for three thousand years, but the external form, the crowning bond of union, is still wanting. A nation must have a country. The old land, the old people. This is not an artificial experiment; it is nature, it is history.[8]

In Edward Fox's words:

his mystical belief in Britain's instrumental role in returning the Jews to Palestine – for the sake of Christianity rather than Judaism – was the ideological force behind Britain's increasing political involvement in Palestine throughout the nineteenth century, an involvement which could be seen to result later in British support for Zionism, as expressed in the Balfour Declaration of 1917, and in Britain itself assuming the government of Palestine in 1921, and holding it for nearly 30 years in the form of the British Mandate. To understand politics it is sometimes necessary to understand the power of such apparently irrational ideas.[9]

Such Christian Zionism continues to be influential through to the present day, with some Christian groups, such as Christian Friends of Israel being specifically dedicated to the cause. Indeed, present-day governments must take popular Zionist opinions into consideration when formulating policies relating to the Middle East (as, for example, with the growing Christian Zionist movement in the USA, which was outspoken regarding the recent conflicts in Iraq).[10]

XV

'SOMEWHERE A PLACE FOR US': MODERN UTOPIAS

... the intricate evasions of as,
In things seen and unseen, created from nothingness,
The heavens, the hells, the worlds, the longed-for lands
Wallace Stevens[1]

Previous chapters have shown how millenarian ideas appealed especially to radical reformers, whether possessed of more, or fewer, Christian convictions. Such ideas and policies could readily be secularised into utopianism. Utopia is either an ideal place (the opposite of dystopia) or a place of the pure imagination that does not exist. The Greek basis of the word 'utopia' provides an explanation for this paradoxical variety of meaning: the first syllable represents either the Greek adverb 'well' (*eu*), or the Greek negative *ou*. This chapter will concentrate on some literary examples, particularly from the nineteenth and twentieth centuries. The title of the chapter is of course a quotation from Leonard Bernstein's *West Side Story*, in celebration of that work's 50th anniversary in 2007.

Nearly 30 years ago Norman Shrapnel wrote in the *Guardian*: 'The new myths are weaving the patterns of fictional foreboding or wish-fulfilment, reaching out beyond *Brave New World* or *Nineteen Eighty-Four*. Utopias are in again and not all of them come in black, which would be tedious.'[2] At about the same time (1979) a book by I.F. Clarke was published under the title *The Pattern of Expectation 1644–2001*.[3] This provided an admirable survey, showing the variety of forms of the new, and not so new, mythology to which Shrapnel referred. The twenty-first-century reader, of course, looks back on these expectations with the benefit of hindsight, and therefore with the possibility of commenting on their accuracy – but that can only add to their fascination, because one is enabled to assess them within the historical contexts that gave birth to such hopes.

Some utopias are the immediate products of new scientific discoveries and represent a popularisation of the advances of science. Some are the nightmares of poetic imagination, perhaps reacting in terror at the applied science and advanced technology of modern warfare. Some still look for a 'happy land', a utopian existence. In the past, particularly in the nineteenth century, this utopia was the logical consequence of contemporary civilisation, according to a widespread theory of progress: 'The whole human race, through alternate periods of rest and unrest, of weal and woe, goes on advancing, although at a slower pace, towards greater perfection.'[4] At another time any utopia is likely to appear like an escapist's paradise; and a pragmatist might instead have a vision of 'dystopia', weeping 'for a world in which man had become the slave of the machine, and self-interest had replaced love'.[5]

By comparison, W.H. Hudson's *A Crystal Age* (1887) contained an allusive expectation of hope, beyond the understandable attitudes of revolution and pessimism:

A sort of mighty Savonarola[6] bonfire, in which most of the things one valued have been consumed to ashes – politics, religions, systems of philosophy, -isms and -ologies of all descriptions; schools, churches, prisons, poorhouses; stimulants and tobacco; kings and parliaments; cannon with its hostile roar, and pianos that thundered peacefully; history, the press, vice, political economy, money and a million things more – all consumed like so much worthless hay and stubble. This being so, why am I not overwhelmed at the thought of it? In that feverish full age – so full, and yet, my God, how empty! – in the wilderness of every man's soul, was not a voice crying out, prophesying the end?[7]

In modern currency 'utopia' has become a vaguer term because of the almost infinite variety of expectation it implies. It can denote the retrospective myths of a Golden Age, or the imminent future of a dire Judgement or a glorious Millennium – in fact anything from Paradise Lost to Paradise Regained. While it is a practical exercise in precision to classify such expectations in the categories of utopia and dystopia, and to maintain a distinction between the two senses of utopia (the ideal and the unreal), there is a further kind of debate to be had between the three language systems that obviously overlap in utopian descriptions: the apocalyptic, scientific fact and science fiction. The question of their relationships is a proper subject for academic debate. Indeed, some universities have run courses on the relationship between 'apocalyptic and science fiction'.

The apocalyptic has played a greater part in this discussion since the middle of the twentieth century, as a result of the language of 'nuclear apocalyptic', defined by the bombing of Hiroshima, and also from the immediacy of *Apocalypse Now* as defined by experiences such as the Vietnam War (and perhaps redefined more recently by military operations in Iraq and Afghanistan). Since the bombing of Hiroshima the existence of much larger nuclear weapons (and a multiplicity of them) led during the Cold War period to the concept of Mutually Assured Destruction (which yields the appropriate acronym MAD), by which the total wipe-out of the planet could happen, it was said, at least 17 times.

Biblical thought had encompassed the idea of a new state or golden age, both as the climax of God's purposes and as an escape from present suffering. In New Testament texts this is expressed as the 'New Jerusalem', descending from heaven to transform the earthly sanctuary (see Rev. 21.2), and also as 'Paradise' (see Luke 23.43). The term 'paradise' derives from a Persian word (*pairidaeza*) meaning an area that is 'walled around', like a walled garden or circumscribed estate. The Hebrew word *pardes* was used, in Nehemiah 2.8, for the Persian king's own 'forest/park' (see also the 'enclosed garden' of S. of S. 4.12; and Eccles. 2.5). The Biblical concept was also focussed on the Garden of Eden, as the paradise that is lost to human beings in Genesis 3.23–4 and will one day be regained, as in the eschatological hopes for the end of time (see also Rev. 2.7; 22). In this sense the End corresponds to the Beginning.

This Biblical language can be expressed in terms of individual salvation, but more frequently as a national, international or social reconstitution:

> The furnace of Gehenna shall be made manifest, and over against it the paradise of delight. (4 Ezra 7.37)

> Then shall the heart of the inhabitants of the world be changed, and be converted to a different spirit. For evil shall be blotted out, and deceit extinguished; faithfulness shall flourish, and corruption be vanquished. And truth ... shall be made manifest. (4 Ezra 6.26–8)

> In the age to come there is no eating or drinking, no begetting of children, or multiplying, but the righteous sit with crowns on their heads, and rejoice in the radiance of the Godhead. (Babylonian Talmud, Ber. 17a)

There are indeed other sayings, which speak of women in the age to come giving birth daily. Clearly, imagination and prejudice has free scope to elaborate the details.

Krishan Kumar, formerly Professor of Social Thought at the University of Kent, commented on millennial ideas in a utopian context:

> The millennium is both restitutive and retributive. It reverses the period of evil and suffering, and it rewards the virtuous for their fortitude, while punishing evil-doers ... The millennium faces the future more than it harks back to the past ... Of all ideal society conceptions, it is the millennium which most forcibly introduces the elements of time, process and history. The millennial Good Time restores something of the glory of the Golden Age, but it is also the End of Time ... The peculiar power of the millennial idea comes from the fact that in it eschatology complements futurology.[8]

Kumar argued that it was desirable to see millennial and other utopias in their place within a specific tradition of social and political thought, recognising them within their historical and cultural boundaries. He identified Utopia as a concept that historically arose in the West as an original way of coping with the problematic aspects of modern Western society. The case is argued that the themes of Utopia are those of power, inequality, democracy and science – all of which are characteristic of modern Western social thought. These themes are treated in a distinctive and compelling way as a form of imaginative fiction. This is no fantasy or wish-fulfilment, but rather a rehearsal in critical terms of the dilemmas of modern society – and it may prescribe the best way of resolving those dilemmas.

Two of the texts most frequently cited or discussed as antecedents of modern utopian statements are *The Republic* of the Classical Greek philosopher Plato, and the *Utopia* of Sir Thomas More.

PLATO: THE REPUBLIC

The idealist Greek philosopher Plato (427–347 BCE) believed in two worlds: the one in which we actually live is claimed to be an illusory shadow of the true and real world that is constituted by ideas (or ideals). This principle of thought is explained most vividly within the celebrated image or simile of the cave, which is to be found in the seventh of the ten books of Plato's dialogue *The Republic*. This whole work was written as a text of philosophical education for those embarking on a political career in Classical Greece. In the words of Socrates, Plato constructs for his readers the perfect city-state.

According to this cave image, the basic human condition is that of men who have been imprisoned in a subterranean cave since childhood. They are chained in such a way that they can only look in one direction, that is, in front of them, towards the cave wall. There is a fire burning behind and above them, which gives them light to see anything at all. But what they see are only the shadows of objects behind them, which are projected by the firelight onto the wall in front of them. Because this is all they can see, therefore, they regard these shadows as the only reality, while it is clear that it is all an imperfect image, or a virtual illusion. But there are also the 'guardians', the philosopher-kings and the rulers-to-be, the ones to possess the wisdom of the ideal state, knowing the ideas of Justice and the Good. These are the people who will succeed in struggling out of the cave into the world of knowledge and wisdom. Good education is therefore to be seen as a liberation. Also, at the end of the ninth book, Socrates describes his ideal society, which is perhaps only a *paradeigma* (example) existing in heaven.

According to Robin Waterfield:

> In *Republic* Plato is not primarily interested in politics in the real world: he is constructing an *imaginary* community, to serve as a paradigm. The primary purpose for any political exploration that will occur in the book is ... to help us understand an individual. ... to demonstrate that morality is beneficial to its possessor – that, in fact, an individual gains in happiness by being moral, whether or not any external advantages accrue to him. ... He therefore proposes to work with a political analogy: perhaps morality will be easier to see if we construct a community, describe its political system, and look for morality in this imaginary community.[9]

SIR THOMAS MORE: UTOPIA

Thomas More lived from 1478 to 1535, being beheaded for high treason on 6 July that year. He had been appointed Lord Chancellor of England in 1529 as successor to Thomas Wolsey, but he resigned from that office in 1532. More sought to prosecute 'heretics' such as followers of Martin Luther or William Tyndale, being fired by the threat to the established Church of the eschatological approach of Antichrist in the persons of such heretics. His most famous literary work, *Utopia*, had been published much earlier, in 1516; it was written in Bruges during a visit to Flanders in 1515 as an envoy from the council of King Henry VIII and the Merchant Adventurers, charged with the renegotiation of commercial and diplomatic treaties.

Utopia is a description of an ideal community or commonwealth that lives in accord with natural law, practising a natural religion. Its original title was 'The Best Condition of a Society' (*De Optimo Reipublicae Statu*). The work abounds in satirical side-swipes at the abuses in contemporary society. It is no accident that the dimensions and geographical position of the island of Utopia, which is described, resembles that of England – just as the number of its city states corresponds to that of the English counties.

The book depicts Thomas More in Antwerp, where Peter Gillis, a close friend of Erasmus, apparently introduces him to a bearded and sunburnt traveller called Raphael Hythlodaeus, who reminds the more modern reader of Coleridge's Ancient Mariner. Hythlodaeus is from Portugal and claims to have travelled extensively with Amerigo Vespucci. Raphael is the name of the guiding angel in the Biblical book of Tobit, but the surname Hythlodaeus is a Greek word meaning someone who is cunning in gossip or nonsense. It is Hythlodaeus who describes the island of Utopia with its laws and customs. Not only does the description raise difficulties because the dimensions of the island are problematic and some customs of the inhabitants seem impractical;[10] the readers are also teased by the names of a river Anydros ('without water') and a governor Ademus ('no people'). But, as often happens with such literature, the satire has a very serious underlying intention, raising as it does a wide range of political and philosophical issue for discussion.

Erasmus stated that Thomas More in his youth had written a dialogue in defence of Plato's *Republic*. In Peter Ackroyd's description of the resemblances to Plato's work in *Utopia*:

> More devises a republic like that of Plato ... More's work is less profound, more hastily written and altogether less satisfying than Plato's great discourse; nor does More address those philosophical questions on the nature of happiness or the principles of harmony that are at the centre of the earlier work. Yet clearly More has taken certain aspects of *The Republic* ... and proceeded to examine how they might work in practice. Plato insisted that only a philosopher can properly administer his republic, and at the beginning of *Utopia* More refers to the founder of the state – Utopus – who trained his people to the highest level of *cultus* and *humanitas*.[11]

OTHER UTOPIAN WORKS

The influence of More's *Utopia* was widespread and profound, being read and interpreted on different levels of satire and reality, and in a variety of contexts. By early in the seventeenth century the word 'utopian' (in both ideal and negative senses) had entered the vocabulary of the main European languages. More's work appeared first in Latin but was translated into English, French, Italian and German. It inspired other utopian works by Anton Francesco Doni (1553),

Johann Valentin Andreae (1619), Tommaso Campanella (1623), Robert Burton's *Anatomy of Melancholy* (1621–38), Francis Bacon's *New Atlantis* (1627) and works of satire such as Jonathan Swift's *Gulliver's Travels* (1726).

A twentieth-century novel very much in the tradition of More's *Utopia* and of Swift's *Gulliver's Travels* is Umberto Eco's *The Island of the Day Before* (Italian 1994; English 1995).[12] The story is set in the year 1643, when Roberto della Griva, a young nobleman who has survived war, the Bastille, exile and shipwreck, is voyaging to a Pacific island that straddles the date meridian. He writes that he is 'the only man in human memory to have been shipwrecked and cast up upon a deserted ship', the Dutch flyboat *Daphne*. He waits alone on the mysteriously deserted (but well-provisioned) ship; he is separated by treacherous reefs from the island that he can see beyond, the 'island of the day before'; he cannot swim and there is no longboat. But he knows that if he could reach the island, time and his recent misfortunes would be reversed. Characteristically, Umberto Eco employs a range of literary theories to tell his story, while reflecting the history of science and the problematic concept of longitude.

* * *

Italo Calvino's novel *Invisible Cities* (Italian 1972; English 1974)[13] derives its theme from the *Travels of Marco Polo*. Marco Polo lived from 1254 to 1324, a member of a patrician family from Venice. Beginning in 1271 he accompanied his father and his uncle on an embassy from the Pope to Kublai Khan, the Grand Khan of Tartary. Marco Polo is reputed to have written an account of his extensive and exotic travels, originally in French. An English translation was made in 1579, and later versions in the nineteenth century. The accuracy of his narrative in whole or part has frequently been disputed, just as happened to Hythlodaeus' accounts of the voyages of Amerigo Vespucci, or the travel romances of Sir John Mandeville.

In Calvino's novel, Marco Polo is invited by Kublai Khan to describe the cities he has visited each time he returns from his travels. The explorer and the conqueror exchange visions, with the difference that for Kublai the world is constantly expanding, while for Marco it is an ever-diminishing place. Calvino has ordered Marco Polo's descriptions of the cities in a range of categories, corresponding to psychological as well as historical states, to possibilities and to transformations, each of which is supposedly designed to stimulate Kublai Khan's imagination. But effectively Calvino is only representing one single city by all of these: Venice. However sordid some aspects may be, and at times the dead seem to outnumber the living, the splendour of Venice stands as substantial evidence of human abilities in creating perfection out of chaos.

* * *

Arthur Koestler said that 'all utopias are fed from the sources of mythology; the social engineer's blueprints are merely revised editions of the ancient text'.[14] His own work *Darkness At Noon* (1940),[15] a novel translated from a German original, has been called an 'anti-utopia' because of the savagery of its attack on twentieth-century socialism. In effect the significant power of the socialist utopia was acknowledged by Koestler's work, as also by Aldous Huxley's *Brave New World* (1932)[16] and George Orwell's *Nineteen Eighty-Four* (1949).[17] Koestler projected the thought forms and structures of the new society of the Soviet Union as a prison-house, clearly drawing attention to the nature of the regime of Josef Stalin.

Darkness at Noon concerns the arrest, imprisonment, trial and execution of an Old Bolshevik, Nicolas Salmanovich Rubashov, within an unnamed dictatorship that is presided over by 'No. 1'. Koestler describes Rubashov, in the book's dedication, as 'a synthesis of the lives of a number of men who were victims of the so-called Moscow Trials'. Kingsley Martin, writing in the *New Statesman*, called this

> One of the few books written in this epoch which will survive it. It is written from terrible experience, from knowledge of the men whose struggles of mind and body he describes. Apart from its sociological importance, it is written with a subtlety and an economy which class it as great literature … Koestler approaches the problems of ends and means, of love and truth and social organization.[18]

Darkness at Noon is given the credit for saving the French state from coming under Communist control when a referendum was held in 1946 on the future form of the constitution. Koestler himself renounced his own previous Communist faith – as a result, he said, of mystical experiences during 'the hours by the window' of the condemned cell in one of Franco's prisons, as he waited moment by moment for death.[19] (As a journalist he had been representing the *News Chronicle* during the Spanish Civil War, when he was captured by Franco's troops and held under sentence of death.)

* * *

Andrew Niccol's film *Gattaca* (1997) demonstrates how an experiment in genetic engineering becomes a divisive force in human society. It tells the story of a society in the near future in which each child is the dream child of their parents, the best combination of their respective genes, provided that the child is conceived in the laboratory. This view of utopia is flawed and illusory (and the artist's concept intended to be dystopian), in that it depends on the creation, and subsequent oppression, of a near-slave underclass.[20] Those children who have been conceived in the natural way are considered defective by members of the ideal society, and so will never be able to rise higher in society than the performance of manual labour. Vincent Freeman is such a natural child, but he sets out to acquire an illegal identity and a new genetically perfect profile, that of Jerome Eugene. This enables him to train as an astronaut in the Gattaca complex for space programmes.

* * *

The subject of genetic engineering is also involved as one of the possible scenarios that were generated by the Economic and Social Research Council during an exercise in 2007 to consider what sort of world – utopian, dystopian or both – might be created by recent advances in technology and the sciences. In assessing social, political and economic impacts, other factors to be reckoned with beside

technology were trends such as climate change, new political align-
ments, and the rise of key players such as Brazil, Russia, India, China
and South Africa to the world stage.

Four visions of the future were generated by the exercise, two
more positive and hopeful, and two more negative and perhaps horri-
bly pessimistic. The first was 'heterarchy', a collaborative world where
science enhanced life and extended the human lifespan to 180 years.
A second merely extended the present situation, with greater out-
sourcing of production to China and Africa; governments struggled
to cope but eventually succeeded in catching up. The third vision
was of 'gridlock', where the left–right split of today's politics became
a radical division between the 'enhanced' (who made fullest use of
all scientific tools) and the 'naturals' (an alliance of science sceptics
and religious fundamentalists, rejecting any meddling with nature).
Fourth came the most negative world view, labelled 'no glue', in
which all financial, political and social bonds came apart, as a result
of a rapid evolution of virtual worlds (attractive because of their effi-
ciency) which outpaced any ability of governments or of international
organisations to cope.[21]

The philosopher John Gray has defined a utopian project as one in
which 'there are no circumstances in which it can be realized'.[22] Under
this definition, Gray argues, the tag of utopianism applies equally to
the ravages of Nazi Germany and to the conflict in Iraq and the 'war
on terror'. The crisis of today is created by fantasies driving the neo-
conservative agenda, fantasies derived from apocalyptic religion or
secularist utopianism (a scenario not unrelated to the vision of 'gridlock' just mentioned). The death of Utopia would not mean peace,
but rather leaves space for the resurgence of ancient myths, seen in
openly fundamentalist forms. Apocalyptic religion returns as a major
force in global conflict, obscurely mixed with geopolitical struggles
for the control of natural resources.

The novelist Ian McEwan spoke about humanity's recurrent hunger for Apocalypse and its expression in terms of 'end-time thinking',
commenting on 'the adaptability and resilience of end-time thought'.
He was delivering a lecture at the University of East Anglia in 2007
during Norwich's annual programme called 'New Writing Worlds'.

He argued that for more than a thousand years the millenarian tradition in Christianity – and to a lesser, but not negligible, extent in Judaism and Islam – has nourished self-electing groups and cults with cataclysmic fantasies of 'salvation for themselves and perdition for the rest'.[23]

On reflection it can be seen that Christian millenarianism has been, and continues to be, the influential pattern behind a significant number of utopian movements. Frequently this happens under conditions in which two cultures meet, 'as in the case of the Melanesian cargo cults, where Christian millennialism was grafted onto tribal beliefs'.[24] Cargo cults are therefore the appropriate concern of the next chapter.

XVI

CHRISTIAN MISSIONS AND THE CARGO CULTS

M odern colonialism, Western culture and the legacy of Christian missions – all of these are either welcomed within the so-called Third World's revolutionary movements as representing 'salvation', or (much more likely) they are rejected, with all the means that primitive, even pre-literate, societies have at their command. The results of this interaction may include millennial movements, cargo cults or drug cultures.

In case this chapter should seem to be venturing too far from the northern hemisphere, some prefatory remarks about the interest in such matters by British sociologists and anthropologists could be reassuring. The academic study of social and political science is naturally concerned with the shaping and development of communities, and the influence, for example, of religious factors in that process. A sociological study of the effects of Methodism on a particular mining community, Quebec, in County Durham in the early decades of the twentieth century, commented as follows:

> Given continuing economic decline, two possibilities are plausible: it would have continued as one of a possibly increasing number of Socialist cells, perhaps contributing to the rise of a nationwide Socialist movement. The interesting problem is then whether it would have become less overtly religious as it attracted wider support and grappled with more wholly secular issues. Or it could have become a wholly religious movement of a sectarian kind, possibly a millenarial movement. [With radical leadership, susceptible to the claims of 'fringe' sects] the group was open to millenarian inspiration.[1]

In a relatively advanced European society, the interaction of religion and politics is evident, as is the potential for movement towards extremes. How much more likely this is in a more primitive society, when the regular pattern is disturbed by outside influences. In the same way the independence movements in Latin America, from the nineteenth century onwards, encouraged New World millennialists. Such influences are also perceptible in the utopianism of Liberation Theology (although this is principally a revolutionary 'bias to the poor').

According to the functional theory first propounded by the British anthropologist Bronislaw Malinowski (1884–1942), the social anthropologist explains institutions in a culture by showing what ends and needs are served by the institution. For example 'rites of passage' and marriage ceremonies signal, display and accordingly reinforce the changes that have taken place in their participants' social roles and status. Similarly the institution of the 'bride price' marks, exhibits and reinforces the changed social role and social worth of the bride, as well as legitimising and stabilising the marriage. In such instances Malinowski's functional theory is frequently criticised as outmoded, a statement of the obvious, or, when addressing something more mysterious, as inherently untestable. In the case of the cargo cult, however, the functional explanation may be regarded as more plausible and informative. Teleological considerations are much more relevant and helpful, when, as with the cargo cult, a culture is changing in response to outside influences.

THE MISSIONARY LEGACY

A bewildering range of religious movements and cults are loosely labelled 'millenarian'. This can be highly misleading, if they really have no link with the belief in an apocalyptic Kingdom of one thousand years' duration. But there are among them some groups that originated in relation to, or in reaction against, the activities of the Christian missionary societies. Such groups are appropriately termed 'millenarian' because they make use of apocalyptic traditions derived from the missionaries. In most cases these traditions have become interwoven with local tribal beliefs; the Millennium takes its place within other ideas of cyclic transformation.

Examples of these kinds of millenarian movements can be identi-fied in Africa, the Americas and Asia. They would include some of the new prophetic churches in Africa, the Ghost Dance among native North Americans, the migrations led by shamans among the Tupi-Guarani in South America, as well as the cargo cults of New Guinea. All of these reflect the consequences of decades of missionary activity by the churches. The impact of modern colonialism, along with the culture and supposedly superior 'civilisation' of the Western world, is usually either welcomed as salvation or rejected by every possible means. Such millennial movements may be expressions of cargo cults, or they may rely on trance-inducing drugs, or perhaps relate to ves-tiges of Judaeo-Christian traditions left by missionaries. We turn next to look particularly at one group, the so-called 'cargo' movements.

THE CARGO CULTS

At the end of Gualtiero Jacopetti's film *Mondo Cane* (1962), eager islanders from Papua New Guinea are shown gathered around a large, roughly constructed model of an aeroplane. They have created an air-strip out of what was forest, high up in the mountains. Here they wait, gazing skyward in eager expectancy, for aeroplanes to land, load-ed with marvellous 'cargo'. Their fate is to be disappointed, however, because no aeroplanes will ever land. Such islanders are the deceived victims of a cargo cult.

The term 'cargo cult' seems to have originated in 1945 and be-came widely adopted by anthropologists, who applied it to particular social movements of the 1940s and 1950s in Melanesia in the South Pacific. Previously the phenomenon had sometimes been referred to as 'Vailala Madness' after a place in Papua New Guinea studied by an anthropologist in the 1920s. The basic idea that characterises a cargo cult is to use different religious rituals in order to obtain *kago* (or cargo). Such cargoes are broadly of two kinds: the immediate sense refers to planes (or ships) loaded with a whole range of manufactured goods that may be particularly desired by a primitive society, or a windfall of money that would enable such 'Western' goods to be obtained. Beyond material goods there is also the metaphorical sense of 'cargo' that denotes a new order of existence, offering independence from colonial exploitation. Either kind of expectation would amount to a miracle of divine intervention in such societies.

Bryan Wilson analysed the circumstances of the Melanesian phenomena in this way:

> Revolutionist religion is a demand for the transformation of the social situation: in the South Seas that demand has been expressed as a search for social betterment and status opportunities … Since trade goods occupied an important place in Melanesian cultures, being the means by which an individual established his status in many societies, the arrival of materially well-endowed Europeans, with many new and useful commodities, was by no means universally unwelcome to the natives. The demand for these goods was quickly developed, and natives were eager for power similar to that of Europeans to conjure up cargoes from beyond the seas.[2]

The role of Christianity, within an essentially polytheistic religious environment, is seen as part of a process of 'trial and error':

> Transference of allegiance from one deity to another when the first had failed to produce material blessings occurred in traditional religion. Christianity was now to be tried out, to see if it would bring cargo for natives as it did for white men. Old customs were given up. There were widespread conversions, and the claims made for Christianity by missionaries fed cargo ideas partly because Melanesians lacked any sense of historical time with which to interpret missionary promises and their own prospects. Christian phrases carried hidden implications concerning cargo, and although native mission helps knew this and fostered these ideas, the missionaries themselves did not, and this contributed to many mutual misunderstandings. In the 1930s many more than 50 per cent of 'the natives of Madang and the Rai coast … subscribed to quasi-Christian cargo doctrines'.[3]

Christian millenarianism, channelled through the educational efforts of missionaries, often provided the resource of ideas for the prophetic leaders of these cargo cults. The day when the promised cargo would arrive could be identified with the Second Coming of Christ, and the Day of Judgement, often referred to as the 'Last Day':

> Mountains would flatten and valleys would rise up. Land would become sea, and the seas would become land. People expected the coming of a new world, with remade people, and many cult rituals included elements of rebirth, or baptism, to mark the creation of a new order. Two very common prophesies were that the dead would come back to life and that the skins of the faithful would turn white. The first of these prophesies reflected the importance of ancestors in traditional religion and their connections with fertility and production. The second responded to the stark racial inequalities of colonialist regimes where Europeans controlled access to money, goods, and education.[4]

A particular kind of fundamentalist Christian preaching on the Second Coming by the missionaries had clearly contributed to this emphasis. Jean Guiart wrote, in relation to the New Hebrides, that

> [the missionaries] laid great stress on the Apocalypse. Over and over again I have seen Presbyterian and Seventh Day Adventist teachers walking about the hills in Espiritu Santo and Malekula to show the heathen sets of brightly coloured pictures of the life of Jesus. The last picture of the set, by contrast in tones of black and red, always depicted the Day of Judgement according to the Book of Revelation of St John.[5]

Obviously the oppressive regimes and exploitation of colonialism could provoke such social and political reactions. These cults were the 'forerunners of Melanesian nationalism'. In addition the lifestyle of the missionary, or even more of the local representative of the colonial power, could generate a sense of envy between the 'have nots' and the 'haves'. Frequently this local momentum of anger and envy was intensified by beliefs among the islanders that these riches were really theirs by right. Either the creativity to produce such goods had originally belonged to their ancestors, but one of them had long ago sailed away to Europe (or America or Australia) and sold their secrets there – or the foreigners had come and stolen the secret knowledge from the ancestors of these Pacific islanders. Alternatively, perhaps the foreigners were intercepting the cargo that their ancestors were trying to send back to the islands. In such circumstances the cults developed ritual means to make contact with these ancestors, to bring them back to life and induce them to return home with the cargoes.

There is an enormous diversity of cargo cults, each reflecting their local settings and political circumstances. Among the most significant are the John Frum and the Nagriamel movements on Vanuatu, the Christian Fellowship Church of the Solomon Islands, and in Papua New Guinea the Paliau and Yali movements, the Hahalis Welfare Society, Pomio Kivung and the Peli Association. The John Frum movement illustrates the aftermath of wartime American involvement in the Pacific; they predicted the return of the American military, and developed rituals involving uniforms and marching drills. Many cargo cults had a very short life, naturally terminating in disillusionment when the cargo failed to arrive, or the world remained the same. By contrast, John Frum is still surviving, under the third generation of leadership, from its origins in the 1930s. Some cults become institutionalised as churches or political parties. The Christian Fellowship Church is a syncretistic church in New Georgia, in the Solomon Islands, for example; equally the Peli Association and Pomio Kivung have become local political organisations in Papua New Guinea.

Since the 1980s there has been an upsurge of Christian missions from Australia, New Zealand and the USA – mostly of a fundamentalist variety – who are developing their work in the Pacific. The effect of this has been to intensify the element of Christian millenarianism among the largely Christian population of Melanesia. The expectations of cargo are now more muted, while the movements are characterised more by the phenomenon of Holy Spirit possession. The aim is to transform the self and society, and to eradicate sorcery. Holy Spirit prophets predict the Last Day and the coming of Christ, rather than of cargo, with the establishment of a new world order.

THE BRAZILIAN EXPERIENCE

Paulo Augusto de Souza Noguiera from São Paulo in Brazil has recently written:

Brazilian culture is profoundly affected by millenarianism. We have inherited from the Portuguese a messianic perspective on history, and, on the basis of indigenous rituals and practices, we have given Messianism more concrete expressions, since Brazilian life is full of utopias and practices that it is hoped will transform mundane existence.[6]

Brazilian culture has a strong sense of divine intervention, even when this is expressed in what we would regard as a more secular context – for example from a Brazilian perspective it is this intervention, and the role of a saviour figure, that would enable Brazil to succeed at football in the World Cup.

There exists a creative tension between magic and the Millennium, between the millenarian expectation represented by the great movements in nineteenth and early twentieth-century history, and magical beliefs and practices, local rituals with direct and immediate impact, experienced today in spiritual gatherings and Pentecostal and neo-Pentecostal (syncretistic) forms of worship services:[7]

Apocalyptic is a framework in which whole sections of our society experience the sacred, drawing together in a creative way dreams of utopia and the expectation of immediate results, hopes for the future and manipulation of the present through magic, the longing for a new era and access to the sacred in the 'here and now' of worship.[8]

In this situation apocalyptic and millenarian ideas can embrace both the radical, political ideas exemplified in twentieth-century theologies of liberation from oppression, and also the intensity of religious experience in the forms of personal visions and mysticism.

The most famous Brazilian prophet of the Millennium was Antônio Conselheiro, who established a community at Canudos in the interior of the backlands of Bahia province. He had been an itinerant preacher for 20 years when, in June 1893, with a few hundred followers, he established a small town to be named Belo Monte on the banks of the river Vaza-Barris. The aim was to create an alternative society to the one offered by the Republic (declared four years previously) and the religious hierarchy of the time. Thousands were attracted to the settlement, which led the forces of law and order to a brutal suppression of the community and a massacre of the inhabitants in 1897. The classic work on this episode, by Euclides da Cunha, cruelly characterises Conselheiro as a 'buffoon carried off into ecstasy in a vision of the Apocalypse'.[9]

A text called *Prophecy* was found in the wreckage of the settlement. It predicted the end of the world for 1901, when the light would be extinguished and the Pastor would reunite his sheep in a single flock. This would not be achieved without conflict, but afterwards there would be much pasture, and only few creatures to feed upon it. Cataclysms will turn the sea into backlands and the backlands into sea. It was concluded that Conselheiro was like Montanus of Phrygia:[10] 'the heresiarch of the 2nd century brought right into modern times, the same extravagant millenarianism, the same fear of the Antichrist emerging in the universal downfall of life, the imminent end of the world'. In a critical assessment of the evidence, Pedro Lima Vasconcellos concludes that the book of Revelation was profoundly influential to Conselheiro's teaching; he clearly believed in the reality of the Antichrist's appearance (with the declaration of the Republic) and placed his hopes in the fulfilment of the vision of the New Jerusalem (now relocated to Belo Monte); but there is little evidence of particular importance attached to the Millennium or of a threat of violence to society as a whole.[11] The caricature of the millenarian extremist may be part of a retrospective justification by the authorities for the brutal massacre. This invites comparison with the experience of David Koresh and the Waco siege.

XVII

FIGURES OF THE MESSIAH: DAVID KORESH AND THE WACO SIEGE

This transatlantic chapter begins with a look at the Jonestown massacre, but its main concern is with David Koresh as a messianic figure, apparently obsessed with the book of Revelation, who led the Branch Davidians until the tragic climax of the Waco siege in 1993. Episodes such as these raise issues about how modern authorities should understand and deal with these kinds of movements.

When Adeline Yen Mah was writing about the Chinese spiritual movement called Falun Gong, led by Li Hongzhi, she compared him to David Koresh, the leader of the Waco Branch Davidians, as well as with Osama Bin Laden of al Qaeda: 'People respond to cult figures differently, depending on their own cultural background and psychological conditioning, and there is but a fine line between devoted follower and fanatical terrorist.'[1]

Anthony Storr has made a comparative study of guru figures (the Sanskrit word guru means 'one that brings light out of darkness'; it is used in India as much for a teacher as for a spiritual guide or leader). Storr has this comment:

> It appears that once a guru has convinced a follower of his Messianic status, his actual behaviour, as judged by ordinary human standards, becomes largely irrelevant. Belief in the guru, while it persists, entirely overrules rational judgement. Dedicated disciples are as impervious to reason as are infatuated lovers.[2]

As a psychiatrist, Storr finds evidence that gurus do indeed suffer from a form of insanity; they may be affected by drugs or alcohol, but the more frequent diagnoses are in terms of manic depression or schizophrenia. In the poetic words of Gerard Manley Hopkins, 'O the mind, mind has mountains / Cliffs of fall frightful…'.[3]

In their book *Prophets, Cults and Madness*, Anthony Stevens and John Price argue that the blame for religious fanaticism should not be attributed to God, but to the very human condition of schizophrenia.[4] In the context of evolutionary biology, their case is supported by recent discoveries in evolutionary psychology and psychiatry. The leader needed to exploit the female cult members to ensure the propagation of the schizophrenic genes. So in the study of cult leaders such as David Koresh the authors focused on the ruthless exploitation of female members of the cult by their leader.

JONESTOWN

Jim Jones was the cult leader who effectively orchestrated the suicide of 912 followers at Jonestown in Guyana in 1978.[5] James Warren Jones (1931–78) was a minister of the Disciples of Christ from Indiana. In 1963 he founded a community in Indianapolis that he named the People's Temple Full Gospel Church. Two years later, warning his congregation of the threat of impending nuclear war, he relocated them to California. He was a political activist, influenced by Marxism, a bold preacher, and had a reputation for faith healing. But rumours circulated about some sexual improprieties and, as a result, he leased some land in Guyana, transferred many of his followers there (to the 'promised land') and established Jonestown as an agricultural colony in the jungle. His retreat preserved his autonomy, but isolated the community and limited proselytising and other interactions with the outside world.

Jones ran the new colony like a dictator, with control over its members' lives, activities and finances. The ideology was a blend of socialism and apocalyptic religion. According to the account by Constance Jones (no relation):

Themes of destruction, redemption, flight and deliverance taken from the book of Isaiah were used to justify a prophecy of the destruction of the fattened nations and escape of the righteousness into a new nation … The United States, its institutions and even its standards of beauty were portrayed as the 'beast' – totally irredeemable. Well-versed in both doctrinal and operational aspects of the opposing forces of good and evil, members of the People's Temple were prepared for sacrifice, struggle and an apocalyptic 'final showdown'.[6]

Jim Jones became unwell and increasingly paranoid and demonic in character in the face of perceived threats from the US government and relatives of community members. The catalyst for the final crisis was a visit by the US Congressman Leo J. Ryan. The visitor and his entourage were murdered, and then on the night of 18 November 1978 more than nine hundred members of the People's Temple either committed mass suicide, or were murdered. Jones' apocalyptic prophecies had been fulfilled quite literally. In the words of Stephen J. Stein, 'The historical record demonstrates that the most likely way for an outsider community to fulfill its apocalyptic vision is for them to take things into their own hands.'[7] Clearly the controlled environment and the oppressive leadership were key factors in this situation. There is no suggestion that other members of the People's Temple, still in the USA, would follow suit and commit suicide.

THE SOLAR TEMPLE

The Order of the Solar Temple (*Ordre du Temple Solaire*) is an off-shoot of the various movements derived from the Knights Templar of the Middle Ages (who had been burned at the stake in France in the fourteenth century).[8] On three occasions in the 1990s they attracted media attention when a significant proportion of their membership committed mass suicide. The Order was led by Luc Jouret and Joseph di Mambro, established grandmasters of the neo-Templar tradition. They owned a farm-cum-commune near Quebec in Canada, as well as other centres in Switzerland. Quebec was regarded as a survival shelter because of its 'granite bedrock', a suitable location for resisting ecological disaster.

The Order had been taught a mystical/apocalyptic doctrine, and believed that their members were immortal but fully conscious beings, coming from the star Sirius, who entered the material world at moments of crisis in order to alert humanity to imminent disaster. According to Susan J. Palmer's account:

> The Order ... espoused an ecofeminist apocalyptic theory ... Luc Jouret, the Quebec Grand Master, claimed it was necessary to balance 'feminine energies' – which they associated with the French culture, art, and nature – with the extant negative 'male energies' – associated with the English, industrial powers, and materialism. To this esoteric end, the OTS imported eleven francophone members from Martinique to Quebec to combat the anglo influence.[9]

During the 1980s the Order had been more optimistic about the survival of humanity, but they became increasingly pessimistic. Not only was the earth destined for an imminent ecological catastrophe, but they believed that as a self-appointed spiritual elite they faced an apocalyptic war of persecution. The leaders visited Australia in 1994 and claimed to have received a revelation at Ayers Rock from the Elder Brothers to the effect that they were abandoning the earth. The suicide letters left by the community show that they saw this as a sign of cosmic judgement, and then the core members had no alternative but to follow their Elder Brothers by resuming their solar bodies and returning to Sirius. This was to be effected in three 'Transits'; the timetable of these may well have been accelerated by the humiliation of a mundane arrest for firearms offences. The first transit took place on 4 October 1994, when a chalet in Quebec was destroyed by fire; the second in December 1995 at Grenoble in France, when fourteen charred bodies were found in a star formation round a campfire; and the third on 22 March 1997 when two family groups committed suicide in Quebec, although three teenagers from one family escaped.

Police and legal investigations raised the possibility that some of the dead had been murdered, as potential defectors from the Order. However, the Transits were also intended as charismatic displays, to reinforce the leadership of the Order and the ultimate authority of the Elder Brothers. It was said that, in the first Transit, the family involved (the Dutoits) had a four-month-old child, Emmanuel, who was denounced as the living Antichrist and killed. One of the leaders, the Swiss Grand Master di Mambro (who had wanted a son to raise as the avatar of the New Age but instead had a daughter Emmanuelle, whom he insisted on bringing up as a boy), had convinced the executioner that he needed to kill the Dutoit's child to expiate a crime, because he was the reincarnation of the soldier who had pierced Christ on the cross with his lance.[10]

DAVID KORESH

David Koresh led the Branch Davidians, until the Waco tragedy of 1993, when their residence was burned and more than 80 lives were lost, following a stand-off with federal government officials.[11] The Branch Davidians are the best known, owing to the media, of those groups who definitively separated from the mainstream of the Seventh Day Adventist church (see Chapter XI), exercising an independent and urgently apocalyptic ministry on the fringes of Adventism. The original Davidians had emerged as a millennial reform movement within the Adventist church in 1929, believing in an imminent return of Christ but fearing that his return might be delayed by the worldliness of the church. The Branch Davidians were created by Ben Roden as a second group who split away from the Davidians in 1955. Their name is based on the text of Isaiah 11.1 with its reference to a 'branch' from the roots of Jesse, identified as Christ (see also Zechariah 6.12). Roden was buried in Jerusalem but he had believed that, following the 1967 war, it would be possible for Revelation's prophecy to be fulfilled when the true church of 144,000 believers gathered on Mount Zion.

The Branch Davidians were now controlled by Lois Roden, the wife of Ben, who popularised more feminist interpretations in a magazine entitled *SHEkinah*. Lois Roden also befriended a new convert, named Vernon Howell (1959–93), who became a Branch Davidian in 1981. Formerly he had been a member of the Seventh Day Adventists and a regular critic of the church. From 1983 he proceeded to recruit and lead a sectarian group, substantially from within the church community. When the leadership of the Branch Davidians passed to Ben and Lois's son George, he tried to expel the Howell faction, but within two years George lost power to Vernon Howell following several altercations, including a shoot-out. In 1990 Howell changed his name to David Koresh: David to perpetuate the messianic link; and Koresh (Hebrew for Cyrus) as the champion of the true Israel against her enemies, just as Cyrus delivered the Jews from the Babylonian Exile. The community centre, Mount Carmel, was renamed Ranch Apocalypse.

Vernon Howell was a semi-literate rock guitarist with a detailed knowledge of the Bible from memorisation. According to Dick J. Reavis he revived this dying sect against all the odds. He was not the charismatic prophet/messiah of traditional expectation, but a laid-back figure with a somewhat contemptuous attitude, who had the ability to preach extempore for hours on end – but in a slangy, conversational style. He obviously attracted attention for the substance, more than the style, of what he said.

David Koresh wrote a commentary on the book of Revelation and seems to have been obsessed with this text. His focus was on the opening of the seven seals (Rev. 6–8), which meant, to him, the breaking open of a coded book. Only a new prophet could open the seals, and he saw himself as the rider on the white horse who appears when the first seal is opened. As Damian Thompson says, in his ministry 'Koresh focused the attention of the Davidians more clearly than ever before on the inevitability of a titanic apocalyptic struggle between the forces of good and evil.'[12] Koresh frequently quoted from Psalm 2.2: 'The Kings of the Earth set themselves, and the rulers take counsel together, against the Lord and his anointed.' In contrast to Seventh Day Adventist exegesis, which regularly sees the present-day church as that of Laodicea in Revelation 3.14–22, Koresh did not relate the Laodicean text to his group.

There is a significant difference between the expectations of David Koresh and those of the majority of fundamentalists who are classified as pre- or postmillennialists. He did not believe in a Rapture of the faithful prior to the Millennium, nor in a ready survival of the Saints through to Armageddon and beyond. Instead these Branch

Davidians anticipated a struggle to survive through the early years of the Great Tribulation, but then they would be slain by the demonic forces before the Tribulation ended, only to return with the Heavenly Host to join in the final conflict of Armageddon. They expected their struggle to the death with the demonic forces of the Babylonians (the USA) to take place in 1995.

Koresh saw himself as one of a sequence of Christ figures (the Lamb in the terms of the book of Revelation) that had begun in the Old Testament with the person of Melchizedek. Whereas Jesus was essentially a pacifist, Koresh's leadership role demonstrated, in Old Testament terms, the need to take up arms and fight for the Kingdom, and so he expanded an already considerable arsenal of guns. In a further contrast with Jesus Christ, David Koresh referred to himself as the 'sinful messiah' (although this must be seen in the context of the Adventist views on the sequence of history, and the deterioration of world and church immediately prior to the End – see Chapter XI). For example, in 1989 Koresh announced that, in order to ensure that he would be the father of all the children in his new kingdom, he alone was to have sexual intercourse with the female members of his movement.

Another echo of Adventist tradition, seen in the Adventist *Testimonies* of Ellen White, is the idea of the heavenly journey, transported in the Throne chariot from Ezekiel 1 (the Merkabah). The leaders of both the Davidians and the Branch Davidians (Ben Roden, for example) had associated this with a belief in flying saucers. So David Koresh, during the siege at Waco, told Federal Bureau of Investigation (FBI) negotiators how, when he was in Israel in 1985, he had been transported into the heavens by angelic beings in a kind of celestial spaceship. He claimed that his travels took him past Orion, to the discovery that God had created an earlier civilisation even before he made the planet Earth.

Matters rapidly came to a head. Texas child protection workers were investigating Koresh because of accusations of rape and child abuse. In particular the federal Bureau of Alcohol, Tobacco and Firearms issued a warrant on 28 February 1993 for the arrest of David Koresh on the charge of possessing illegal weapons. The Branch

Davidians did not react violently, however, until the actual provocation of an air and ground military assault by government forces. The Davidian premises were stormed by 90 federal agents, with resulting deaths on both sides from the gunfire. Clearly from Koresh's point of view this was the anticipated strike of the Babylonians against The Lamb in the last days. There followed a 51-day stand-off with the FBI, after which the Waco residence burned to the ground, and at least 80 people died.

During the siege the government forces followed established negotiating procedures and tactics, but these merely confirmed for Koresh their identity as the Babylonians and his chiliastic interpretation of the stand-off. Two academic scholars of religion attempted to make contact with Koresh via taped messages, offering an alternative interpretation of the prophecy regarding the seals in Revelation. They suggested that, after the fifth seal, there was a delay before the destructive opening of the sixth seal (Rev. 6.9–12), to enable the completion of the messianic work. Koresh responded to this offer of a 'way out' and sent a message claiming a new revelation, and a promise to surrender once he had completed a fresh exposition of the seals. Koresh started writing but the FBI lost patience, seeing this as yet another delaying tactic. The government forces advanced on the compound with armoured vehicles equipped with rams. Was this to be the final murderous assault of the Babylonians? They broke through the walls and inserted CS gas. Fires erupted (whether pre-set for mass suicide, or triggered by the flammable gas) and most of the Branch Davidians in that community, including the children, perished.

Although the Branch Davidians were shaken apart by the event of Waco, and several survivors were sent to prison, the movement nevertheless continues to attract a small community of followers, split into at least three factions, each with their own leader. As a result of the deaths several militias were formed, and the Murrah building in Oklahoma was destroyed by a bomb blast on the second anniversary of the Waco disaster. The New York film-maker Hal Hartley presented a musical, *Soon*, at the Salzburg Festival in 1998, based on the apocalyptic hopes of the Branch Davidians and the events of the Waco siege. Michael Barkun warned that there would be more Wacos if law-enforcement officials 'naively become co-participants in millenarians' end-time scripts'.[13]

One disciple of Koresh who survived the Waco siege, Livingston Fagan, was sentenced to 40 years' imprisonment. He has continued to write in the Branch Davidian tradition and produced a commentary on Revelation.[14] His interpretation of the letters to the seven churches in Revelation 2–3 regards them as entirely concerned with the church in the past, not the present. They 'give us, who are living today, some insights into how Christ dealt with his church in the past'. The conclusion can be drawn that, while the Waco chapter is regarded as closed, a new chapter is just beginning for the Branch Davidians. The emphasis has shifted from the message Koresh preached onto the person of Koresh himself. Some of the sect expected the return of Koresh, together with those who had died at Waco, on the basis of calendrical calculations drawn from Daniel 12.12 (1,335 days) or Daniel 8.14 (2,300 days) and the sixth seal of Revelation 6.16–17, which speaks of the 'wrath of the Lamb'. Thus the dates were set for December 1996 and August 1999.

XVIII

'APOCALYPSE NOW': CELEBRATING THE MILLENNIUM ON OR AFTER 2000 CE

When the world is ending, the golden angel on St Fin Barre's Cathedral will blow its horn. At least that's what they say in Cork, the city that grew up around the monastery of Fin Barre (the 'fair haired') in 606.

Around the middle of the twentieth century the following eschatological tag was common, at least among schoolboys: 'Someday, somewhere, someone will be called by God and blessed by the Pope. He'll tell this world that it's about to end, but nobody will believe him – until proved right.' It is possible that this idea of a mysterious secret, entrusted to an ignored prophet, may be influenced by the relatively large amount of attention paid by the news media at that time to the discovery of the Dead Sea Scrolls and their evidence for a previously unknown group of religious extremists based at Qumran. But what a difference 50 years makes! As the clock ticked towards the start of the new Millennium (whether strictly in 2000 or 2001) the news media, and the popular imagination as well as the serious minds of religious devotees, became focused on the signs of the End (or perhaps the prospects of a new beginning), to be marked by the climactic dawn of the twenty-first century.

Four centuries earlier, in 1587, John Foxe (the author of the well-known *Book of Martyrs*) had written a commentary on the Apocalypse (the book of Revelation) in which the seven ages were interpreted as successive millennia, the first six of which were scheduled to give way to the seventh and final millennial Kingdom, sometime before AD

2000.[1] Michel de Nostredame (1503–66), or Nostradamus as he is known, wrote that 'in the year 1999 and seven months' a 'great and frightening King will come from the sky'. He specifies neither any day of the month nor Armageddon. An accompanying reference to 'the great King of the Mongols' has been interpreted of Osama bin Laden, and the whole prophecy deferred to relate to 11 September 2001.[2]

The artist Wassily Kandinsky (1866–1944) shared similar theosophical and spiritualist beliefs to those of other artists such as Mondrian, Klimt and Beuys in the early twentieth century:

> It is often suggested that Kandinsky's early abstractions contain not only intimations of disaster, but premonitions of the coming first world war. The artist was himself not immune to apocalyptic speculations and thought the world might end around the year 2000.[3]

'Are we living in the Endtimes?' was a typical question posed to advertise one of an exploding number of facilities on the Internet that were preoccupied with these issues – 'Our website is devoted to this question.' (See the appendix to this chapter which lists a number of these Web addresses, current at the time of writing.) One might have expected that, a few years into the twenty-first century, the acute sense of urgency in these matters might have begun to fade. The opposite appears to be the case, however, at least in certain parts of the Judaeo-Christian world. Nor is this sustained, or growing, momentum entirely to be explained by political pressures (such as those between the USA and Iraq, or the War on Terror following 11 September 2001). To quote but one example, from a news item in *The Times* on 13 July 2002:

> The largest ever single group of US immigrants arrived in Israel this week. The 371 Americans made the move with the financial support of Evangelical Christians. Bishop Huey Harris of the First Pentecostal Tabernacle Church in Elkton, Maryland, said his congregation had given money to the immigrants in order to see the fulfilment of the Scriptures. 'I'm looking for the church to be raptured,' he said, 'Jesus returning to the church – and the Jews would receive him as their messiah.'

Dr Robert Wuthnow, director of the Centre for the Study of Religion, based at Princeton University, New Jersey, comments on American attitudes: 'We are in some ways a very religious country, especially compared with Western Europe.'[4] On this basis further significant rises can be seen in the statistics relating to religion within the months immediately following the attacks on the World Trade Center and the Pentagon. It was claimed, following the attacks, that now nearly half the population was attending church or synagogue each week, and that Christian music was selling particularly well. The Revd Jim McClurkan, pastor of West Point Baptist Church in Alabama, observes:

> Just going to church doesn't do it. Sitting in church doesn't turn you into a Christian any more than sitting in a garage turns you into a car. The difference I am seeing since September 11 is in the hearts of people. They are much more serious than before. They are more and more sold out to the Lord.

The sign outside his church reads: 'Church closing soon due to Rapture.' He explains:

> Any moment, Jesus is going to split the sky open and take us back to live with him at his side, and we will not be worrying about terrorists or anything like that any more, because we'll be with Jesus.[5]

Right-wing Christians in the USA have been encouraged to believe that the 'End time' is near, at which point Jews will be confronted with the stark choice between accepting Christ as their Messiah or facing eternal damnation.

To indicate a sense of balance, it is fair to say that by no means would all the world's Christians share this apocalyptic scenario for the Millennium and its aftermath. As a contrast, here is the measured statement of Dean John Simpson about the service in Canterbury Cathedral at the very end of 1999:

> On 31 December the passing of the second millennium was marked by a silent vigil of prayer in semi-darkness in the Nave. At midnight, a candle was lit and a procession proclaiming the 'Light of Christ' moved from the west end of the Cathedral to the Nave Altar, where

special prayers were said to usher in the new millennium, all the while candles being lit throughout the congregation of nearly a thousand people. It was a moving experience, which for all present focused the need of the world for the Christ who came to bring salvation to all.[6]

To return to the end of the world, the Internet offers a Rapture Index (*www.raptureindex.com*), which Richard Morrison, writing in *The Times*, described as 'a kind of Dow Jones for the Apocalypse'.[7] This is a listing of 'End-time activities', updated weekly so that those who consult the pages can calculate how much time they have remaining. The Index evaluates the traditional Biblical portents of doom, such as plagues, famine and drought, but it also employs more up-to-date indicators: for example, 'drug abuse', 'liberalism', 'false prophet' (identified with the Pope), 'government by the Beast' (any international power base, such as the United Nations or the European Union) and 'the mark of the Beast' (any unified currency such as the Euro). The Index also calculates a figure to show the closeness to the time of Rapture. The all-time high of 182 was recorded shortly after the attack on the World Trade Center in 2001, but even in mid-September a year later the Index stood at 170. Anything below 85 on the RI is regarded as 'slow prophetic activity' (which allows a measure of relaxation); above 110 on the scale is 'heavy prophetic activity', while a figure above 145 is a warning signal of imminent Rapture.

The origins of the concept of Rapture were examined in Chapters III and IV of this history, with special reference to the Thessalonian correspondence and the book of Revelation. In the current situation, particularly in those parts of the USA collectively known as the Bible Belt, the emphasis is on 'Dispensational Premillennialism' (as Rapturism is more properly known). Modern exposition of this concept is rightly said to derive largely from the work of a nineteenth-century British evangelist, John Nelson Darby (see Chapter XI). He believed that human history was divided into seven divine phases or 'dispensations'. History would end with a seven-year Tribulation, followed by Armageddon and the millennial reign of Christ, all of which were regarded as imminent. Darby's influence in Britain was restricted within the sectarianism of the Exclusive (Plymouth) Brethren, but in America his scheme has proved highly popular among evangelical Christians.

In a recent survey it was found that a quarter of all Americans believe that Jesus will return within their lifetimes, and approaching two-thirds of all Americans (including, apparently, President Bush) believe in the broad accuracy of this application of Biblical prophecies. According to the Dispensational Premillennialists, Christ's Second Coming or return to earth will happen when most people least expect it. He will sweep the believers up towards heaven on clouds of glory (this is the Rapture) and will leave the evil-doers, unbelievers and agnostics on earth to endure a period of seven years of catastrophe (the prophesied Tribulation). This earthly period will be presided over by the most evil person in history (the Antichrist); it will culminate in a colossal battle on the land of Israel (at Armageddon), following which the triumphant Christ will rule in peace for a thousand years (the Millennium) and the world will end.

As we have seen in this volume, the timing of the world's end has often been subjected to intense speculation and considerable ingenuity. One factor which recurs in such calculations is the special significance of the number 14,000. Accordingly, the End was predicted for 4 October 2005, since this would have been 14,000 days after Israel's capture of the Old City of Jerusalem in the Six-Day War. This event was regarded as a milestone in the full return of the Jews to the Promised Land. According to Darby's original insights, the plan of Biblical prophecy had been disrupted by the Jews' rejection of Christ. In today's view of the Rapture, the Jews' return to their Promised Land is essential to the fulfilment of God's will. The modern state of Israel might well be regarded as a sign of Christ's return; but implicit in such a relatively secular state is the acknowledgment that the Jews now see that they were wrong, and must convert to Christianity for the fullest realisation of the End.

Further evidence for the vogue in this apocalyptic expectation is provided by the Left Behind series of thrillers, written by Tim LaHaye, a 'prophecy scholar' in his seventies and a Christian evangelist from California, in collaboration with the novelist Jerry B. Jenkins. In July 2002 the tenth volume in this series, *The Remnant*, was published and went immediately to first place in the bestseller list of the *New York Times*. The previous volume *Desecration: Antichrist Takes the Throne* became the bestselling American novel of 2001 after the 11 September attack. In only nine years these two authors have accumulated sales of 40 million copies. The principal market for such publications is vast among born-again Christians in Bible-Belt America. According to the FBI there are no fewer than 1,500 apocalyptic cults now flourishing in the USA as well as the mainstream, but fundamentalist, Christian churches. The Left Behind series has already produced one film and video, with another to come, and a related website for merchandise including calendars (to enable one to count the days?).[8]

This series of novels begins with the Rapture and ends with Armageddon. It depicts the experiences of those 'left behind' in the aftermath of the Rapture, when Christ removes the true believers, leaving everyone else to suffer seven years of Tribulation under Satan's proxy, the Antichrist. The message and the prejudices are explicit: in Richard Morrison's words, 'it's up to right-minded Americans to get out there and show them, at gunpoint if necessary (and it usually is), that God is boss'.[9] The Antichrist figure, Nicolae Carpathia, happens to be Secretary General of the United Nations, whose wicked stormtroopers are called 'Peacekeepers' and have their headquarters in Baghdad. All international organisations are equally regarded as suitable cover for secular humanists who do 'the Devil's work'. The Roman Catholic Church is heavily criticised, as are all liberals, ecumenists and believers in global peace. Women in authority are crude caricatures, appearing as foolish or sadistic; Europeans are mostly unreliable and not to be trusted; and the only acceptable Jew would seem to be the Christian Jew, converted by 'Jews for Jesus'. This recommendation for converting Jews corresponds to the seventeenth-century millennial perspective of the Puritan, Cotton Mather: 'to be the means of converting a Jew was not merely a matter of personal glory, but another step accelerating the establishment on earth of the Kingdom of God'.[10]

A much more sophisticated literary exploration of these ideas is provided in John Updike's novel *Toward the End of Time*.[11] The central theme is the winding down or the wearing out of the world, a sense of cosmic chaos and futility. The book is set in the year 2020 (a significant number that denotes perfect eyesight). There has been a nuclear conflict between the USA and China that has left cities such as Boston battered, scavenged over by predators, and with its social order broken down. The apocalyptic machinery is further enhanced by the presence of an abandoned spaceship somewhere in space, circling with the bodies of its crew, and a strange starcraft visits the planet like a warning sign. But the space with which Updike is primarily concerned is that which exists between this cosmic scenario and the seasonal/diurnal rhythm of nature and human existence, in which the agony of ageing takes place.

It is clear that neither John Updike's work nor the Left Behind series of novels – nor for that matter the Rapture Index on the Internet – are anchored definitively to the celebration of the new Millennium in 2000 (or 2001). If that had been the case, their originators would have needed to explain why such a significant date had apparently passed without any cataclysmic event. In the past such a failure of prophecy (if failure it was) demanded alternative explanation – in a process known to modern sociologists as cognitive dissonance – if anyone was to go on believing in the essentials of a (modified) prophecy. An explanation of that order was the Seventh Day Adventists' interpretation of 'The Great Disappointment' of the Millerites.[12] For us to develop this aspect more fully from our vantage point (some small distance after the actual turning point of the Millennium), we should look back to those movements which, in the years before 2000, were building up expectations of some cataclysmic intervention around this critical point in time.

References to the Millerites – and other religious predictions of the End – recall the frequent association of these predictions with astronomical data. Today's preoccupation in the scientific world is with predictions of asteroids on a collision course with earth. One such was the announcement by NASA in September 2003 of the possibility that a lump of rock, 1,300 yards wide and code-named 2003 QQ47, could strike the earth on 21 March 2014.[13] Individual calculations of this kind are today refined on numerous occasions before the event. If the odds on the impact were to be confirmed, the result could be a cosmic catastrophe similar to that which is conjectured to explain the fate of the dinosaurs. From both scientific and humanitarian points of view it makes sense to utilise the latest technology in projects such as the Spaceguard centre, to give the most accurate warning of any significant impacts by objects from space that may threaten the future of the earth.

To return to the religious dimension of the Millennium, it is a fact that Pope John Paul II paid a week-long visit to the Holy Land in March 2000. The Vatican had declared that it was a 'sacred duty' for Christians to visit the Holy Land in the years 1998–2001. The expected increase in the flow of Christian visitors to Israel was certainly disrupted in the latter part of this period. The Intifada, suicide bombing and Israeli military retaliation effectively brought about the collapse of the tourist industry. Even now our historical perspective is still too short for a reconstructed prophecy to take account of such a political crisis within the Middle East peace process and to present a convincing religious overview of the direction of these events, however catastrophic.

The previous papal visit to Israel was the 11-hour flying visit to the Jewish state by Pope Paul VI in 1964. On this occasion he met President Shazar of Israel and Prime Minister Levi Eshkol at Mount Megiddo (the Biblical site of Armageddon). The archaeological site of Megiddo overlooks the Jezreel Valley; its strategic importance lies in the fact that it controls the great trunk road that leads from Egypt in the south to Syria and Mesopotamia in the north, the road that the Romans knew as Via Maris. Through the centuries it has been the site of major battles: in the fifteenth century BCE between the forces of Pharaoh Thutmose III and a coalition of Canaanite kings; of the clash between the Israelites and the Canaanites, recounted in the Bible in the Song of Deborah (Judges 5); of the confrontation with Pharaoh Necho II, in which the celebrated reforming king Josiah was killed in 609 BCE; and of the defeat of the Turks at the end of the First World War by General Edmund Allenby, later to become Lord Allenby of Megiddo. It is scarcely surprising that in the prophecy of the book of Revelation it marks the site of the world's ultimate battlefield. As far as we know, the name Armageddon does not appear in any source before the New Testament; it is a corrupted combination of the Hebrew word (*har*) for mountain and the place name Megiddo. The bus bombing by Islamic Jihad at Megiddo Junction in June 2002, which claimed the lives of 17 people, was clearly in the tradition of this area.

Horrifying though such suicide bombing undoubtedly is, it still falls short, however, of that ultimate conflict that is prophesied.

On 1 August 2000 members of the international society for New Testament studies (*Studiorum Novi Testamenti Societas*), including me, visited the site of Megiddo as part of their academic conference based in the University of Tel Aviv. Near the shaded tennis court, created for the team from the University of Chicago, which carried out the pioneering archaeological dig at Megiddo between 1925 and 1939, we had an evening banquet and listened to a lecture by Professor Joel Marcus (a Jew who converted to Roman Catholicism at the age of 24) with the title 'The Setting of Armageddon: Waiting for the Messiah in early Christianity and Chabad'.[14]

On that occasion I saw no sign of the project, planned by the Israeli Government Tourist Office in collaboration with the computer giant IBM, to transform the site into an 'intellectual theme park' for the Millennium so that pilgrims could experience a 'virtual Armageddon' – the final battle between good and evil that signals the end of the world for many Christians. As one newspaper headline had celebrated the plan: 'Israel plans a hell of a party at Armageddon'. There was to be a combination of computer graphics, created in a system known as 'magic windows', with holograms, *son et lumière*, and the siting of 14 new multimedia visitor centres.

The aim was to bring the past alive and to project the future, in terms such as the prophecy of Joel 2.1–2:

> Let all the inhabitants of the land tremble, for the day of the Lord is coming ... Like blackness spread upon the mountains a great and powerful army comes; their like has never been from of old, nor will be again after them in ages to come.

(Joel's prophetic language is based on the natural realism of the locust plague, with its capacity to devour all in its path. Such language readily gives rise to human or superhuman fears.) I do not know what happened to this Millennium project: perhaps the money ran out, or it was feared that the apocalyptic plans might be overtaken by events.

Reports appearing in the Jerusalem press in the period before the new Millennium suggested that the Israeli security services were in a high state of readiness, particularly in expecting the arrival of members of various millennialist cults. Specialist units were also in training, including those dealing with psychiatric problems among pilgrims. Dr Yair Bar-El had identified some years previously what became known as the 'Jerusalem syndrome' – that is, the belief by some visitors that they are Biblical figures or have a divine mission.

In October 1998, 60 members of such a millennialist cult, calling itself Concerned Christians, disappeared from Denver in Colorado, where their leader Monte Kim Miller had predicted (inaccurately) the destruction of Denver in an earthquake; they were thought to be travelling to the Holy Land in an attempt to commit mass suicide before the start of the new Millennium. Mr Miller claimed to be both God and the final prophet on earth before Armageddon. He claimed that like Jesus he will rise from the dead after three days; he had talked about dying on the steps of Jerusalem in December 1999. An American commentator said: 'I do not think they are going to Jerusalem to cheer-lead. My fear is that, if Miller's prophecy does not happen, he is liable to do something bizarre to ensure his place in history.'[15] The mass-suicide cult was becoming an increasing feature of such a religious scenario, as for example with the 39 members of the Heaven's Gate cult who killed themselves near San Diego in 1997.

The *Jerusalem Post* reported on 21 October 1998 that Israeli security detained two Christian pilgrims when they landed at Ben Gurion airport in Tel Aviv, and deported them without trial. They were said to be on their way to carry out an attack on the Temple Mount in Jerusalem, 'to precipitate Armageddon'. Intelligence sources identified them as members of a US fundamentalist group which supports the construction of the Third Temple on the site of the present Al Aqsa mosque, as a means of accelerating the Second Coming of Jesus. The anti-terrorism unit of the Israeli Prime Minister's office estimated there would be in the region of 5 million Christian pilgrims in the Holy Land for the Millennium, and predicted that some could become involved in terrorist violence on the Temple Mount. A central motivation for the activity of Christian radicals was the 'apocalyptic inclinations that view the year 2000 as the end of the world, at which time believers wish to find their death in places holy to Christianity'.[16]

Richard Landes, head of the Centre for Millennial Studies at Boston University, was on record as saying that he expected tens of thousands of Christians with end-of-the-world visions to flock to Jerusalem for the Millennium:

> Do not let anyone in without a round-trip ticket and a place to stay. I would say to Israeli security: the Mount of Olives might be taken over by squatters waiting for Jesus to return. If, in their disappointment, they dig in, you have an impossible situation.[17]

Some born-again Christians from the USA had indeed taken up residence on the Mount of Olives already by 1998, in the expectation that Christ's return would inaugurate a thousand-year reign of peace. A hotel with 61 rooms, run by Palestinian Muslims, circulated publicity to 2,000 Christian groups in the USA to ask them: 'How would you like to be staying at the Mount of Olives Hotel the day that Jesus returns?' Some US Christian groups certainly were convinced that the state of Israel was a God-given institution, renewing the covenant with God's Chosen People, and therefore that the 50th anniversary in 1998 of its inauguration was a clear signal of the nearness of the Second Coming. An alternative view, but with the same end result, is the Zionist theory of 'catastrophic Messianism' – the idea that the secular Jewish state is merely a precursor to the promised and triumphant recreation of the Biblical state of Israel. This Kingdom will be established with the victorious military advent of the Messiah.

One detail that may have caused complications for this symbolic coming together of Christians and Jews at the time of the Millennium was the fact that 31 December 1999 fell on a Friday. Strictly religious Jewish organisations and the ultra-orthodox rabbis would accordingly impose restrictions on any celebrations of the Millennium during the hours of the Sabbath (which began at sunset on the Friday evening). That Friday was also the last Friday of the Muslim fast of Ramadan, the day when up to 400,000 Muslims flood into the old city to pray at the Al Aqsa mosque. Christian anticipation of the passing of the old century was accompanied by the sound of fire crackers as Muslims celebrated the end of Ramadan.

So what did happen in the Holy Land at the dawn of the new Millennium? The Israeli authorities closed the site of Armageddon, to prevent fanatics from triggering the End times with suicides or terror attacks. The director of the Megiddo National Park, Ahmed Agbaria, spoke of staff being on duty 24 hours a day, but experiencing only 'normal tourists'. In Jerusalem in the weeks of December dozens of Christian tourists, mainly from the USA, had been arrested on suspicion that they were planning suicide on the eve of the Millennium. One man was arrested trying to jump off the top of the Church of the Ascension on the Mount of Olives. And shortly before midnight another zealot was led away from the sealed-up Golden Gate to Jerusalem's old city as he began to declaim about the sign of the Beast, the impending catastrophe and the subsequent Rapture awaiting humanity.

James Meek reported for the *Guardian*:

> Just before midnight, led by the flashing blue lights of a police van and flanked by heavily armed Israeli troops, a column of several thousand Christian pilgrims, tourists and local Palestinians, carrying candles and a heavy wooden cross, marched along the hills from the Mount of Olives to the grounds of a guest house where they celebrated the coming of 2000 ... The Christians gathered round the cross to sing hymns before counting down the seconds to midnight and marking the passing of the old century with champagne and fireworks. But there was no Messiah.[18]

A Texan called Sean, waiting on the Mount of Olives, commented: 'We are most certainly living in the End times and the Messiah will come. He just didn't choose last night for Armageddon.' Fr Micallef, a Franciscan friar from Malta working at the Church of the Holy Sepulchre, said: 'A new millennium means something. It means the 2,000th birthday of Jesus. But it doesn't mean it's the end of time or anything like that. He will come again, but let's stick to what he said himself: nobody knows when.'[19]

APPENDIX: INTERNET ADDRESSES

www.leftbehind.com (merchandise related to the book series)
www.raptureindex.com (the Rapture Index of End-time activities)
www.rapturewear.com (for clothes/accessories bearing a Rapture logo)

XIX

Epilogue

The healthiest antidote for American millennialism might be a return, by mainline Protestants and Catholics alike, to the theology of Saint Augustine, whose *City of God* (426 CE) inspired the rejection of millennialism by the Catholic Church at the Council of Ephesus in 431.[1]

The recurrently literal readings of the book of Revelation, especially those of the second century CE and of the later Middle Ages, had never found much favour within the Catholic tradition of the mainstream churches. Here the tendency was to stress the allegorical rather than the literal meaning of the text. In such allegorical interpretation the Millennium symbolises the temporal life span of the Church, throughout the age that lasts from the Resurrection of Christ to the Last Judgement. As particular examples of this tendency, one can cite Augustine's *City of God* 20.7–9 and Thomas Aquinas' *Summa Theologiae* 3.77.1–4.

R.J. McKelvey's emphasis is similar, in his study appropriately timed for the beginning of the new Millennium in 2000 CE:

> It is time to strip the millennium of the utopian fantasies that it has acquired through the centuries. Visions of the lion lying down with the lamb, revolutionary millenarian movements and the popular identification of the millennium as the kingdom of God on earth are all based on the mistaken view that John's millennium is to be taken literally. It cannot be too strongly emphasized that the thousand-year reign of Christ and the martyrs should not be taken literally any more

than the descent to earth of the enormous cube-shaped holy city. The millennium is metaphor. It stands for the triumph of God and the cause of truth and justice. It means the end of deception, idolatry, exploitation and injustice. But although the millennium should not be taken literally the truth it portrays confronts a world which suffers from idolatry and its ruinous consequences.[2]

McKelvey is arguing on the basis of the text of the final chapters of the book of Revelation. He identifies inconsistencies between 19.11–21 (the Second Coming) and 20.4–10 (the Millennium), if these were to be read as the account of a chronological sequence – as they must be in the premillennialist type of interpretation. One difficulty, for example, is how there could be any adversaries left for Gog and Magog, if all evil-doers have already been annihilated. Instead of a literal and chronological reading, McKelvey advocates seeing the text as metaphor in a context that uses the literary and theological device of recapitulation. This might remind one of the modern idea in the film *Groundhog Day* (Harold Ramis, 1993), but it is not exactly the same. Instead of someone being caught in a loop of time and being fated to repeat the same experience indefinitely, this literary device explains a single happening by superimposing several different perspectives on that same happening. So the descriptions of Second Coming and Millennium, no longer taken literally or as a prophetic projection, are to be regarded as metaphorical variants conveying the same spiritual truth.

For a particular kind of reader this certainly avoids the problem and lets them off the hook of commitment to premillennialism. Ironically, other types of literary-critical reading, applied to these texts, can yield different results.

One theory, which had a wide appeal in the first half of the twentieth century, saw these texts as damaged and corrupted – for example, by the pages being jumbled and reassembled in the wrong order. So it would be the responsibility of the commentator, as in the classic two-volume work by R.H. Charles,[3] to reconstruct the text, so that the events occurred more consistently and in the correct order. However, to achieve this result the commentator must employ not only the corrupted text but also his preconceived ideas of what constitutes the correct order. Thus a premillennialist text can become an example of postmillennialism, or vice versa.

The text as it stands provides a series of snapshots for the theological album. These can be reassembled in any preferred order on the album pages. Perhaps they actually represent a more haphazard and uncoordinated set of impressions of this religious experience of the end of time. As such they have permitted (even encouraged) throughout history the diversity of theories that we have been examining. Only by the application of our own instincts and preconceived ideas do they allow us to declare prophetically that one theory is right and all the rest must be wrong.

The Christian believer might well declare that the vital emphasis is contained in the Aramaic phrase *Maranatha* (to be found in the New Testament at 1 Cor. 16.22 and Rev. 22.20). This is either a statement ('Our Lord comes') or a prayer ('Come, Lord') and it was a very important eschatological slogan for the earliest Christians. Given the inherent ambiguity within a phrase that can be construed as either a statement of fact or an exclamatory invocation, it is clearly not to be settled upon as a matter of any human (mis)calculation.

NOTES

PREFACE

1 R.H. Charles, *A Critical and Exegetical Commentary on the Revelation of St John* (Edinburgh: T. and T. Clark, 1920).

I   INTRODUCTION

1 From the hymn 'I cannot tell' by W.Y. Fullerton (*b.*1857–*d.*1932).

2 J.F.C. Harrison, *The Second Coming: Popular Millenarianism (1780–1850)* (London: Routledge and Kegan Paul, 1979), p.208.

3 See John G. Gager, *Kingdom and Community: The Social World of Early Christianity* (Englewood Cliffs, NJ: Prentice-Hall, 1975).

4 Charles Allen, *God's Terrorists: The Wahhabi Cult and the Hidden Roots of Modern Jihad* (London: Little Brown, 2006), pp.73–4.

5 Ibid.

6 Ibid., p.294.

7 See Anthony Stevens and John Price, *Prophets, Cults and Madness* (London: Duckworth, 2000).

8 Albert I. Baumgarten (ed.), *Apocalyptic Time*, Numen Series: Studies in the History of Religions 86 (Leiden: Brill, 2000), pp.viii–ix. Cf. Morton Smith, 'What is implied by the variety of Messianic figures?', in *Journal of Biblical Literature* 78 (1959), pp.66–72.

9 Albert I. Baumgarten, 'The pursuit of the Millennium in early Judaism', in Graham N. Stanton and Guy G. Stroumsa (eds), *Tolerance and its Limits in Early Judaism and Early Christianity* (Cambridge: CUP, 1998), pp.38–60.

10 Leon Festinger, Henry Riecken and Stanley Schachter, *When Prophecy Fails: A Social and Psychological Study of a Modern Group that Predicted the Destruction of the World* (New York: Harper and Row, 1956).

11   Alison Lurie's novel *Imaginary Friends* (London: Heinemann, 1967) is an effective illustration of internal and external perspectives on a millennial group and of a sociologist's involvement.

II   THE ROOTS OF THE IDEA

1   Edmund Gosse, *Father and Son: A Study of Two Temperaments* (London: William Heinemann, 1907 [reissued by Nonsuch Publishing, 2007]). See also Ann Thwaite, *Edmund Gosse: A Literary Landscape, 1849–1928* (reissued by Tempus, 2007).

2   Denis Baly, *The Geography of the Bible* (London: Lutterworth Press, 1964), p.49.

3   Jack Fruchtman, *The Apocalyptic Politics* (Philadelphia: American Philosophical Society, 1983), p.8.

4   Eusebius of Caesarea, *Ecclesiastical History*, trans. G.A. Williamson, rev. by A. Louth (London: Penguin Books, 1989 edn), p.1. (*Eccl. Hist.* 1.1)

5   See R.A. Markus, *Saeculum: History and Society in the Theology of St. Augustine* (New York: Cambridge University Press, 1970).

6   Eusebius of Caesarea: *Ecclesiastical History*, pp.3, 17 (*Eccl. Hist* 2.3; 5.5).

7   Stephen Clark, 'Deep time: does it matter?', 16th Eric Symes Abbott Memorial Lecture, King's College, London, 11 May 2001.

8   Zoe Oldenbourg, *The Corner-Stone*, trans. Edward Hyams (London: Victor Gallancz, 1954), p.187.

9   Cousin de Granville, *Le Dernier Homme* (1805), quoted in I.F. Clarke, *The Pattern of Expectation 1644–2001* (New York: Basic Books, 1979), pp.43.

10   Teilhard de Chardin, *The Phenomenon of Man* (London: Collins, 1955), pp.259–60.

11   C.S. Lewis, *The Last Battle* (London: Puffin, 1964), p.165.

12   Clark: 'Deep time: does it matter?'.

13   Jurgen Moltmann, *Theology of Hope* (London: SCM Press, 1967), p.155.

III   THE BIBLICAL BASIS

1   Jack Fruchtman, *The Apocalyptic Politics* (Philadelphia: American Philosophical Society, 1983), p.8.

2   See Dieter Sänger (ed.), *Das Ezechielbuch in der Johannesoffenbarung*, Biblisch-theologische Studien 76 (Neukirchen-Vluynn: Neukirchener Verlag, 2006). I have quoted briefly here from my review of this book for the *Review of Biblical Literature*.

3   Cited by H.H. Rowley in *The Faith of Israel* (London: SCM Press, 1956), p.177 and n.

4   Tat-siong Benny Liew, *Politics of Parousia: Reading Mark Inter(con)textually*, Biblical Interpretation Series 42 (Leiden: Brill, 1999), pp.108, 132.

5   Timothée Colani, *Jésus Christ et les Croyances Messianiques de Son Temps* (Strasbourg: Treuttel et Wurtz,1864), p.204.

6   Some of this material first appeared in Grace Emmerson and John Parr, *Guidelines* (Oxford: The Bible Reading Fellowship, 1993). Its original source is acknowledged with thanks.

7   Ramsey MacMullen, *Paganism in the Roman Empire* (New Haven: Yale University Press, 1981), p.55.

8   Emmerson and Parr: *Guidelines*.

9   See Martin Karrer, *Die Johannesoffenbarung als Brief* (Göttingen: Vandenhoeck and Ruprecht, 1986).

10 David E. Aune, *Word Biblical Commentary*, vol.52, Revelation (Dallas: Word Books, 1997), pp.lxxxix–xc.

11 J. Webb Mealy, *After the Thousand Years* (Sheffield: Sheffield Academic Press, 1992), pp.247–8.

IV   THE RETURN OF CHRIST

1   Maurice Wiles in John McManners (ed.), *The Oxford Illustrated History of Christianity* (Oxford/New York: OUP, 1990), p.566.

2   Martin Marty in McManners (ed.): *Oxford Illustrated History of Christianity*, pp.397, 412.

3   Jack Fruchtman, *The Apocalyptic Politics of Richard Price and Joseph Priestley: A Study in Late Eighteenth-Century English Republican Millennialism* (Philadelphia: American Philosophical Society, 1983), p.5, commenting on the work of Ernest Tuveson in *Millennium and Utopia* (Gloucester, MA: Peter Smith, 1972).

4   See for example Bryan R. Wilson, *The Social Dimensions of Sectarianism: Sects and New Religious Movements in Contemporary Society* (Oxford: OUP, 1990).

5   Uncredited report in *The Times*, 25 May 1998.

6   Rachel Campbell-Johnston, *The Times*, T2, 29 January 2003, p.14.

7   1 Clement 7.6; Justin, *Apologia* 2.5; Theophilus of Antioch, *Ad Autolycum* 3.19.

8   *Adversus Haereses* 5.29.

9   Compare this with the literary presentation in the work of Dante (see Chapter IX).

10 Not an insignificant date, related to the year 1500 CE and agitation in Italy at this time (see also Chapter IX).

V   MILLENARIANS AMONG THE
       CHURCH FATHERS

1   Cited in Eusebius, *Historia Ecclesiae* [*H.E.*] 5.18.2.

2   Ibid.

3   William Hazlitt, *The Classical Gazeteer: A Dictionary of Ancient Sites* (London: Whittaker, 1851).

4   William Tabbernee and Peter Lampe, *Pepouza and Tymion: The Archaeological Discovery of Two Lost Cities in Phrygia* (Münster/Hamburg: LIT, forthcoming).

5   William Tabbernee, 'Portals of the Montanist New Jerusalem: the discovery of Pepouza and Tymion', *Journal of Early Christian Studies* xi/1 (2003) pp.92–3.

6   W.M. Calder, *Philadelphia and Montanism* (reprinted from *Bulletin of John Rylands Library* 7.3) (Manchester: MUP, 1923), pp.13, 35 and facing illustration.

7   Didymus, *De Trin.* 3.41.3; Jerome, *Ep.* 41.4.

8   Epiphanius, *Haer.* 51.33; see Calder: *Philadelphia and Montanism*, pp. 37, 46.

9   Adolf von Harnack, *The Mission and Expansion of Christianity in the First Three Centuries*, vol.2, trans. James Moffatt (London: Williams and Norgate, 1908), p.356.

10   *Non enim nos et milites sumus? Eo quidem maioris disciplinae, quanto tanti imperatoris.* Tertullian, *De Exhort.* 12.

11   Epiphanius, *Haer.* 51.33.

12   *The Martyrdom of Polycarp* is the account of the execution of Polycarp, Bishop of Smyrna. See J.B.Lightfoot and J.R.Harmer (eds), *The Apostolic Fathers*, 2nd edn (Grand Rapids, MI: Baker Book House, 1992).

13   See Robert M. Grant (ed.), *Theophilus of Antioch: Ad Autolycum* (Oxford: OUP, 1970).

14   Jean Danielou, *The Theology of Jewish Christianity: A History of Early Christian Doctrine before the Council of Nicaea*, vol.1 (London: Darton Longman and Todd, 1980), pp.34–5, 110–14. This interpretation is heavily criticised by Nicole Zeegers in 'Théophile d'Antioche est-il Millénariste?', *Revue d'Histoire Ecclésiastique* xci/3–4 (Jul–Dec 1996), pp.743–84.

15   As in Irenaeus, *Adv.Haer.* 5.33–5.

16   Justin Martyr, *Dialogue with Trypho*, chapters 51, 80–1, 109, 110, 113, 139.

17   J. Pelikan, *The Christian Tradition*, vol.1, The Emergence of the Catholic Tradition (Chicago: University of Chicago Press, 1971), p.125.

18   Gaius in his *Dialogue* against the Montanist Proclus.

19   Origen, *De Principiis* 2.11.2–3.

20   Methodius of Olympus, *Symposium* 9.1.

21   Commodianus, *Instructions* 2.3.6–9; 2.39.15.

22   Augustine, *De Civitate Dei* 20.

23   Pelikan: *The Christian Tradition*, vol.1, p.129.

24   Charles E. Hill, 'Millenarianism', in Stanley E. Porter, *Dictionary of Biblical Criticism and Interpretation* (London/New York: Routledge, 2007), p.227; see also Charles E. Hill, *Regnum Caelorum: Patterns of Future Hope in Early Christianity* (Oxford: OUP, 1992).

VI   APOCALYPSE THEN: THE YEAR 1000

1   As reported in *The Times*, 23 October 2002, p.14.

2   Stephen Bann, 'How we got our Millennium', *Canterbury Cathedral Chronicle* (2000), p.41.

3   MacKay, Charles, *Extraordinary Popular Delusions and the Madness of Crowds* (1841), available online at the Litrix Reading Room (*www.litrix.com/madraven/madne001.htm*), 2001, pp.257–8. The French quotation is from Lucien Buonaparte's *Charlemagne: Poëme Épique*.

4   In contrast, a draftsman of charters in the name of King Edgar in the 960s had cited the imminent end of the world, to justify the act of giving.

5   Glaber, R., *Opera*, trans. A. Orchard (Oxford: OUP, 1989), Book II, pp.75, 93, 111.

6   Ibid., Book III, pp.115.

7   Ibid., Book IV, pp. 171, 193, 205.

8   Ibid., Book IV, pp.4–6.

9   See Richard Landes, *Encyclopedia of Millennialism and Millennial Movements* (New York/London: Routledge 2000), pp.299–301.

10   *Sermo Lupi ad Anglos*, trans. A. Orchard, from Kevin Crossley-Holland (ed.), *The Anglo-Saxon World – An Anthology* (Oxford: OUP, 1982).

11   The German Emperor reinterred the bones of Charlemagne on the feast of Pentecost, 1000, in Aachen, as part of a conscious *Renovatio imperii Romanorum*.

12   Richard Landes (ed.), *Encyclopedia of Millennialism and Millennial Movements* (London: Routledge, 2000), p.447.

13   Victoria Clark, *The Far-Farers* (London: Pan, 2003).

14   Ibid.

VII   JOACHIM OF FIORE (C.1135–1202 CE)

1   Norman Cohn, *The Pursuit of the Millennium – Revolutionary Millenarians and Mystical Anarchists of the Middle Ages* (London: Secker and Warburg, 1990 [1957]), p.282.

2   See Chapter IX, pp.98–9.

3   Damian Thompson, *The End of Time: Faith and Fear in the Shadow of the Millennium* (London: Sinclair-Stevenson, 1996), pp.63–4.

4   See Chapter V on Theophilus of Antioch, pp.56–7.

5   See Chapter II, pp.17–18.

6   *As You Like It*, II. vii. 138–65, fo. of 1623.

7   *The Two Cities: A Chronicle of Universal History to the Year 1146 AD*, trans. Charles C. Mierow; edited by Austin P. Evans and Charles Knapp (2002).

8   The term derives from Ephesians 1.10 (where God sums up all things). The Church Fathers applied it to a totalling-up of past events and revelations in an ultimate climax.

9   Marjorie Reeves, *Joachim of Fiore and the Prophetic Future* (London: SPCK, 1976), p.10.

10   Beryl Smalley, *The Study of the Bible in the Middle Ages*, 3rd edn (Oxford: Basil Blackwell, 1983), p.xiii.

11   Reeves: *Joachim of Fiore*, p.6.

12   Marjorie Reeves and Warren Gould, *Joachim of Fiore and the Myth of the Eternal Evangel in the Nineteenth and Twentieth Centuries* (Oxford: Clarendon Press, 2001).

13   Joachim features in George Eliot's novel *Romola* (1863), which is set in late fifteenth-century Florence at the time of Savonarola: 'Abbot Joachim prophesied of the coming time three hundred years ago, and now Fra Girolamo has got the message afresh' (London: J.M. Dent, 1999), p.26.

14   Cited in Brian Arkins, Builders of My Soul: Greek and Roman Themes in Yeats (Lanham, MD: Rowman and Littlefield, 1990), p.187.

15   The year 1260 is an interpretation, on the basis of a year for a day, of the time interval of 1,260 days or 42 months, as prophesied in Revelation 11.3, 12.6 and 13.5.

16   See Sophie de Sède, *La Sainte Chapelle at la politique de la Fin des Temps* (Paris: Julliard, 1972). The theme of the Apoclaypse is maintained in the fifteenth-century glass of the Rose Window.

17   Katie Grant, 'We are all doomed – so what's new?', *Sunday Telegraph*, 3 June 2007, p.27.

18   In Richard Landes (ed.) *Encyclopedia of Millennialism and Millennial Movements* (London: Routledge, 2000), p.207.

19   See Chapter VIII.

VIII   THE BLACK DEATH AND OTHER PLAGUES

1   Ronald Blythe, *Church Times*, 16 March 2001, p.28.

2   Philippa Gregory, *Earthly Joys* (London: Harper Collins, 1999), pp.245–6.

3   Daniel Defoe, *A Journal of the Plague Year* (London: J.M. Dent, 1957), p.276. Originally published in 1722, after the 1720–1 plague in Marseilles.

4   A transcript of Pepys' diary is available on line at *www.pepys.info*.

5   See the report by Mark Henderson, 'Bubonic plague "did not cause the Black Death"', *The Times*, 13 April 2002.

6   Giovanni Boccaccio, *The Decameron* (Florence, *c*.1350–3).

7   Gabriele de' Mussis, *Historia de Morbo*, as in Rosemary Horrox, *The Black Death* (Manchester: MUP, 1994), p.25.

8   *Breve Chronicon Clerici Anonymi*, as in Horrox: *The Black Death*, p.41.

9   Cortusii Patavini Duo, *Historia de Novitatibus Padueae et Lombardiae*, as in Horrox: *The Black Death*, p.35.

10 John Clynn, *Annalium Hibernae Chronicon*, as in Horrox: *The Black Death*, p.84.

11 Michele da Piazza, *Cronaca*, as in Horrox: *The Black Death*, p.38.

12 Thomas Burton, *Chronica Monasterii de Melsa*, as in Horrox: *The Black Death*, pp.69–70.

13 Johannes Nohl, *The Black Death*, trans. C.H. Clarke (London: George Allen and Unwin, 1926), p.57.

14 *Historia Roffensis*, as in Horrox: *The Black Death*, p.73.

15 *Annalium Hibernae Chronicon*, as in Horrox: *The Black Death*, p.83.

16 According to a letter of William of Blofield, as in Horrox: *The Black Death*, pp.154–5.

17 Bernard Cornwell, *Vagabond* (London: Harper Collins, 2002/3), pp.443–4.

18 Johan Huizinga, *The Waning of the Middle Ages* (London: Penguin, 1955), p.31.

19 Julian of Norwich, *Revelations of Divine Love*, chapter 31.

IX   APOCALYPSE AND CIVIL WAR (1500 CE AND AFTER)

1   *Bonfire of the Vanities* is the title of a 1987 novel by Tom Wolfe; it echoes the 1497 call by Savonarola for the 'burning of the vanities'.

2   Jonathan Jones, 'Heavenly art', *Guardian*, G2, 6 March 2006, p.9.

3   Ibid.

4   A word is missing here; it has been conjectured as 'him buried' (i.e. the devil) or 'heaven'.

5   Lugduni Batavorum, I.928 E (Leiden edition of the works of Erasmus, edited by Leclerc, 1703).

6   Stephen Bann, 'How we got our Millennium', *Canterbury Cathedral Chronicle* (2000), p.42.

7   Nicholas Crane, *Mercator, the Man who Mapped the Planet* (London: Weidenfeld and Nicolson, 2002), pp.26–7.

8   Byzantine Emperor Constantine VII Porphyrogenitus, cited by Anthony Bryer, 'Do they know it's Christmas?', *History Today*, li/1 (January 2001), p.16.

9   Andres Bernaldez, *The Voyages of Christopher Columbus, Being the Journals of his First and Third, and the Letters Concerning his First and Last Voyages*, to Which is Added the Account of his Second Voyage, now newly translated and edited by Cecil Jane (London: The Argonaut Press, 1930), available at *www.mith2.umd.edu/eada/html/display.php?docs=columbus_4thvoyage.xml &action=show*.

10   See Chapter VII.

11   As n. 9.

12   Samuel Eliot Morison, *Journals and Other Documents on the Life and Voyages of Christopher Columbus* (New York: Heritage Press, 1963), dated October 1500, p.291.

13   Marilena Chaui (1998), quoted in Pedro Lima Vasconcellos, 'Apocalypses in the History of Brazil', *Journal for the Study of the New Testament* xxv/2 (2002), p. 236.

14   Scott Mandelbrote in Jim Bennett and Scott Mandelbrote, *The Garden, the Ark, the Tower, the Temple* (Oxford: Museum of the History of Science/ Bodleian Library, 1998), pp.34–5.

15   B.S. Capp, *The Fifth Monarchy Men* (London: Faber and Faber, 1972), p.35.

16   Simon Schama, *A History of Britain: The British Wars 1603–1776* (London: BBC Worldwide, 2001), p.180.

17   See P.G. Rogers, *The Fifth Monarchy Men* (Oxford: OUP, 1966).

18   Hans-Jürgen Goertz, *Thomas Müntzer: Apocalyptic Mystic and Revolutionary* (Edinburgh: T. and T. Clark, 1993) [German original: München: Beck, 1989].

19   Quotation from John Carew the regicide, as cited in Austin Woolrych, *Britain in Revolution, 1625–1660* (Oxford: Oxford University Press, 2002), p.617. Carew was referring to the beginning of the Protectorate in 1653.

20   Schama: *A History of Britain*, pp.195–6, 222.

21   See Chapter VII.

22   Gerrard Winstanley, *Law of Freedom in a Platform* (1652).

23   See Jaqueline Eales, 'Provincial preaching and allegiance in the first English Civil War, 1640–1646', in Thomas Cogswell, Richard Cust and Peter Lake (eds), *Politics, Religion and Popularity in Early Stuart Britain: Essays in Honour of Conrad Russell* (Cambridge: CUP, 2002), pp.185–207.

24   Schama: *A History of Britain*, p.228.

25   William Prynne, *A Brief Description of the Future History of Europe, from Anno 1650 to Anno 1710* (London: 1650), p.5.

26   Keith Thomas, *Religion and the Decline of Magic* (London: Penguin, 1991), p.170.

27   Bill Bryson, *A Short History of Nearly Everything* (London: Doubleday, 2003), p.71.

X   EDWARD IRVING AND THE CATHOLIC APOSTOLIC MOVEMENT

1   J.F.C. Harrison, *The Second Coming: Popular Millenarianism (1780–1850)* (London: Routledge and Kegan Paul, 1979), p.208.

2   B.F. Streeter, *The Four Gospels* (London: Macmillan, 1924), p.477.

3   The Catholic Apostolic Church was the proper name; the title 'Irvingites' was conferred by a government official enquiring into them as part of the 1851 census of religion.

4   The liturgies of the Catholic Apostolic Church were chiefly prepared by John Bate Cardale.

5   See Chapter XVII for Waco. Edward Norman was reviewing (in the *Church Times*, 28 May 1993, p.12) the book by Columba Graham Flegg, *Gathered Under the Apostles: A Study of the Catholic Apostolic Church* (Oxford: Clarendon Press, 1993).

6   See review by Edward Norman, *Church Times*, 28 May 1993, p.12.

7   Sheridan Gilley, 'Edward Irving: prophet of the Millennium', in Jane Garnett and Colin Matthew (eds), *Revival and Religion since 1700: Essays for John Walsh* (London: Hambledon Press, 1993), p.105.

8   Alec R. Vidler, *The Church in an Age of Revolution: 1789 to the Present Day* (Harmondsworth: Pelican, 1961), p.11.

9   Published in London by Seeley in 1827 as two volumes.

10   Gilley: 'Edward Irving', p.106

11   Quoted in Mrs M. Oliphant, *The Life of Edward Irving, Minister of the National Scotch Church, London*, 2 vols. (London: Hurst and Blackett, 1862), vol.1, p.247.

12   Ernest Sandeen, *The Roots of Fundamentalism: British and American Millenarianism, 1800–1930* (Chicago: University of Chicago Press, 1970), p.14.

13   See Chapter III, p.35.

XI   ACROSS THE POND

1   David L. Rowe in Richard Landes (ed.), *Encyclopedia of Millennialism and Millennial Movements* (New York: Routledge, 2000), p.266.

2   William Miller, *Evidence from Scripture and History of the Second Coming of Christ: About the Year 1843* (Boston: J.V. Himes, 1842), p.145.

3   Alice F. Tyler, *Freedom's Ferment: Phases of American Social History from the Colonial Period to the Outbreak of the Civil War* (New York: Harper Torch, 1944), p.73.

4   Rowe in Landes (ed.): *Encyclopedia of Millennialism*, p.267

5   Ibid., p.265.

6   George M. Marsden, *Jonathan Edwards: A Life* (New Haven and London: Yale UP, 2003), p.485. I am indebted to the review of this book by Frank Whaling in the *Expository Times* 115.1, October 2003.

7   See Jennifer Martin, 'The rise of premillennial dispensationalism as the cornerstone of American fundamentalism', in John M. Court (ed.), *Biblical Interpretation: The Meanings of Scripture – Past and Present* (London: T&T Clark International, 2003), pp.202–09.

8   See *http://en.wikipedia.org/wiki/Christian_Zionism*, accessed 10 May 2008.

9   Cited online at *www.zionism-israel.com/dic/Christian_Zionism.htm*.

10   The full text of this letter to Prime Minister Tony Blair from Rowan Cantuar and David Ebor is available online at *www.cofe.anglican.org/news/news_item.2004-10-19.9713606593*. See also Chapter XIV.

11   James White, 'An earnest appeal', *Review & Herald*, 2 September 1873, p.92.

12   Ellen White, *Testimonies for the Church*, vol.1, an Adventist publication, November 1857, p.186.

13   Harold Bloom, *Omens of Millennium* (London: Fourth Estate, 1996), p.223

14   *The Watch Tower*, 1 November 1914, p.61.

15   See North Seattle Bible Students, 'Special times and seasons divinely appointed', Study 1, available at *www.nsbible.org/sits_v2/v2s1.htm*, accessed 10 May 2008.

XII   JOANNA SOUTHCOTT (1750–1814 CE) AND HER FOLLOWERS

1   Jane Shaw in the *Church Times*, 11 October 2002.

2   Joanna Southcott to a friend, 8 October 1803 (University of Texas, Southcott Collection), 339, f.118.

3   Joanna Southcott, *Strange Effects of Faith*, Part 1 (Exeter, 1801), p.29.

4   Frances Brown, *Joanna Southcott: The Woman Clothed with the Sun* (Cambridge: Lutterworth Press, 2002), p.9.

5   William H. Oliver, *Prophets and Millennialists* (Auckland: Auckland UP, 1978).

6   Cited in Fiona Robertson, *Women's Writing 1778–1838* (Oxford: OUP, 2001).

7   From preaching by Joanna Southcott.

8   See Chapter IV, pp.44–5.

9   James K. Hopkins, *A Woman to Deliver Her People: Joanna Southcott and English Millenarianism in an Era of Revolution* (Austin: University of Texas Press, 1982), p.xix.

10   Quoted in Brown: *Joanna Southcott*.

XIII   J.J. JEZREEL: THE TRUMPETER AND HIS TOWER

1   P.G. Rogers, *The Sixth Trumpeter: The Story of Jezreel and His Tower* (London: OUP, 1963), p.38.
2   *Flying Roll*, vol.1, Preface, pp.xvi, 24, 84.
3   Rogers: *The Sixth Trumpeter*, p.37.
4   Inscription on the cornerstone.
5   Personal letter from Miss A. Vincent, dated 25 April 1977.
6   See their website at *www.maryscityofdavid.org/index.html*.
7   See their website at *www.israelitehouseofdavid.org*.
8   Advertisement in *The Times*, 15 and 22 February 1913.
9   See Chapter IX, p.106.
10 P.G. Rogers, *Battle in Bossenden Wood: The Strange Story of Sir William Courtenay* (Oxford: OUP, 1961), p.93.

XIV   AN ANGLICAN ISRAEL AT THE END OF TIME

1   From a speech opening a Palestine exhibition at Basingstoke in 1908; reprinted in Earl Curzon of Kedleston, *Subjects of the Day* (London: George Allen and Unwin, 1915).
2   Thomson chaired the first general meeting of the Palestine Exploration Fund. See Edward Fox, *Palestine Twilight* (London: Harper Collins, 2001), pp.54–5.
3   Barbara W. Tuchman, *Bible and Sword: England and Palestine from the Bronze Age to Balfour* (London: Alvin Redman, 1956), pp.114, 117.
4   Edwin Hodder, *Life and Works of the Seventh Earl of Shaftesbury*, 3 vols (London, 1886).
5   Mission statement of the Palestine Exploration Fund, London.
6   Conder's field notes were included in *Memoirs of the Survey of Western Palestine*, 3 vols (London: Palestine Exploration Fund, 1881).
7   Palestine Exploration Fund, *Palestine Exploration Fund Quarterly*, 1875.
8   Palestine Exploration Fund, *Palestine Exploration Fund Quarterly*, 1876.
9   Edward Fox, *Palestine Twilight* (London: Harper Collins, 2001), p.58.
10 See also Chapter XI, p.125.

XV   'SOMEWHERE A PLACE FOR US': MODERN UTOPIAS

1   Quoted in Sir William Golding and Harold Bloom, *Wallace Stevens: The Poems of Our Climate* (New York: Cornell University Press, 1980), p.331.
2   Norman Shrapnel, 'New fiction reviewed: the survival path', *Guardian*, 17 May 1979.

3   I.F. Clarke, *The Pattern of Expectation 1644–2001* (New York: Basic Books, 1979).

4   A.R.J. Turgot, 'A Philosophical Review of the Successive Advances of the Human Mind' (1750), as quoted in Clarke: *The Pattern of Expectation*, p.25.

5   The words of Emile Souvestre on dystopia, as quoted in Clarke: *The Pattern of Expectation*, p.128.

6   For information on Savonarola see Chapter IX, pp.93–4.

7   W.H. Hudson, *A Crystal Age* (1887), as quoted in Clarke: *The Pattern of Expectation*, p.148.

8   Krishan Kumar, *Utopianism (Concepts in the Social Sciences)* (Milton Keynes: Open University Press, 1991), p.7.

9   Robin Waterfield, *Plato: Republic* (Oxford: Oxford University Press, 1993), p.xvii.

10   See also the woodcut *The Island of Utopia* (1518) by Ambrosius Holbein from the Offentliche Kunstsammlung, Basel.

11   Peter Ackroyd, *The Life of Thomas More* (London: Chatto and Windus, 1998), p.168.

12   Umberto Eco, *The Island of the Day Before* (London: Secker and Warburg, 1995).

13   Italo Calvino, *Invisible Cities* (London: Secker and Warburg, 1974).

14   Arthur Koestler in Richard Crossman (ed.), *The God That Failed* (New York: Bantam Books, 1965), p.12.

15   Arthur Koestler, *Darkness at Noon* (London: Jonathan Cape, 1940).

16   Aldus Huxley, *Brave New World* (London: Chatto and Windus, 1932).

17   George Orwell, *Nineteen Eighty-Four* (London: Secker and Warburg, 1949).

18   Endorsement cited by the publisher at *www.randomhouse.co.uk/vintage/vintageclassics/title.htm?command=Search&db=/catalog/main.txt&eqisbndata=0 099424916*.

19   Arthur Koestler, *Spanish Testament* (1938), published as *Dialogue with Death* (London: Penguin Books, 1942).

20   Compare this to the theme of Margaret Atwood's *The Handmaid's Tale* (McClelland and Stewart: Toronto, 1986).

21   Acknowledgments to Kevin Anderson in *Guardian*, Technology, 28 June 2007, p.2.

22   John Gray, *Black Mass: Apocalyptic Religion and the Death of Utopia* (London: Allen Lane, 2007), quoted at *www.independent.co.uk/arts-entertainment/books/reviews/black-mass-by-john-gray-455059.html*, 29 June 2007.

23   Lecture entitled 'End of the world blues' by Ian McEwan, University of East Anglia, Norwich, June 2007.

24   Kumar: *Utopianism*, p.11.

XVI CHRISTIAN MISSIONS AND THE CARGO CULTS

1 Robert Moore, *Pit-men, Preachers and Politics: The Effects of Methodism in a Durham Mining Community* (Cambridge: CUP, 1974), p.181.

2 Bryan Wilson, *Magic and the Millennium* (St Albans: Paladin, 1975), pp.311–12.

3 Wilson: *Magic and the Millennium*, pp.330–1, quoting Peter Lawrence in 'The Madang District cargo cult', *South Pacific* viii/1 (1955), pp.6–13.

4 Lamont Lindstrom in Richard Landes (ed.), *Encyclopedia of Millennialism and Millennial Movements* (London: Routledge, 2000), p.59.

5 J. Guiart, 'Conversion to Christianity in the South Pacific', in Sylvia L. Thrupp (ed.), *Millennial Dreams in Action* (The Hague: Mouton, 1962), p.127.

6 Paulo Augusto de Souza Noguiera, 'Introduction', *Journal for the Study of the New Testament* xxv/2 (2002), p.123.

7 Popular practices such as *pajelanças* and *umbanda* meetings, for example.

8 *JSNT* 25.2 (2002) p.124.

9 Euclides da Cunha, *Rebellion in the Backlands* (Chicago: University of Chicago Press, 1944), p.221 (English translation of Portuguese original).

10 See Chapter V, pp.52–4.

11 Pedro Lima Vasconcellos, 'Apocalypses in the history of Brazil', *Journal for the Study of the New Testament* xxv/2 (2002), pp.241–54.

XVII FIGURES OF THE MESSIAH: DAVID KORESH AND THE WACO SIEGE

1 Adeline Yen Mah, *A Thousand Pieces of Gold* (London: Harper Collins, 2002), p.144.

2 Anthony Storr, *Feet of Clay: A Study of Gurus* (London: Harper Collins, 1996).

3 Gerard Manley Hopkins (1844–89), from the poem 'No worst, there is none'.

4 Anthony Stevens and John Price, *Prophets, Cults and Madness* (London: Duckworth, 2000).

5 See David Chidester, *Salvation and Suicide: An Interpretation of Jim Jones, the People's Temple and Jonestown* (Bloomington: Indiana University Press, 1988).

6 Constance H. Jones, 'Exemplary dualism and authoritarianism in Jonestown', in Moore and McGehee (eds), *New Religions, Mass Suicide and the People's Temple* (Lewiston: Edwin Mellen, 1989), p.212.

7 Stephen J. Stein, *The Encyclopedia of Apocalypticism*, vol.3 (New York: Continuum 1999), p.136.

8   See Roland J. Campiche, *Quand les sectes affolent: Ordre du Temple Solaire, médias et fin de millénaire* (Geneva: Labor et Fides, 1995).

9   Susan J. Palmer, 'Woman as world savior: the feminization of the Millennium in new religious movements', in Thomas Robbins and Susan J. Palmer (eds), *Millennium, Messiahs and Mayhem: Contemporary Apocalyptic Movements* (New York/London: Routledge, 1997), p.168.

10 See John 19.34.

11 See particularly the volume by Kenneth G.C. Newport, *The Branch Davidians of Waco: The History and Beliefs of an Apocalyptic Sect* (Oxford: OUP, 2006).

12 Damian Thompson, *The End of Time* (London: Sinclair-Stevenson, 1996), p. 293.

13 'Reflections after Waco: Millennialism and the state', in J. Lewis (ed.), *From the Ashes* (Lanham, MD: Rowman and Littlefield, 1994), p.49.

14 *The Price of Faith*, privately published c.1994.

XVIII 'APOCALPYSE NOW'

1   John Foxe, *Eicasmi seu Meditationes in Sacram Apocalypsin* (London: Bishop, 1587), p.60.

2   See Nostradamus, *Century 10,* quatrain 72.

3   Adrian Searle, 'Mysteries and mush', *Guardian*, 21 June 2006.

4   Cited online at *www.freerepublic.com/focus/f-news/583523/posts*, 4 December 2001.

5   Revd Jim McClurkan, quoted in the *Sunday Telegraph*, 2 December 2001.

6   Quoted in *Canterbury Cathedral Chronicle* (1999).

7   Richard Morrison in *The Times*, T2, 20 September 2002, pp.2–3.

8   See Glenn W. Shuck, *Marks of the Beast: The Left Behind Novels and the Struggle for Evangelical Identity* (New York: New York University Press, 2004).

9   Morrison in T2, pp.2–3.

10 Quoted from L.M. Friedman, 'Cotton Mather's ambition', in *Jewish Pioneers and Patriots* (Philadelphia: Jewish Publication Society of America, 1942), p.98.

11 John Updike, *Toward the End of Time* (London: Hamish Hamilton, 1998).

12 See Chapter XI, pp.119–22.

13 The date recalls the day in March 1843 calculated by Miller for the end of the world.

14 Chabad is the name of the Lubavitcher movement of Hasidic Judaism.

15 Bill Honsberger, reported in *The Times*, 22 October 1998.

16 From the report leaked in the Jerusalem weekly *Kol Hair*, cited by Christopher Walker, 'Israelis on alert for millennium suicide invasion', *The Times*, 22 October 1998, p.23.

17 In *The Jerusalem Report*, cited by Walker: 'Israelis on alert', p.23. Richard
    Landes is the editor of *The Encyclopedia of Millennialism and Millennial
    Movements* (London: Routledge, 2000).

18 James Meek, 'Still to come: The Second Coming', *Guardian*, 1 January
    2000.

19 Ibid.

XIX   EPILOGUE

1   Harold Bloom, *Omens of Millennium* (London: Fourth Estate, 1996),
    p.222.

2   R.J. McKelvey, 'The Millennium and the Second Coming', in Steve Moyise
    (ed.), *Studies in the Book of Revelation* (Edinburgh: T. and T. Clark, 2001),
    p.98. See also R.J. McKelvey, *The Millennium and the Book of Revelation*
    (Cambridge: Lutterworth Press, 1999).

3   R.H. Charles, *A Critical and Exegetical Commentary on the Revelation of St
    John* (Edinburgh: T. and T. Clark, 1920).

GLOSSARY

Antichrist – The exact term is used of an opponent of Christ in the Bible only in the letters of John, or in the plural of the writer's opponents. A variety of synonyms are found in apocalyptic texts for this incarnation of opposition and evil who will emerge before the end of the world.

Apocalypse – The Apocalypse usually refers to cataclysmic circumstances at the end of the world and places an equal emphasis on the existence of secret information hidden away and on the ultimate revelation of foretold mysteries. Biblical books known as Apocalypses are Daniel in the Old Testament and Revelation in the New Testament, and there are many Apocalypses in places other than the Bible.

Apocalyptic – This comes from a Greek word meaning to uncover or reveal and refers to revelations or prophecies relating to the destruction of the world at the end of time.

Armageddon – Armageddon is named in Revelation 16.16 ('the place that in Hebrew is called Armageddon') as the symbolic site of the battle which will take place at the end of the world. The name is a corruption of the Hebrew word for mountain and the place name of Megiddo. Megiddo is 18 miles south of Haifa, in an historically or militarily strategic situation, guarding a gap in the mountain range of Carmel. Modern references to Armageddon are, by analogy to the Biblical idea, denoting an ultimate and catastrophic conflict elsewhere.

Biblical prophecy – The term prophecy comes from the Greek word which means to forecast or predict, as well as to be a spokesman on behalf of an authoritative figure, such as God. Both the Old and New Testaments of the Christian Bible contain substantial prophecies or future prediction. Some texts interpret immediate political situations and their consequences as they affected Israel or the early

Biblical prophecy (cont.)

Christian communities. Other texts are apocalyptic in nature, looking much further ahead and interpreting whole sequences of historical events and future ages, leading up to expectations of the world's end.

Cargo cult – A religious movement appearing in tribal societies, often following interaction with technologically advanced cultures. Typically these cults focus on rituals designed to speed the arrival of ancestral spirits who will bring cargoes of food and other goods.

Charismatic – Charismatic derives from the Greek word *charisma*, meaning a gift, and thence a spiritual endowment (see Paul's list in 1 Corinthians 12). Religious leaders are often referred to as charismatic, for different reasons: they are celebrities seen as divine or divinely inspired; they have revolutionary prophetic gifts; they work miracles; they interact with others to attract or repel.

Chiliasm, chiliastic – This term comes from the Greek numeral *chilioi* for one thousand. It is used to refer to the period of one thousand years (*see* Millennium) during which Christ and his saints (or the Church) are expected to reign before the final climax of the world's end. Those sectarian groups that are preoccupied with this expectation are often referred to as chiliastic. *See also* Millenarian.

Four Horsemen of the Apocalypse – The Four Horseman are perhaps most familiar as illustrated in the fifteenth-century woodcuts of Albrecht Dürer (*see* Chapter IX). The four horses and riders are described in Revelation 6 as they are called forth one after another as the first four of the seven seals are opened. The colours of the horses (white, red, black and livid green) and the characterisations of the riders, with reference to the objects they carry, have led to a range of speculations as to what they represent.

Glossolalia – Glossolalia is a Greek word meaning literally 'speaking with tongues'. In the Biblical tradition this can be either a remarkable facility with foreign languages (see for example Acts of the Apostles 2.11), or the use of otherwise unknown spiritual languages (*see* 1 Corinthians 12.10).

Kingdom of God – The Kingdom of God, sometimes referred to in more Jewish terms as the Kingdom of Heaven, is a way of denoting the kingly rule or effective reign of God. Much of Christian theology sees it in this somewhat more general or abstract way, rather than referring to a particular geographical location. Millenarian groups in contrast tend to particularise the Kingdom, located within their immediate community. Through history the Kingdom has been identified with the Millennium, either as fulfilled following Christ's return, or as an earthly anticipation of a heavenly reality. *See also* Pre- and postmillennialism.

Last Judgement – The apocalyptic tradition took up prophecies from the Hebrew Bible of God's judgement on Israel's enemies and on Israel herself. These were made into a projection of the End Time, which would be preceded by a sequence of judgements and woes (sequences of seven judgements and of three woes, according to the book of Revelation). The final Day of the Lord, when Christ will sit in judgement on mankind, paradoxically combines the ideas of a dreadful day of judgement and of the dawn of the golden age of God's Kingdom.

Messiah, or messianic leader or prophet – The root meaning of the Hebrew word Messiah is of a person who is anointed, and therefore empowered. The equivalent in Greek – the title 'Christ' – means the same. These are the Biblical prototypes, which are reapplied in many later situations. In a context that is fraught politically, because a group is without power or marginalised, it is natural to look for an inspired and charismatic leader of the group who will interpret the situation positively and look for a successful outcome. Such is the role adopted by James Jezreel (*see* Chapter XIII) and David Koresh (*see* Chapter XVII), although they took the initiative rather than waiting to be chosen.

Millenarian – Millenarian describes that which pertains to the Millennium. It is formed from the Latin adjective *millenarius* (of a thousand) and as this does not refer specifically to a period of years (*anni*) it is not spelled with a double 'nn'. The term is used, as an alternative to chiliastic, to denote the activities and beliefs observed in a variety of sectarian groups, or to label those groups and their members.

Millennium – The Millennium literally refers to a period of one thousand years, or ten centuries; the word is formed from the Latin *mille* (thousand) and *annus* (year), hence the spelling with a double 'n'. Millennium is used as a specific term to denote the thousand year reign of the saints with Christ, following his Second Coming, or the same period controlled by the Church leading up to Christ's return. It is sometimes used less precisely of a coming golden age.

New Jerusalem – The final vision, in chapter 21 of the book of Revelation, describes the descent from heaven of the holy city, Jerusalem, in terms resembling the glorious arrival of a bride at a wedding ceremony. The image of the New Jerusalem is an ideal, built up from the transformed realities of the earthly Jerusalem. The vision makes clear that its immediate origin is heaven itself. It signifies the inauguration of the new age, or the dawn of a new created order of existence.

Parousia – Parousia is a Greek word, used to denote the Second Coming or return of Christ. The original meaning of the word was 'presence' or 'arrival'. In its Biblical applications it was used to refer to the cloud and

Parousia (cont.)

fire of God's presence (as in the wilderness wanderings of Exodus), or to the return of Christ in glorious triumph and absolute judgement (comparable to the state visit of an emperor or monarch).

Pre- and postmillennialism – These two terms are used to distinguish two different expectations of the Millennium, depending on whether the awaited Second Coming or return of Christ will happen before the actual Millennium, or at its conclusion. The premillennialist expects Christ to return first, in order to reign with his saints. The postmillennialist believes that the Christian community should apply itself with added vigour, as God's Kingdom on earth, before Christ's return. Both views are supported by texts from the book of Revelation, in chapters 19 and 20 respectively.

Rapture – The idea of a heavenly Rapture – literally, an elevation towards heaven – of believers has become increasingly popular, especially among evangelical Christian groups, up to the present day. The foundation of the idea is found in Paul's first letter to the Christians at Thessalonica: 'We who are alive … will be caught up in the clouds … to meet the Lord in the air' (1 Thess. 4.17). The survivors, greeting the return or Second Coming of Christ, will not wait for him on the ground but will be empowered to meet him halfway to heaven.

Revelation, book of (or Apocalypse of John) – The last book in the New Testament, supposedly written by a person named 'John' (who may or may not be the author of the Gospel or Letters of John). It is a highly symbolic work, full of imagery relating to the present circumstances of Christian groups and their expectations of the future.

Second Coming – *See* Parousia.

Utopia – Utopia is the word for an ideal place, the description of which may be the fulfilment of religious dreams or the goal of a secular revolution. The original word in Greek maintains the essential ambiguity about whether the place can actually exist, for the first syllable either means positively 'well', or negatively 'no'.

Zionism – In Judaism Zionism relates to a movement of some, but not all, Jews who are committed to the return of the Jewish people to the land of Israel. Movements of Christian Zionism, now found particularly in the USA, maintain the concept of a 'Greater Israel' and its role in the Ingathering of people at the End Time. Necessarily such Zionists believe that the restoration of Israel to its fullest historical boundaries is a fulfilment of Biblical prophecies, in accordance with God's plan. In modern times the ideology of Zionism has become significant in political terms.

SELECT BIBLIOGRAPHY

Allison, Dale, *Jesus of Nazareth, Millenarian Prophet* (Minneapolis: Fortress Press, 1998).

Balleine, George Reginald, *Past Finding Out: the Tragic Story of Joanna Southcott and her Successors* (London: SPCK, 1956).

Barr, James, *History and Ideology in the Old Testament: Biblical Studies at the End of a Millennium* (Oxford: OUP, 2005).

Bauckham, Richard and Trevor Hart, *Hope Against Hope: Christian Eschatology at the Turn of the Millennium* (London: Darton Longman and Todd, 1999).

Baumgarten, Albert I. (ed.) *Apocalyptic Time*, Numen Book Series: Studies in the History of Religions 86 (Leiden: E.J. Brill, 2000).

Bloom, Harold, *Omens of Millennium* (London: Fourth Estate, 1996).

Bowie, Fiona and Christopher Deacy (eds), *The Coming Deliverer: Millennial Themes in World Religions* (Cardiff: University of Wales Press, 1997).

Briggs, Asa and Daniel Snowman (eds), *Fins de Siècle: How Centuries End, 1400–2000* (New Haven/London: Yale University Press, 1996).

Bruce, Susan (ed.), *Three Early Modern Utopias (Thomas More: Utopia; Francis Bacon: New Atlantis; Henry Neville: The Isle of Pines)*, Oxford World's Classics Series (Oxford: OUP, 1999).

Bull, Malcolm (ed.), *Apocalypse Theory and the Ends of the World* (Oxford: Blackwell, 1995).

Burridge, Kenelm, *New Heaven, New Earth: A Study of Millenarian Activities* (Oxford: Basil Blackwell, 1980 [1969]).

Butler, Rex D., *The New Prophecy and 'New Visions': Evidence of Montanism in the Passion of Perpetua and Felicitas* (Washington, DC: Catholic University of America Press, 2006).

Carey, Frances (ed.), *The Apocalypse and the Shape of Things to Come* (London: British Museum Press, 1999).

Carey, John (ed.), *The Faber Book of Utopias* (London: Faber and Faber, 1999).

Clark, Stephen, 'Deep time: does it matter?', 16th Eric Symes Abbott Memorial Lecture, King's College, London, 11 May 2001.

Clark, Stephen, *God's World and the Great Awakening* (Oxford: Clarendon Press, 1991).

Cohn, Norman, *Cosmos, Chaos and the World to Come: The Ancient Roots of Apocalyptic Faith* (New Haven/London: Yale University Press, 1993).

Cohn, Norman, *The Pursuit of the Millennium – Revolutionary Millenarians and Mystical Anarchists of the Middle Ages* (London: Secker and Warburg, 1990 [1957]).

Collins, Adela Yarbro, *Cosmology and Eschatology in Jewish and Christian Apocalypticism*, Scholars' List (Leiden: Brill, 2000).

Collins, John J., *The Apocalyptic Imagination: An Introduction to the Jewish Matrix of Christianity* (New York: Crossroad, 1984).

Daley, Brian E., *The Hope of the Early Church: A Handbook of Patristic Eschatology* (Cambridge: CUP, 1991).

Daniélou, Jean, *The Development of Christian Doctrine Before the Council of Nicaea*, vol.1, The Theology of Jewish Christianity (London: Darton Longman and Todd, 1964).

Dick, Everett N., *William Miller and the Advent Crisis* (Berrien Springs, MI: Andrews University Press, 1994).

Edwards, David L., *The Last Things Now* (London: SCM Press, 1969).

Ehrman, Bart D., *Jesus, Apocalyptic Prophet of the New Millennium* (Oxford: OUP, 2001).

Emmerson, Richard Kenneth, *Antichrist in the Middle Ages: A Study of Medieval Apocalypticism, Art and Literature* (Manchester: MUP, 1981).

Firth, Katharine R., *The Apocalyptic Tradition in Reformation Britain 1530–1645* (Oxford: OUP, 1979).

Forrester, Duncan B., *Apocalypse Now? Reflections on Faith in a Time of Terror* (Aldershot: Ashgate, 2005).

Fruchtman, Jack Jr, *The Apocalyptic Politics of Richard Price and Joseph Priestley: A Study in Late Eighteenth-Century English Republican Millennialism* (Philadelphia: American Philosophical Society, 1983).

Furedi, Frank, *Culture of Fear: Risk-taking and the Morality of Low Expectation* (London/New York: Continuum, 2002 [1997]).

Gager, John G., *Kingdom and Community: The Social World of Early Christianity* (Englewood Cliffs, NJ: Prentice-Hall, 1975).

Goertz, Hans-Jürgen, *Thomas Müntzer: Apocalyptic Mystic and Revolutionary* (Edinburgh: T. and T. Clark, 1993).

Gould, Stephen Jay, *Questioning the Millennium* (London: Jonathan Cape, 1997).

Hanson, Paul D. (ed.), *Visionaries and their Apocalypses* (Philadelphia/London: Fortress Press/SPCK, 1983).

Harland, Peter J. and Robert Hayward, *New Heaven and New Earth: Prophecy and the Millennium*, essays in honour of Anthony Gelston: *Vetus Testamentum*, Supplements 77 (Leiden: E.J. Brill, 1999).

Harrison, J.F.C., *The Second Coming: Popular Millenarianism (1780–1850)* (London: Routledge and Kegan Paul, 1979).

Hill, Charles E., *Regnum Caelorum: Patterns of Future Hope in Early Christianity* (Oxford: OUP, 1992).

Hill, Christopher, Barry Reay and William Lamont, *The World of the Muggletonians* (London: Temple Smith, 1983).

Hillyer, Philip and members of the Foundation of Concilium (eds), *On The Threshold of the Third Millennium*, special issue of Concilium (London/Philadephia: SCM Press/Trinity Press International, 1990/1).

Holstun, James, *A Rational Millennium: Puritan Utopias of Seventeenth-Century England and America* (New York: OUP, 1987).

Horne, Brian, *Imagining Evil* (London: Darton Longman and Todd, 1996).

Hunt, Stephen (ed.), *Christian Millennialism: From the Early Church to Waco* (London: Hurst, 2001).

Jameson, Fredric, *Archaeologies of the Future: the Desire called Utopia and other Science Fiction* (London: Verso Books, 2007).

Jeppesen, Knud, Kirsten Nielsen and Bent Rosendal (eds), *In The Last Days: On Jewish and Christian Apocalyptic and its Period* (Aarhus: Aarhus University Press, 1994).

Keller, Catherine, *Apocalypse Now and Then: A Feminist Guide to the End of the World* (Boston: Beacon Press, 1996).

Kermode, Frank, *The Sense of an Ending: Studies in the Theory of Fiction* (Oxford/New York: OUP, 1967).

Knight, George R., *Millennial Fever: A Study of Millerite Adventism* (Boise, ID: Pacific Press, 1993).

Kreuziger, Frederick A., *Apocalypse and Science Fiction: A Dialectic of Religious and Secular Sociologies*, A.A.R. Academy Series 40 (Chico, CA: Scholars Press, 1982).

Kumar, Krishan, *Utopianism*, Concepts in the Social Sciences Series (Milton Keynes: Open University Press, 1991).

Lacey, Robert and Danny Danziger, *The Year 1000: What Life was Like at the Turn of the First Millennium (An Englishman's World)* (London: Little, Brown and Co., 1999).

Landes, Richard (ed.), *Encyclopedia of Millennialism and Millennial Movements* (London: Routledge, 2000).

Liew, Tat-siong Benny, *Politics of Parousia: Reading Mark Inter(con)textually*, Biblical Interpretation Series 42 (Leiden: E.J. Brill, 1999).

MacKay, Charles, *Extraordinary Popular Delusions and the Madness of Crowds* (1841), available online at the Litrix Reading Room (*www.litrix.com/madraven/madne001.htm*), 2001.

Mackey, James, *The Scientist and the Theologian: On the Origin and End of Creation* (Dublin: Columba, 2007).

Marsden, George M., *Fundamentalism and American Culture* (New York: OUP, 1980).

McGinn, Bernard (ed.), *Apocalyptic Spirituality* (New York: Paulist Press, 1979; London: SPCK, 1980).

McKeating, Henry, *God and the Future* (London: SCM Press, 1974).

Moltmann, Jürgen, *The Coming of God: Christian Eschatology* (London: SCM Press, 1996).

Monloubou, Louis (ed.), *Apocalypses et Théologie de l' Espérance* (Paris: Cerf, 1977).

Newport, Kenneth G.C., *The Branch Davidians of Waco: The History and Beliefs of an Apocalyptic Sect* (Oxford: OUP, 2006).

Newport, Kenneth G.C., *Apocalypse and Millennium: Studies in Biblical Eisegesis* (Cambridge: CUP, 2000).

Newport, Kenneth and Crawford Gribben (eds), *Expecting the End: Millennialism in Social and Historical Context* (Waco: Baylor University Press, 2006).

Oldroyd, Drina, 'Dante and the medieval prophets', in John C. Barnes and Jennifer Petrie (eds), *Dante and His Literary Precursors: Twelve Essays* (Dublin: Four Courts Press, 2007).

Pate, C. Marvin and Douglas W. Kennard, *Deliverance Now and Not Yet: The New Testament and the Great Tribulation*, Studies in Biblical Literature 54 (New York: Peter Lang, 2003).

Patrides, C.A. and Joseph Wittreich (eds), *The Apocalypse in English Renaissance Thought and Literature: Patterns, Antecedents and Repercussions* (Manchester: MUP, 1984).

Pearson, Simon, *A Brief History of the End of the World: From Revelation to Eco-Disaster* (London: Constable and Robinson, 2006).

Peterson, Eugene, *Reversed Thunder: The Revelation of John and the Praying Imagination* (San Francisco: Harper, 1991).

Reeves, Marjorie, *Joachim of Fiore and the Prophetic Future* (London: SPCK, 1976).

Reeves, Marjorie, *The Influence of Prophecy in the Later Middle Ages: A Study in Joachimism* (Oxford: Clarendon Press, 1969).

Reeves, Marjorie and B. Hirsch-Reich, *The 'Figurae' of Joachim of Fiore* (Oxford: Clarendon Press, 1972).

Reeves, Marjorie and W. Gould, *Joachim of Fiore and the Myth of the Eternal Evangel in the Nineteenth Century* (Oxford: Clarendon Press, 1987).

Reventlow, Henning Graf (ed.), *Eschatology in the Bible and in Jewish and Christian Tradition*, Journal for the Study of the Old Testament Supplements 243 (Sheffield: Sheffield Academic Press, 1997).

Riddlebarger, Kim, *A Case for Amillennialism: Understanding the End Times* (Leicester: Apollos/IVP, 2003).

Robbins, Thomas and Susan J. Palmer (eds), *Millennium, Messiahs, and Mayhem: Contemporary Apocalyptic Movements* (New York/London: Routledge, 1997).

Rowe, David L., *Thunder and Trumpets: Millerites and Dissenting Religion in Upstate New York, 1800–1850* (Chico, CA: Scholars Press, 1985).

Rowland, Christopher and Andrew Bradstock, *Radical Christian Writings* (Oxford: Blackwell, 2002).

Rowland, Christopher and Paulo Augusto de Souza Nogueira (eds), 'Brazilian studies in early Christian apocalyptic', *Journal for the Study of the New Testament* xxv/2 (2002), pp.123–264.

Rudd, E. Gordon, *Principalities and Powers: Studies in the Christian Conflict in History* (London: Epworth Press, 1963).

Russell, D.S., *Prophecy and the Apocalyptic Dream* (Peabody, MA: Hendrickson, 1994).

Russell, D.S., *Apocalyptic: Ancient and Modern* (London: SCM Press, 1978).

Sandeen, Ernest R., *The Roots of Fundamentalism: British and American Millenarianism 1800–1930* (Chicago: University of Chicago Press, 1970).

Schwarz, Hans, *Eschatology* (Grand Rapids, MI: Eerdmans, 2000).

Stein, Stephen J. (ed.), *Encyclopedia of Apocalypticism*, vol.3, Apocalypticism in the Modern Period and the Contemporary Age (New York: Continuum, 1999).

Stevens, Anthony and John Price, *Prophets, Cults and Madness* (London: Duckworth, 2000).

Stone, Jon R., *Expecting Armageddon: Essential Readings in Failed Prophecy* (New York/London: Routledge, 2000).

Taithe, Bertrand and Tim Thornton (eds), *Prophecy: The Power of Inspired Language in History 1300–2000*, Themes in History Series (Stroud: Sutton, 1997).

Thompson, Damian, *The End of Time: Faith and Fear in the Shadow of the Millennium* (London: Sinclair-Stevenson, 1996).

Thrupp, Sylvia L. (ed.), *Millennial Dreams in Action* (New York: Schocken, 1970).

Toon, Peter (ed.), *Puritans, the Millennium and the Future of Israel: Puritan Eschatology 1600 to 1660* (Cambridge: James Clarke, 1970).

Tuveson, Ernest Lee, *Millennium and Utopia: A Study in the Background of the Idea of Progress* (New York: Harper Torchbooks, 1964).

VanderKam, James C. and William Adler (eds), *The Jewish Apocalyptic Heritage in Early Christianity* (Compendia Rerum Iudaicarum ad Novum Testamentum) (Assen/Minneapolis: Van Gorcum/Fortress Press, 1996).

Weber, Eugen, *Apocalypses: Prophecies, Cults and Millennial Beliefs Through the Ages* (London: Pimlico, 2000).

Wilson, Bryan, *Magic and the Millennium* (London: Heinemann, 1973).

Zamoyski, Adam, *Holy Madness: Romantics, Patriots and Revolutionaries, 1776–1871* (London: Weidenfeld and Nicolson, 2000).

Zeegers, Nicole, 'Théophile d'Antioche est-il Millénariste?', *Revue d'Histoire Ecclésiastique* xci/3–4 (Jul–Dec 1996), pp.743–84.

INDEX